The Psalter is a most important book  of its testimony to Christ. Richard
against the background of his wide]
scholarship while successfully avoidir
language. His love for Christ and Scripture are evident and he
expounds psalms representative of particular genres, considering
various ways each has been handled in terms of its application to
Christ. He is convinced that every psalm contains a Messianic
element, although not all will agree with his identification of this
in every instance.

Geoffrey W. Grogan

Dr. Richard "Dick" Belcher Jr. is Professor of Old Testament at Reformed Theological Seminary, Charlotte, North Carolina. He is an ordained minister in the PCA and pastored an urban nondenominational church in Rochester, New York for ten years before pursuing his PhD. He graduated from Covenant College and received his MDiv. from Covenant Seminary. He also received an S.T.M. from Concordia Theological Seminary and his PhD. is from Westminster Theological Seminary.

The Messiah and the Psalms:

Preaching Christ from All the Psalms

Richard P. Belcher, Jr.

MENTOR

Dedicated to my wife

Lu
who is a gift from the LORD

Proverbs 19:14

Copyright © Richard Belcher 2006

ISBN 978-1-84550-074-0

10 9 8 7 6 5 4 3 2 1

Published in 2006
Reprinted 2008, 2012, 2016, 2019 and 2021
in the
Mentor Imprint
by
Christian Focus Publications, Ltd.,
Geanies House, Fearn, Ross-shire,
Scotland, IV20 1TW, UK.

www.christianfocus.com

Cover design by moose77.com

Printed by Bell & Bain, Glasgow

CONTENTS

Particular Psalms

Preface

Seeing more of the majesty of Christ in the pages of Scripture should be an encouragement to God's people and should lead to praise and thanksgiving. The basic thesis of this book is that all the psalms have a relationship to the person and/or work of Christ, not just the traditional Messianic psalms. The goal is not to find Christ in every verse, but to understand how the major concepts and ideas in the Old Testament are foundational for understanding the person and work of Christ. The justification for this approach is laid out in Chapters 1–3. The benefit of this approach follows in the rest of the book. Different types of psalms are examined to show how those psalms relate to Christ and what those psalms might teach us about Christ. The basic structure of a psalm, its use of key concepts and themes, and its basic message in its Old Testament setting are first analyzed as a foundation for making connections to Christ. It is important for the reader to have a Bible open to the psalm that is being discussed, and then to be willing to explore the New Testament connections that are brought out in relationship to Christ. Most technical matters are dealt with in the notes.

Unless otherwise stated, the quotations of Scripture come from the English Standard Version (esv). As Hebrew students quickly realize, many times the Hebrew verses are off by a verse or two in comparison with the English verses. The Hebrew includes the title of the Psalm as the first verse. The English versification is followed except where specific comment may be made on a Hebrew word. The verse in the Hebrew will always follow in brackets the verse in the English. For example, Psalm 8:2 [3] means that verse 2 is the English verse and verse 3 is the Hebrew verse. There is very limited discussion of Hebrew words, but when the Hebrew is commented on, English transliteration is always given. Most of the transliteration is straightforward, but the lay person may want to take note of the following pronunciations: w = v (as in vine); h = ch (as in Bach); t = t (as in tall); s = ts (as in nets); $ś$ and s = s (as in set); $š$ = sh (as in shine); $ā$ and a = a (as in father); $ē$ = ey (as in they); $î$ and i = e (as in she); $ô$ and $ō$ = o (as in row). Also, behind the covenant name Lord stands the Hebrew *yhwh* (יהוה), a name so sacred the Jewish people would not pronounce it. The older pronunciation is Jehovah, but more recent scholars use Yahweh. This name for God becomes prominent in the Exodus event. Yahweh is the covenant name that reminds the people of his saving power to deliver. Many times I will use both to remind the reader of the connection – Lord (Yahweh) – but sometimes I may only use one or the other.

I would like to thank Christian Focus for the opportunity to pursue this topic and for their patience while I finished the project. I was able to complete the basic approach and structure of the book while on sabbatical several years ago. Thanks also to the Board of Reformed Theological Seminary for the sabbatical and for providing a great place to teach.

Part of the joy of teaching at RTS Charlotte is the good relationship among the faculty members. I would especially like to thank my colleagues Dr. Robert J. Cara and Dr. Michael J. Kruger for their encouragement and stimulating discussions concerning Scripture, hermeneutics, and theology (yes Jill, it is 'work' and we do love it!!). Dr. Cara has made several helpful suggestions along the way. I would also like to thank Dr. Tremper Longman III, who has greatly influenced my approach to the psalms. However, I take full responsibility for any shortcomings in the book.

I am grateful to members of Christ Ridge Church who regularly prayed for this book to be completed, especially Grady and Carol Hope.

I thank my parents for the good foundation they laid for me in the Christian faith. As a 'preacher's kid' I never felt like I lived in a glass bowl or was held to a higher standard than others.

I especially thank my wife Lu, to whom this book is dedicated. Without her tireless efforts on behalf of our family I would not be where I am today, and I would not have been able to finish this book. Thank you for your Christ-like spirit.

I pray that this book will help others to see more of the majesty of Christ in the Psalms.

Richard P. Belcher, Jr., Ph.D.
Reformed Theological Seminary, Charlotte, North Carolina
January 2006

Abbreviations

AB	Anchor Bible
ANE	Ancient Near East
BECNT	Baker Exegetical Commentary on the New Testament
BibSac	*Bibliotheca Sacra*
chap	chapter
chaps	chapters
diss.	dissertation
ed.	editor
eds.	editors
ESV	English Standard Version
ff	following
FOTL	Forms of Old Testament Literature
IBS	*Irish Biblical Studies*
ICC	International Critical Commentary
Int	Interpretation
JAOS	*Journal of the American Oriental Society*
JETS	*Journal of the Evangelical Theological Society*
JBL	*Journal of Biblical Literature*
JSOT	*Journal for the Study of the Old Testament*
KJV	King James Version
LXX	Septuagint
n.	note (footnote)
NASB	New American Standard Bible
NCB	New Century Bible
n.d.	no date
NICNT	New International Commentary on the New Testament
NIDOTTE	New International Dictionary of Old Testament Theology and Exegesis
NIGTC	New International Greek Testament Commentary
NIV	New International Version
NIVAC	New International Version Application Commentary
NKJV	New Kings James Version
ns	new series
NT	New Testament
NTC	New Testament Commentary
Num	Numbers
OT	Old Testament
OTL	Old Testament Library
pft	perfect
PNTC	Pillar New Testament Commentary
RTR	*Reformed Theological Review*

trans.	translator
TrinJ	*Trinity Journal*
TynBul	*Tyndale Bulletin*
vol.	volume
vols.	volumes
VT	*Vetus Testamentum*
v	verse
vv	verses
WBC	Word Biblical Commentary
WSC	Westminster Shorter Catechism
WTJ	*Westminster Theological Journal*

Chapter 1

Key Issues in Interpreting the Psalms

There has always been debate concerning which psalms are Messianic. What is it that makes a psalm Messianic? Are there certain concepts that set some psalms apart as Messianic? Must a Messianic psalm have a predictive element in it that the New Testament recognizes is a reference to Jesus Christ? What relevance do Messianic psalms have to their own historical context? Certain psalms have been historically recognized as Messianic because they speak more directly of Christ and are used as such in the New Testament (Pss. 2, 16, 22, 110), but does that mean that other psalms do not have any relationship to Christ?

The significance of these questions can be seen in how commentators have dealt with Psalm 1. Psalm 1 sets forth the blessedness of 'the man'[1] who avoids wickedness and lives a fruitful life because he meditates on the law of God. Such a man is contrasted with the wicked, who are unstable and have no future. Nothing distinctly Messianic is found in this psalm. There is no mention of a king or a kingdom (as Pss. 2 and 110) and there is nothing that ties the psalm directly to the ministry or suffering of Jesus Christ (as Ps. 22). Calvin's exposition of this psalm focuses entirely on the blessedness of God's devout servants, with no mention of Christ.[2] Luther, on the other hand, begins by noting that the 'first psalm speaks literally concerning Christ'. The blessed man is Christ, who did not consent to the design of the Jews (walked not in the counsel of the ungodly).[3] An analysis of these two approaches raises important issues for interpreting the psalms, especially the traditional Messianic psalms.

Calvin's commentaries are an extraordinary testimony to sober, historical exegesis.[4] His first concern is to try to understand the Old Testament passage in its historical context. Calvin emphasizes the human author and is in constant search for the intention of the human author.[5] This emphasis keeps Calvin from jumping to Christ before he has explored the meaning of the passage in its original Old Testament setting. He is thus very reserved at times in making direct application to Christ from the psalms. Even in psalms that are more traditionally Messianic, he seeks to understand the psalm in reference to David and the Old Testament kingdom before examining how it relates to Christ. Thus at the beginning of Psalm 72 Calvin sets forth this caution:

> Those who would interpret it simply as a prophecy of the kingdom of Christ, seem to put a construction upon the words which do violence to them; and then we must always beware of giving the Jews occasion of making an outcry, as if it were our purpose, sophistically, to apply to Christ those things that do not directly apply to him.[6]

Even for Psalm 22, which opens with the cry that Jesus uttered on the cross (Matt. 27:46), Calvin wants to speak first of how this psalm and the distress expressed in the psalm relates to David.[7] Calvin's emphasis on the intention of the human author and the historical situation limits the number of psalms that he considers Messianic.[8] Yet the benefit of his emphasis on the historical situation and the intention of the human author cannot be overestimated as foundational to the interpretation of Scripture.

Although Calvin stresses the human author and the historical situation, he does recognize another dimension to the psalms. The psalms do speak of the future coming of the Messiah and his kingdom. In one psalm at least, there is a direct reference to Christ without any attention given to the historical situation. In the introduction to Psalm 110 Calvin comments:

> In this psalm David sets forth the perpetuity of Christ's reign, and the eternity of his priesthood . . . Having the testimony of Christ that this psalm was penned in reference to himself, we need not apply to any other quarter for the corroboration of this statement . . . the truths here stated relate neither to David nor to any other person than the Mediator alone.[9]

Here Calvin sounds very much like Luther in Psalm 1 where Luther takes the man in Psalm 1 to be a direct reference to Christ.

It is more common, however, for Calvin to understand a psalm in reference to David and his kingdom, but then to recognize that what is said about David and his kingdom cannot be fulfilled except in Jesus Christ. For example, the submission to the king in Psalm 47:1 does not fit either David or Solomon's reign:

> Many nations were tributary to David, and to his son Solomon, but while they were so, they ceased not at the time, to murmur and bore impatiently the yoke which was imposed upon them . . . it follows that this language is applicable only to the kingdom of Christ.[10]

Here David and his kingdom are a type of Christ and his kingdom. In these situations the words of the psalm point beyond the historical situation to the coming of the Messiah. Thus Calvin recognizes that something more than historical interpretation is appropriate.[11] Calvin understands that such a typological reference is related to the divine author of Scripture as he refers repeatedly in Psalm 47 to the 'inspired writer' and stresses the 'design of the Holy Spirit'.[12] Although Calvin emphasizes the human author and the meaning of a text in its historical situation, he also recognizes that the meaning of a text may go beyond the historical situation because of the divine author of Scripture.

Luther's approach to the Psalms is best understood in his interaction with the interpretive questions of his day. Thomas Aquinas had developed the four-fold sense of Scripture with an emphasis on the literal sense as foundational to the other senses. The allegorical sense (the spiritual meaning), the tropological sense (the moral meaning), and the anagogical sense (the eschatological meaning) are all rooted in the literal sense.[13] Luther develops the literal sense in his approach to interpreting Scripture, although he gives recognition to the other senses, especially in his early comments on the Psalms. In his interpretation of Psalm 1:1 he sets forth the literal sense that Jesus Christ made no concessions to the designs of the Jews. The allegorical sense is related to the church, which means that the holy church did not agree to these evil designs of the Jews against Christ. There is also a tropological, or moral sense, which means that the spirit of man should not give in to the persuasions of the flesh and the ungodly strivings of the body.[14] Although Luther's early comments on the Psalter followed this pattern, he also laid the foundation for the abolishment of this four-fold approach by his emphasis on Christ as the literal sense. If Christ is the literal sense, then there is no need to find Christ in some spiritual or allegorical sense in the Old Testament. Luther argued that the whole Bible is about Christ and that Christ is the true spiritual sense of Scripture, and that sense is communicated through the historical character of the text.[15] By emphasizing that the literal sense of a psalm speaks of Christ, Luther laid the foundation for the abolishment of the four-fold sense of Scripture and the need for allegory to see Christ in the Old Testament.[16]

This raises an important question: If the whole Bible is about Christ, as Jesus himself in Luke 24:44 seems to say, then how do psalms that are not directly Messianic relate to Christ? Is it appropriate to jump directly from the psalms to Christ, as Luther does when he makes the man in Psalm 1:1 to refer to Jesus Christ?

More recent developments in psalm study fill in the gap between Calvin's historical emphasis and Luther's Christological emphasis, especially as they relate to the identification of 'the man' in Psalm 1. There has been a movement toward a literary approach to the psalms that emphasizes the importance of the editing and structure of the Psalms. The structure of the Psalms has significance for the meaning of individual psalms and reflects the concerns of those who edited the Psalter. Although a number of different proposals set forth various reasons for the structure of the Psalms,[17] there is general agreement that the Psalms are divided into five books,[18] that Psalms 1 and 2 serve as an introduction to the Psalter, and that Psalms 146–150 act as a conclusion.[19] Many also believe that the Psalter came into existence over a period of time, with the first three books being earlier than books IV and V.[20] The structure of the Psalter seems related to kingship and the Davidic covenant. Psalms near the seams of the first three books deal with the king. Psalm 2 stands at the beginning of the Psalter and emphasizes that the king is God's son. Psalm 72, which concludes Book II, is a royal psalm which suggests that the promise of God to David is good for Solomon and for all other descendants of the throne. It focuses on the righteous government expected of the king. Book III, however, ends with Psalm 89, which rehearses the promises of the Davidic covenant (vv. 1-38), but concludes with questions related to the effectiveness of the covenant because the covenant with David seems to have failed (vv. 39-52). Books IV and V may be an answer to the questions raised at the end of Psalm 89. Book IV opens with the Mosaic Psalm 90, taking Israel back to her foundations, and is followed by Psalm 91, one of the boldest expressions of confidence in the Scriptures. There then follows a group of psalms (93–100) that stress the reign of the LORD (Yahweh) . Even if the monarchy is in trouble (Psalm 89) Yahweh reigns as their king.[21] Book IV ends with the plea of Psalm 106:47: 'save us... and gather us from among the nations.' Book V begins with Psalm 107, a psalm of thanksgiving offered to the LORD for gathering his people from the lands of exile, no doubt a response to Psalm 106. Book V then has several groupings of psalms that are significant. There are two groups of Davidic psalms that appear near the beginning and the end of Book V: 108–110 and 138–145. These psalms ultimately show the triumph of the Davidic king and set forth a model of the type of king God's people need.[22] Then there are two groupings of psalms that are connected to the liturgy of Israel. Psalms 113–118 are the Egyptian Hallel psalms which focus on the theme of deliverance and the Exodus event. They may be related to the Passover celebration.[23] The other group is Psalms 120–134, sometimes called the Songs of Ascents, which are pilgrim psalms sung by people on their way to the feasts at Jerusalem. The focus is on Jerusalem (122), the temple (127), and David (132), with a climax reached in Psalms 135–136 where the LORD is proclaimed as the universal king. At the very heart of Book V is Psalm 119, emphasizing the importance of the law for the community. The final editing of the Psalter reflects the concerns of the post-exilic community related to the promises of the Davidic covenant.[24] Because the structure of the Psalter is concerned with the king and the promises of the Davidic covenant, it has Messianic implications.

So, how should we understand 'the man' in Psalm 1? To whom does 'the man' refer? It is hard to determine the origin of Psalm 1 and whether it was composed specifically to serve as an introduction to the Psalter to emphasize the need to meditate on the psalms as Torah (God's instructions).[25] It is appropriate to conclude that 'the man' who is blessed because he meditates on the law of God refers to any Israelite. Calvin's analysis, which emphasizes the human author and the historical situation, stresses this meaning for the psalm. He makes no connection to Christ.

However, Psalm 1 did become a part of the Psalter and within that context takes on fuller meaning. Book I has a strong Davidic flavor. All the psalms in Book I, except 1–2, 10, and 33, are attributed to David. Psalm 2 is a psalm that explicitly deals with royal themes. Since Book 1 has a strong Davidic emphasis, one must entertain the possibility that 'the man' of Psalm 1 is a reference to the Davidic king.[26] Without denying that Psalm 1 applies to common Israelites, the emphasis on meditating on the law of God for a fruitful life coincides well with the emphasis that the king is to keep a copy of the law with him and read it all the days of his life (Deut. 17:19). Thus if 'the man' in Psalm 1 includes the king, it is a small step to see that 'the man' in Psalm 1 is finally fulfilled in the righteous king, Jesus Christ. A foundation is thus laid for Luther's jump from 'the man' in Psalm 1 to Jesus Christ.

The basis for the development of meaning from 'the man' to any Israelite, to the Davidic king, to Jesus Christ is found in the divine author, who is necessary for a text to have meaning beyond the immediate historical situation.[27] The unfolding of progressive revelation and the unity of the message of Scripture is rooted in the divine author. Since the fullness of revelation did not come until Christ, any Old Testament passage or concept may develop in the unfolding of progressive revelation and the fullness of revelation in Christ. There is great overlap in meaning between the divine author and the human author, but the human author may not fully comprehend the full meaning of his writing because he stands at a point before the completed revelation in Christ.[28]

Although some are concerned that bringing in a divine author in relationship to the meaning of a text opens the door to allegory, or making an Old Testament text say anything that one wants,[29] such fears can be adequately addressed. There are proper limits or controls on the meaning of the text so that an appeal to the divine author in light of the fullness of revelation is not an open door for chaos in meaning.[30] The meaning of a psalm in its original context, whether historical or literary, is foundational for not only understanding the psalm, but also for making correct connections to Christ. One should not bypass the meaning in the original context. But how the concepts of a psalm develop in later revelation is also important. It is thus appropriate to contemplate the meaning of a psalm, or any other Old Testament text, in light of the Old Testament canon. And finally, it is appropriate to analyze the meaning of a psalm in light of the coming of Christ, not because Christ is to be found in every verse of the Old Testament, but because Christ is the goal toward which the Old Testament moves.[31] The major message of the Old Testament, its concepts and ideas, find their fulfillment in Christ.

The next chapter is a more technical chapter that defines the different approaches to the Messianic psalms and reviews the concept of the Messiah in the Psalms. One could skip Chapter 2 and go directly to Chapter 3, where the foundation for the basic thesis of this book is laid out. However, it might be helpful to read 'The Historical Grammatical Approach' in Chapter 2 as background to the Christological Approach that is developed in Chapter 3.

Chapter 2

Different Approaches to the Messianic Psalms

There has not been a consensus among interpreters concerning which particular psalms should be classified as 'Messianic'. Most limit the term 'Messianic' to a particular number of psalms, but the criteria used to define a psalm as 'Messianic' and the psalms that are included within that definition vary greatly among scholars. It is helpful to review a number of proposals in order to understand the issues involved in preaching and teaching Christ from the psalms. What characteristics are necessary for a psalm to be a 'Messianic' psalm?

The Historical-Critical Approach ①

A large number of scholars argue that none of the psalms should be classified as Messianic if the term Messiah refers to a great king that will come in the future. This view received great impetus in the work of Sigmund Mowinckel[1] and has almost reached a consensus[2] among those who follow the historical-critical method of interpreting Scripture.[3] One of the main reasons the psalms are not understood to be Messianic is that the so-called Messianic psalms in their historical context deal only with the king of Israel.

Any hope for the future was centered in an historical king, and after the exile, in the restoration of the monarchy. Kingship always focused on a present or future *historical* king. On the other hand, the Messiah as a future, eschatological figure did not develop until Judaism. The Messiah became the kingly ideal entirely transferred to the future and should not be identified with a specific historical king. Thus the future hope of the Old Testament related to historical kingship is different from the eschatological hope, which looked for a new order on a cosmic scale in the last days. Although the Messianic, eschatological hope developed from ideas connected to the historical king, expectations of a future great king only arose in later Judaism and early Christianity. Thus the Psalms cannot be Messianic.[4]

The Old Testament term for messiah (*māšiaḥ*), which refers to an anointed one, does not historically refer to a future, eschatological ruler. It is used of the anointing of the historical king with oil at the time of his coronation, which was an act of consecration, setting the king aside as a sacred person (1 Sam. 24:6; 26:11).[5] J. J. M. Roberts notes that not one of the 39 occurrences of *māšiaḥ* in the Hebrew canon refers to an expected figure of the future whose coming will coincide with the inauguration of an era of salvation. In the noun form all the occurrences except one refer to the contemporary Israelite king. The use of the term *māšiaḥ* underscores the close relationship between Yahweh and the king whom he has chosen and installed.[6] The reference, however, is to a present, historical king.

Most of those who deny that the psalms are Messianic do see some kind of connection between the future, historical hope expressed in the psalms and the later development of the eschatological Messianic concepts.[7] However, the eschatological *Messianic* hope that developed later was not a concern of the Psalms. John Barton argues that there is a difference between the original meaning of the text of the psalm and the theological doctrine that has been *read back into it*.[8] Joachim Becker claims that a preexilic Messianism is almost a contradiction in terms, because the savior king is in fact present. The immediate historical possibilities are not transcended in the psalms.[9] S. E. Gillingham concludes that the term 'messiah' in the six royal psalms concern the living, reigning monarch and his successors so that its meaning is entirely political and immediate, not prophetic.[10] Aage Bentzen is willing to apply the term 'messiah' to the pre-exilic Israelite king, but he asserts that neither Psalm 2 nor Psalm 110 is concerned with Jesus, because the warlike figure in these psalms has nothing to do with the crucified Mediator of the New Testament. The king in Psalms 2 and 110 might be a type of the Messiah, but the psalms do not deal directly with Christ.[11]

The view that none of the psalms are Messianic would seem to run into a problem because the New Testament looks back to the psalms and understands them as being fulfilled in Jesus the Messiah.[12] It is interesting to see how various scholars try to bridge the gap between the original meaning of the psalm in the context of the Old Testament and the later Messianic meaning given to the psalm. Barton comments that even though the psalms were not originally intended to be Messianic, such Messianic concepts were not totally alien to Judaism. Such concepts developed from earlier insights, such as the realization that God is concerned with political reality and the world order, and the belief that God would in the last days include the Gentiles in the deliverance of Israel.[13] Becker acknowledges that the historical-critical method seems to eliminate the traditional, Messianic expectation of the New Testament because the historical-critical method rules out supernatural manifestations; however, the 'embarrassment' of prophetic prediction in the New Testament cannot be explained away. He tries to hold on to both the historical-critical method and the traditional, Messianic understanding of the New Testament by appealing to the light of faith and the exegetical methods of the New Testament. Thus to find Christ at every step of the way is not only necessary, but a duty imposed on us by the authority of the New Testament.[14] David J. Reimer draws a strong dichotomy between the historically conditioned witness of the Old Testament, which excludes a christological understanding of it, and the anticritical act of faith which finds Christ in the Old

Testament. The Old Testament has to do with history and the New Testament understanding of it has to do with religion. Although a Messianic understanding offends our historical sensibilities, the Old Testament must nourish a Christian understanding of its Messiah because it is primarily a question of religion and not history.[15]

The problem with an approach that denies any Messianic elements in the psalms is that it disconnects the original meaning of the Old Testament from the New Testament.[16] What the psalm intended in its historical setting is not what the New Testament authors understand the psalm to mean. The historical-critical method denies the divine author, which not only destroys the possibility of a prophetic element in the psalms, but also destroys any unified unfolding plan in the Old Testament that could act as a basis for the development of Messianic ideas. On this view it would be very hard to preach Christ from the psalms in a direct way.[17]

The Literary Critical Approach (2)

Most Bible interpreters from the past, and a good number of modern scholars, do acknowledge that there is a Messianic element in the Psalms.[18] However, there is a variety of views concerning the basis for finding a Messianic element in the Psalms and the number of psalms that should be considered Messianic. The literary critical approach moves away from a strictly historical view and emphasizes a more literary view that takes into account the editorial shaping of the Psalter. Although the historical dimension is important, and the usual historical critical approach has many valid observations, James Mays charges the approach with being confined to the historical dimension, which fails to take into account the capacity of literature to shape and recreate reality. The historical critical approach separated David from the psalms and largely dismissed 'the David of the Psalms' as a valid subject of study. To simply negate the Davidic element of the Psalms because it is unhistorical, or to eliminate texts like the psalm titles because they are secondary, destroys the literary context for understanding the psalms.[19]

The literary critical approach finds a legitimate Messianic reference in the psalms in the person of David the king and in the emphasis on the kingdom of God. Thus the royal psalms are key to this view.[20] There is an emphasis on the reinterpretation of the psalms in light of the historical situation of the exile. Clements asks what purpose is served by retaining such a large number of royal psalms for a religious community that had no king and was compelled to live under the jurisdiction of foreign rulers. He answers that these psalms were reinterpreted in the expectation of a time when a new Davidic ruler would appear.[21] Brevard Childs argues that the royal psalms are given an eschatological ring by their position in the Psalter. Thus the psalms were treasured as a witness to the Messianic hope which looked to the consummation of God's kingship through his Anointed One.[22] Mays believes that the relation of David to the psalms is important for the organizing and unifying subject of the Psalter, which he understands to be the kingdom of God. The songs David sponsored are Messianic not because all of them are about the anointed of Israel, but because they are spoken in the knowledge that God has chosen a Messiah and that God will surely keep his promises. Thus David's life itself becomes an illustration of one who lived his life in the hope of the reign of God.[23]

Although the literary critical approach hopes to 'reduce the confused bewilderment that arises when critical study of the Old Testament ignores or refutes popular expectations of OT messianic expectations',[24] it still suffers from a dichotomy between the original meaning of the psalms and the New Testament interpretation. Clements concludes that the way the New Testament interprets the Messianic prophecies of the Old Testament is not precisely the meaning that had come to be attached to them before the New Testament era.[25] There is an attempt to overcome the continuing tension between the historical understanding of the psalm and the later meaning attached to it by the New Testament through the literary angle. The inclusion of the psalms in the Psalter means they ascend to another genre, the genre of Scripture texts. Their new hermeneutical context is the book of Psalms and the other books of the Old Testament. Although in this way they can be understood in relation to Christ, the psalms themselves still do not speak about Jesus of Nazereth because the Jesus of history was not a reference for the psalms. They only speak about the LORD (Yahweh) and his purposes through the Messiah of God. However, this lays the groundwork for the knowledge of the Messiah in the Old Testament, which is important for the later work of Christology.[26] In this view Christ can be preached from the psalms, but only from the royal psalms or from psalms that are directly connected to David or the kingdom of God in some way. Although the literary critical approach opens up avenues in which to preach Christ from the psalms, it still limits the number of psalms which speak of Christ.

The Historical Grammatical Approach

Although there are a variety of views of how to handle the psalms in this approach, they are united by several common ideas. This approach affirms the importance of the divine element in the psalms. Thus there is no problem in acknowledging an aspect of prediction in the psalms as they relate to Christ. Franz Delitzsch argues that Psalm 110 is directly predictive of the Messiah.[27] E. W. Hengstenberg notes the importance of Messianic prediction from the way Christ and the apostles interpreted the psalms. Christ rebuked the Jews for not understanding the Old Testament in reference to him.[28] Even though there is an acknowledgement of a predictive element in the psalms, there is also an emphasis on the historical context in which the psalms were written, especially as they focused on David and his experiences. Hengstenberg comments that many things relate only to David's natural posterity, such as the building of the temple and chastisement for disobedience, but others relate exclusively to the Messiah, such as the repeated assurance of the endless duration of his kingdom.[29] Kaiser especially emphasizes the historical and grammatical elements in interpreting a psalm. He argues that the meaning of an Old Testament passage must reflect the author's own times and historical circumstances, and that the meaning must be grounded in the grammar and syntax of the Old Testament text.[30] Payne notes that a number of psalms receive their accomplishment in David and should not be labeled Messianic just because similar thoughts may appear in the New Testament. Thus Psalm 18:43 only refers to David's foreign conquests, even though Ephesians 2:11-12 may sound similar; and Psalm 24:7 probably only refers to the bringing of the Ark into Jerusalem by David, even though it may be suggestive of the Lord's triumphal entry.[31]

The relationship between the meaning of a psalm in its historical context and its meaning in the New Testament must take into account the unity of the purposes of God and the development of ideas that take place between the Old Testament and the New Testament. Delitzsch argues that the promise of hope related to the seed assumed a Messianic character in relationship to the king of Israel. A decline in the kingship led to an eschatological outlook. Thus he develops five different ways that the Messianic psalms relate to Christ. Many of these ways focus on David and his experiences as typical of the Messiah, especially when the experience of David, or what is said about his kingdom, clearly goes beyond what occurred in the Old Testament context.[32] Kaiser argues that there is a unity to the plan of God that entails both immediate historical fulfillment and a final, climactic fulfillment in the last days. The content of the Old Testament promise grew in accordance with seed thoughts that were contained within its earliest statements.[33] Thus this approach tries to balance the meaning of the psalm in the historical context with its meaning in the New Testament. There is not a dichotomy between the Old Testament meaning and the New Testament meaning, but a real connection.

In the historical grammatical approach Christ can be preached from certain psalms, but not necessarily every psalm.[34] Hengstenberg divides psalms that are legitimately prophetic of the Messiah into two classes. One class of psalms celebrates Christ in his glory and his dominion, which are described by images drawn from the theocracy. These psalms include 2, 45, 72, and 110. In these psalms the Messiah is contemplated as already exalted to glory. The second class of psalms sets forth the suffering of the Messiah. They detail the way in which the Messiah will attain his glory. Psalms in this class include 16, 22, and 40.[35] H. C. Leupold also limits the psalms which are Messianic. He believes Psalms 8, 16, 22, 31:5, and 69:21 are Messianic, and he sees a strictly prophetic element only in Psalms 2, 45, 72, and 110.[36] Both Kaiser and Payne argue that there are 13 Messianic psalms, but their lists are a little different. Kaiser includes Psalms 2, 16, 22, 40, 45, 68, 69, 72, 89, 109, 110, 118, and 132. He deals with Psalms 89 and 132 in connection with the promises to David in 2 Samuel 7. In the section of his book on the Messiah where he deals with the Psalms, he covers Psalms 2 and 110 in general, then examines the rest of the Messianic psalms in light of the predictions they make in the life of the Messiah: the rejection of the Messiah (118), the betrayal of the Messiah (69, 109), the death and resurrection of the Messiah (22, 16), the written plan and marriage of the Messiah (40, 45) and the triumph of the Messiah (68, 72).[37] Payne identifies the Messianic Psalms as 2, 8, 16, 22, 40, 45, 69, 72, 89, 102, 109, 110, and 132. He arrives at the number 13 on the basis of unambiguous New Testament statements concerning these psalms, or, as in Psalm 72, by clear Old Testament reference to the ruler of the eternal Messianic kingdom. Psalms which are cited in the New Testament for the sake of general teaching, illustration, or mere phraseology, or psalms in which the terms of Yahweh's theocratic rule are laid out (96:13), are not included. Only the psalms that are intended to foretell the person and work of Jesus are included.[38]

Although there is much that is positive in the historical grammatical approach, there is no agreement on how to determine whether a psalm is Messianic or on the number of psalms that are Messianic. Leupold lists nine psalms while Kaiser and Payne include thirteen psalms. Even though both Kaiser and Payne have a methodology for determining which psalms are Messianic, they do not agree on which psalms are Messianic. Their lists overlap, except that Payne includes Psalms 8 and 102 in the list, whereas Kaiser has Psalms 68 and 118 instead. Delitzsch, Hengstenberg, and Payne are very dependent on the New Testament for which psalms should be classified as Messianic, whereas Kaiser stresses much more the meaning of the psalm in its historical situation; but ultimately, none of these approaches can explain all the evidence. More psalms than just those listed as Messianic in this approach refer to Christ. This can be demonstrated in how the New Testament uses other psalms than the traditional Messianic psalms to refer to Christ. In other words, Christ can be preached from more than just these Messianic psalms.

In order to show the difficulty of limiting the number of psalms which refer to Christ, the comprehensive work by Gerard Van Groningen will be reviewed.[39] He analyzes the concept Messiah (*māšiaḥ*) and distinguishes a narrower view from a wider view. The narrower view relates to the king as the anointed one. A psalm can be considered Messianic if it deals with the person of the king. However, if only psalms that deal with the person of the king are Messianic, then the number of Messianic psalms is limited severely. The wider view of Messiah refers to any additional aspects involved in the reign of the king, including the promises of salvation, the work that must be done to carry out those promises, the persons required in addition to the king, the realm over which the Messiah reigns, and the results of his reign. Thus passages that deal with the wider work of the Messiah should also be considered Messianic.[40] Because this wider view includes the work of the Messiah, which entails priestly as well as prophetic aspects, Messianic psalms are broader than the royal psalms, which deal specifically with the person of the king.[41] Van Groningen analyzes the following psalms as Messianic: 2, 8, 12, 16, 20, 21, 22, 40, 41, 45, 68, 69, 101, 102, 109, 110, 118, and 129. He also has a section entitled 'Kingdom Psalms,' which includes a brief discussion of 2, 22, 93, and 72.[42]

Even with such a detailed analysis of which psalms are Messianic, some psalms seem to fall through the cracks. Psalm 97:7 is directly applied to Jesus in Hebrews 1:6: 'Let all the angels of God worship Him.' Psalm 31:5 is spoken by Jesus from the cross in Luke 23:46, 'Into your hands I commit my spirit.' Psalm 31 does not have any of the characteristics of a Messianic psalm noted above, and yet it is found in the mouth of the Messiah in the context of his work of salvation. Perhaps the omission of Psalm 31 from the above lists is an oversight, but there seems to be something else that is important for understanding the psalms in relationship to the Messiah. Not just those psalms that directly mention the king or aspects of his reign and kingdom are Messianic psalms. The New Testament implies that all psalms have a relationship to Jesus Christ. Thus Psalm 31, which in its Old Testament context does not seem to have a Messianic emphasis, is messianic in the sense that it refers to the person or work of Jesus Christ, as is clearly shown in its use in Luke 23:46. This does not mean we are dependent on the New Testament for which psalms are Messianic because a broader principle is at work, a principle rooted in Jesus' statements in Luke 24:44-47. The next chapter will develop this principle, which is the basis for the view that all the psalms relate to the person and/or work of Jesus Christ.

Chapter 3

The Christological Approach (4)
to the Messiah in the Psalms

The approach developed here has much in common with the historical grammatical approach. It sees the importance of the historical context, the grammar of the Old Testament text, the literary characteristics of the text, and what the text teaches about God (theology). What is distinctive about this approach is that it recognizes the significance of the divine author for interpreting the Old Testament, not just the human author, and sees the New Testament as a guide to how we can approach the psalms.[1]

An Analysis of Luke 24:
How Jesus Understood the Old Testament

The view that all the psalms have some relationship to Christ is based on several factors. An important one is Jesus' own statements about his relationship to the Old Testament. A key text is Luke 24:26-27, 44-47, where Jesus helps two disciples on the road to Emmaus, and then the rest of the disciples, to understand the Scriptures. They still had not understood the significance of the events they had witnessed in the life and death of Jesus and how those events related to the Scriptures. Jesus rebukes the two on the road to Emmaus for being 'slow of heart to believe' (24:25) and instructs them concerning the right way to understand the Old Testament. Because these verses set forth Jesus' hermeneutical approach to the Old Testament, they are foundational for any methodology for preaching Christ from the Old Testament.[2]

It is significant that when Jesus speaks about the Old Testament in relationship to himself, he speaks about the Old Testament in a comprehensive way. There is the repeated use of the word 'all', twice in relationship to the prophets (Luke 24:25, 27), and twice in reference to the Scriptures (24:27, 44). Jesus mentions the three-fold section of the Old Testament canon (24:44), which makes it clear that all the Old Testament is included: the law of Moses, the Prophets, and the Psalms.[3] Because Jesus does not mention any specific Old Testament texts there is discussion concerning which Old Testament texts Jesus had in mind. I. Howard Marshall emphasizes that Jesus has in view the texts in the Old Testament that are specifically Messianic.[4] Others underscore the texts in Luke and Acts that are foundational for the ministry of Jesus.[5] Although it is important to call attention to these texts, the comprehensive nature of Jesus' reference to the Old Testament is meant to demonstrate that all the Old Testament speaks of Jesus in some way,[6] not merely those texts commonly accepted as 'Messianic'. Thus Jesus himself gives the divine authorization for reading all the Old Testament in reference to him.[7]

There is also an emphasis in Jesus' words on the divine necessity of the events of his life, seen in the use of *dei* twice in these verses. In Luke 24:26 Jesus asks a rhetorical question that expects a 'yes' answer and in 24:44 he states that the things written in the Old Testament *must* be fulfilled. The crucifixion and the resurrection were not haphazard events but were part of God's plan already revealed in the Old Testament. This has tremendous implications for how the Old Testament should be approached. If there is a divine necessity attached to the Old Testament revelation in relationship to the events of Jesus' life, then one would expect that the Old Testament would exhibit a fair degree of unity related to the outworking of God's plan and purposes. In other words, we should approach the Old Testament with the expectation that God is working out his plan in preparation for the coming of Christ. The critical approach of seeing in the Old Testament diverse theologies that do not always fit together is not an approach that fits with Jesus' words. Also, if all the Old Testament relates to Jesus, then narrowly defining the concept of the Messiah and limiting it to the historical king is necessarily faulty.[8] The argument that there is in the Old Testament no concept of a suffering Messiah[9] fails to see how the various concepts in the Old Testament relate together. Certainly Jesus in Luke 24:46 understands the Old Testament to speak of the Christ who must suffer.[10]

If Jesus is the fulfillment of the Old Testament Scriptures, then the Old Testament itself must be seen as preparatory and incomplete, moving toward the coming of the One who would fulfill all things. Thus the Old Testament is anticipatory and always looking ahead. If the Old Testament is anticipatory and preparatory, then one would expect to see development in the Old Testament related to the coming of the Messiah. God's plan progresses throughout the redemptive history of the Old Testament, finding its culmination in Christ. This implies that the Old Testament cannot be fully understood apart from the fulfillment of it in Jesus Christ. Jesus rebukes the disciples for not understanding the Old Testament in light of his ministry, which fulfilled the Old Testament. Thus we cannot properly understand the Old Testament apart from the work of Jesus Christ, and so it is appropriate to read the Old Testament through Christological lenses. Such an approach does not mean that the grammar of the Old Testament is unimportant, nor does it mean the historical and literary contexts of the Old Testament should be ignored, but it does mean that the Old Testament is not fully understood until it is read in light of its fulfillment in Jesus Christ.[11]

It follows from the above that Jesus can be preached from all the Old Testament, and thus from the entire Psalter. But how can Christ be preached from all the Psalms? In Luke 24:25-27 and 44-47 Jesus relates the fulfillment of the Old Testament primarily to his work, that is, his suffering, death, resurrection, and entrance into glory. But he also connects the witness of the disciples to the Old Testament. They would preach repentance and remission of sins *in His name*. This witness is also a fulfillment of the Old Testament Scriptures. The mention of Jesus' name is important, for in the Old Testament the name LORD (Yahweh) is full of authority, which is now fully exercised by the glorified Jesus.[12] In other words, not just what Jesus does but who Jesus is becomes significant. If one accepts the New Testament witness that Jesus is equal to the Father, and therefore is God,[13] then whenever the Psalms speak of God, or use the covenant name Yahweh, they also speak of the person of Christ. Thus in preaching from the Psalms, it is important to understand a particular psalm in its historical and literary context, and then to think how the psalm relates to the person and/or work of Christ. The person of Christ refers to his humanity and deity, and all aspects of the work of Christ can be summarized in his role as prophet, priest, or king.

The use of the Old Testament term 'anointed' or 'messiah' lays a foundation for the importance of prophet, priest, and king in relationship to Jesus. The verb *māšak* means 'to anoint with oil', an activity associated with inauguration and dedication. It initiated a person or object into a new form of service or use, which set that person or object apart from other forms of service or use. The verb is used in the inauguration of the tabernacle and priesthood (between Exod. 25:6 and Num. 7:88 it is used 54 times), as well as the anointing of kings (between 1 Sam. 2:10 and 1 Kings 5:1 it is used 34 times). The noun *māšiaḥ* refers to someone who has been set apart and empowered by God for service. It is used of priests (Lev. 4:3) and prophets (Ps. 105:15), but is mainly used of the king.[14] The LXX translated *māšiaḥ* with *Christos* (Χριστός), which is used of Jesus in the New Testament. These Old Testament offices were preparatory for the full work of salvation and the fullness of revelation that would come in Jesus, the Messiah.

The New Testament Use of the Psalms

The approach that all the psalms relate to Christ, not just the traditional Messianic psalms, is the way the New Testament treats the psalms. The traditional Messianic psalms are considered Messianic by scholars because they are explicitly quoted in the New Testament. The following chart shows how the New Testament uses the traditional Messianic psalms:

Psalm	New Testament Citation
2:7	Acts 13:33
8:2	Matthew 21:16; Mark 12:36
8:4-6	Hebrews 2:6-8; Mark 14:62
8:6	1 Corinthians 15:27; Luke 20:42-43
16:8-11	Acts 2:25-28; Luke 22:69
16:10	Acts 13:35; Acts 2:34-35
22:1	Matthew 27:46; Hebrews 1:13; Mark 15:34
22:18	John 19:24; Luke 20:17
22:22	Hebrews 2:12; Acts 4:11
40:6-8	Hebrews 10:5-7;
45:6-7	Hebrews 1:8-9
68:18	Ephesians 4:8; Mark 12:10-11
69:4	John 15:25
69:9	John 2:17; Mark 11:9-10; Romans 15:3; John 12:13
69:25	Acts 1:20
89:20	Acts 13:22; Luke 13:35
109:8	Acts 1:20; Luke 19:38
110:1	Matthew 22:44; Hebrews 1:5; 5:5; Matthew 26:64
110:4	Hebrews 5:6; 7:17, 21
118:22-23	Matthew 21:42; 1 Peter 2:7
118:25-26	Matthew 21:9
118:26	Matthew 23:39
132:11	Acts 2:30

But there are other psalms cited in the New Testament that do not make the official Messianic list, which demonstrates that any list is short-sighted, especially in light of Luke 24:44. The following chart lists psalms besides the traditional Messianic psalms that are specifically cited in the New Testament in relationship to Christ.

Psalm	New Testament Citation
31:5	Luke 23:46
35:19	John 15:25
41:9	John 13:18
78:2	Matthew 13:35
102:25-27	Hebrews 1:10-12

Someone might argue that the Messianic psalms should be limited to the two lists above, but then what does one do with all the allusions to the Psalms in the New Testament which relate to Christ? Here is a partial list of some of those allusions: 6:3 in John 12:27; 7:9 in Revelation 2:23; 10:16 in Revelation 11:15; 17:15 in Revelation 22:4; 18:4 in Acts 2:24; 23:1 in John 10:11; 28:4 in Matthew 16:27; 34:29 in John 19:36; 38:11 in Luke 23:49; and 41:9 in Matthew 26:23. Many more allusions from psalms that are not considered to be traditionally Messianic psalms could be listed.[15] If the Scripture is our standard of authority for what we believe, the New Testament should be our standard of authority for the methodology we use to interpret the Old Testament.[16]

The Psalms as the Prayers of Jesus

Another dimension that gives insight into the relationship of the psalms to Jesus is to reflect on the psalms as the prayers of Jesus. There is a general consensus that the psalms were part of the worship of Israel.[17] It is also evident that the psalms were prayers prayed by God's people.[18] The use of the Psalter by the Jewish community has implications for a Messianic understanding of the psalms because the Messiah himself would have sung and prayed the psalms. Mark 14:26 and Matthew 26:30 state that before Jesus and the disciples left the Passover to go to the Mt. of Olives, they sang a hymn. It is possible that the Hallel Psalms (113–118) were used as a part of the Passover celebration for they focus on the Exodus (Psalm 114) and general themes of deliverance.[19] It is interesting to read these psalms in light of the events that faced Jesus. As William Lane points out, Jesus would have pledged to keep his vows in the presence of all the people (116:12-19), called upon the Gentiles to join in the praise of God (117), and would have concluded with steadfast confidence in his ultimate triumph, 'I shall not die, but live, to declare the works of the Lord.' Jesus would go to Gethsemane with Psalm 118 on his lips.[20] As our mediator he sang and prayed the psalms.

The book of Hebrews represents the psalms as the words of Jesus in 2:12 and 10:5-7.[21] Hebrews 2:12 puts Psalm 22:22 on the lips of Jesus. The first part of Psalm 22 is a lament and is used in the New Testament as a description of the death of Christ. Psalm 22:1 is his cry from the cross (Matt. 27:46; Mark 15:34). Psalm 22:22 comes from the section of the psalm that moves from lament to praise, and is used in Hebrews to stress the solidarity of Jesus with those he came to save. It was necessary for him to take on flesh and blood in order to secure our salvation (2:14), but also to act as our high priest (2:17-18). It is also interesting that the words of Isaiah the prophet are put into the mouth of Jesus (2:13 quotes from Isa. 8:17b-18).[22] In Isaiah 7–12 the names of Isaiah's children underscore the necessity of trusting in God as King Ahaz and Judah face the threat of invasion (Isa. 7). The experience of Isaiah and Jesus are parallel in that they trust in God in the midst of a crisis. Both the prophet and his children and Christ and his brothers stand before God.[23]

Hebrews 10:5-7 puts Psalm 40:6-8 (vv. 5-7 in the Hebrew) on the lips of Jesus in connection with his incarnation,[24] which is viewed as an act of submission to God's will. In contrast to the ineffectiveness of the Old Testament sacrifices of bulls and goats, Christ offered his body[25] in submission to the will of God[26] as a complete and effective sacrifice.[27] There is an emphasis in Hebrews 2 on the humanity of Jesus and his role as prophet (at least indirectly with the Isaiah connection). His work as priest is at the heart of the quotation from Psalm 40:6-8 in Hebrews 10:5-7. The fact that the book of Hebrews places some psalms on the lips of Jesus lays the basis for understanding all the psalms as the prayers of Christ in his role as our Mediator.[28] This aspect will be developed further in the discussion of how Christ can pray the psalms of confession (see Chapter 5).

A Methodology for Preaching and Teaching the Psalms in relationship to the Person and Work of Christ

The purpose of this section is to briefly lay out a way the psalms can be studied that gives the proper emphasis to the Old Testament context, but also reflects on how the psalm is connected to Jesus Christ. The first step in understanding a psalm is to become familiar with the psalm. The psalm should be read and reread in a variety of translations.[29] As the psalm is read through a number of times, any questions or comments that come to mind should be written down. The following questions are particularly helpful in studying a psalm: (1)Where do the structural breaks in the psalm occur? This will help divide the psalm into its major sections. (2)What is the mood of the psalm? (3)Since all the psalms are poetry, one should ask whether there are any word pictures (metaphors) or any other poetic devices in the psalm.[30] (4)Are there key words or concepts that are repeated in the psalm? (5)What seems to be the major idea in the psalm? These questions will help define the type of psalm it is (see the discussion concerning genre in the next chapter), which will aid in understanding the message of the psalm.

Commentaries are invaluable to help answer some of the above questions, to help point out things that may have been missed in the study of the psalm, or to help refine one's thinking in relationship to a psalm.[31] Commentaries may also help answer the following questions: (1)What is the setting of the psalm? Can the psalm be related to a particular historical situation? Is there evidence for how the psalm is used in the worship of Israel? (2)Is there any significance to the literary placement of the psalm in the Psalter? Are there significant connections with other psalms that are adjacent to the psalm under study? These questions can give further understanding of the meaning of a psalm in its Old Testament context.[32]

Once the psalm is understood in its Old Testament context it is appropriate to reflect how the psalm relates to Christ. There are a variety of ways this can be done. One can think of the person of Christ and ask the following questions: (1)Does the psalm describe God in ways that relate to the deity of Christ? Here the connection between the Old Testament LORD (Yahweh) and the New Testament Lord (*kyrios*) can be significant, especially as it relates to the concepts of Creator or Redeemer. (2)Does the psalm describe the proper role of a human being as created by God, or does it set forth human response to a particular situation? There may be appropriate connections to the humanity of Christ as he faced a variety of life situations. Reflecting on the psalm as the prayer of Christ can be very fruitful in order to see even more clearly his humanity (Heb. 5:7).

One can also think on the redemptive work of Christ and ask the following questions: (1)Are the major concepts of the psalm related to the work of Christ as king? Here the royal psalms become very significant. (2)Are the major concepts of the psalm related to the work of Christ as prophet? Any psalm that emphasizes the Word of God or the teaching of the Word of God would be important here, particularly the wisdom psalms. (3)Are the major concepts of the psalm related to the work of Christ as priest? Psalms that stress sacrifice, obedience, or confession could relate to this aspect of the work of Christ.[33]

The above questions are only guidelines to help a person think through ways that a psalm could relate to Christ. There may be overlap between some of the categories. For example, thinking of how a psalm relates to the person of Christ in his humanity may overlap with thinking of how a psalm relates to the person of Christ as priest. It is also important to emphasize that there is not just one way to relate a psalm to Christ. Several avenues may be appropriately developed, which is in line with the way the New Testament uses the psalms. For example, Jesus quotes

Psalm 8:2 in Matthew 21:16 to support the cry of the children in the temple, 'Hosanna to the Son of David,' over against the objection of the chief priests and scribes. The title 'son of David' has clear Messianic implications, setting Jesus apart as the one from the line of David who would be the king.[34] The book of Hebrews quotes from Psalm 8:5-6 to show that Jesus fulfills the original creation purposes for human beings and that he has human solidarity with those he came to save (Heb. 2:11: 'he is not ashamed to call them brothers'). Thus one psalm can relate to various aspects of Jesus' work, but so can one verse. Psalm 2:7 ('You are my Son, today I have begotten you') is quoted in Acts 13:33 as fulfilled in the resurrection of Jesus. The book of Hebrews uses Psalm 2:7 to show Jesus' superiority to the angels, and then in 5:5 to answer the objection of how Jesus can be high priest if he was from the tribe of Judah: he was called and appointed by God. The sonship of Christ in Psalm 2:7 is not only connected with the resurrection and exaltation of Jesus, but is also related to the priesthood, corresponding to the combination of deity and humanity in the person of the Mediator.[35] The complexity of the person of Christ as both human and divine allows a psalm to relate to Christ in more than one way.[36] In the expositions of the psalms in the following chapters, the goal is not to be exhaustive, but suggestive, as to how a psalm relates to Christ.

One of the main goals of this chapter has been to demonstrate that Christ can be preached from all the psalms. All the psalms relate in one way or another to the person and/or work of Christ. This approach does not deny that there are some psalms that speak more directly of Christ, and they have traditionally been called the Messianic psalms. But if all the psalms relate to the person and/or work of Christ, then all the psalms are messianic (with a small 'm').[37] These can be called indirect messianic psalms. Although there is no absolute agreement about which psalms are directly Messianic (with a capital 'M'), the precise number is not all that significant if all the psalms relate to the person and/or work of Christ. However, it may be helpful to use Messianic (with a capital 'M') when referring to psalms that traditionally have been considered directly Messianic,[38] and to use messianic (with a small 'm') for other psalms. It is also a useful way to deal with the psalms in the rest of this book. The next several chapters will show how to preach Christ from psalms that traditionally have not been considered to be Messianic.

Chapter 4

Indirect Messianic Psalms: Psalms of Orientation

If all the psalms are related to the person and/or work of Christ, an exposition of all the psalms would be appropriate; however, that is beyond the scope of this book. Enough sample psalms will be examined to lay a foundation for preaching Christ from all the different types of psalms. The psalms will be approached through the concept of genre because genre helps to understand the meaning of a psalm.

The Genres of the Psalms
The psalms are commonly grouped into literary categories called genres according to their structure, mood, and content.[1] Most people engage in genre analysis even if they are not aware of it. For example, if you pick up a piece of paper and it begins 'Dear Sally' you know that you are reading a letter. Letters have a certain structure. If what you are reading begins 'Once upon a time' you know that you are reading a fairy tale, and you already know how it will end – 'and they lived happily ever after'.[2] The significance of genre is that a letter will be read differently from a fairy tale. A particular genre produces certain expectations in the reader and

so is related to how a text is understood.[3] The meaning of the Song of Solomon is affected by the genre determination of allegory or love poetry. A genre analysis of the psalms can help someone better understand a psalm. Grouping psalms together that are similar in structure, mood, and content can aid the understanding of individual psalms in that particular group.[4]

There are several different ways one can approach the genres in the Psalms.[5] One approach identifies seven distinct types of genres. These types are the hymn, the lament, thanksgiving psalms, psalms of confidence, psalms of remembrance, wisdom psalms, and royal or kingship psalms.[6] It is also helpful to divide these seven genres into three broader categories related to their outlook on life: psalms of orientation, disorientation, and new orientation.[7] Although the focus will be on how the psalms relate to Christ, it should be evident that the psalms are beneficial for our use as prayers, hymns, and for purposes of meditation and instruction. The rest of this chapter will examine sample psalms under hymns, wisdom psalms, and psalms of confidence to show how psalms in each category can be related to the person and/or work of Christ.

Psalms of Orientation: The Blessings of Life

Psalms of orientation emphasize that life is oriented toward God and a person is experiencing seasons of well-being that evoke gratitude for the constancy of God's blessing. These psalms articulate joy, delight, goodness, the coherence of life, and the reliability of God. The types of psalms that fall into this broad category are the hymns, the psalms of confidence, and some wisdom psalms.

The Hymn[8]

Hymns are full of praise to the LORD from beginning to end and display a universal and cosmic dimension.[9] Hymns generally follow a three-fold structure: exhortations to praise God, reasons given why God should be praised, and then further exhortations to praise God.[10] Some psalms which are hymns are 8, 29, 33,

46–48, 93, 94–100, 103, 104, 111, 113, 114, 117, and 145–150. The hymns can be further delineated according to subject matter, usually focusing on God as Creator, Redeemer, or Lord of history.[11]

Psalm 103: Covenant Blessings for God's Covenant People

Psalm 103 is a straightforward hymn that calls on all creation to praise God for his covenant faithfulness. Although some label this psalm a song of thanksgiving,[12] it is not a response to a specific situation[13] and exuberant praise dominates the psalm. There is a call to praise the LORD (Yahweh) in verses 1-2, reasons for why the LORD should be praised dominate verses 3-19, and the psalm ends with a call for the LORD's works to praise him in verses 20-22. The psalm begins with the psalmist exhorting himself to praise (vv. 1-2), it broadens into exhortations for all creation to praise God (vv. 21-22), and it ends with a final self-exhortation to praise God. Such exhortation shows how easy it is to forget to praise God for his benefits and to fall into a non-praising attitude of life.[14] Praise should be a constant response on our part as we remember the great things God has done. With our whole being we are to join with all creation to offer to God the totality of praise[15] that is due him. May our whole lives be an offering of praise.[16]

The major section of Psalm 103 that highlights the reasons the Lord should be praised (vv. 3-19) focuses on the benefits he pours out on his people, which flow from his character. These benefits are blessings that flow from a covenant relationship with God, covenant blessings poured out on his covenant people.[17] Forgiveness (v. 3) is the plea of Moses in Exodus 34:9 after the golden calf incident and characteristically comes as a result of the sacrifices offered at the tabernacle (Lev. 4–5; 1 Kings 8:30, 34). The healing of diseases (v. 3) is a promise God makes to his people after the Exodus from Egypt. If they obey him he will heal their diseases (Exod. 15:26). Covenant curse is presented as not being healed (Deut. 28:27, 35). Redemption (v. 4) is a key term that describes God's deliverance of his people from Egypt (Exod. 6:6; 15:13). Although the meaning of the phrase 'satisfies your mouth with good things' (v. 5) is debated,[18] eating to full satisfaction is a covenant blessing promised God's people (Lev. 25:19; 26:5) and not eating to full satisfaction is a part of covenant curse (Lev. 26:26).

These covenant blessings flow from the character of the covenant-keeping God. Three times God is called a God of mercy (vv. 8, 11, 17). The Hebrew word is *ḥesed*, an important word in the Old Testament that stresses God's covenant loyalty. He faithfully fulfills his covenant promises, which is demonstrated in the way he treats his covenant people. The incident referred to in verses 7-8 is the plea of Moses after the golden calf episode where God displayed his abundant faithfulness by not destroying the people of Israel. Just as he treated his people in gracious ways that they did not deserve, so he treats covenant sinners the same way. In a series of comparisons the psalmist demonstrates God's ways (vv. 11-14). He does not treat us as we deserve and removes far from us that which causes offense. This response of God is not an isolated event, but is rooted in his everlasting character and is demonstrated to future generations of covenant children (vv. 17-18).

Psalm 103 is a hymn of praise to the God who demonstrates faithfulness to his covenant by pouring out covenant blessings on his undeserving people. Once the meaning of this psalm is developed in its Old Testament context, connections to Christ can be seen. Concerning the person of Christ, everything said about the LORD (Yahweh) can be said about Christ. Christ is worthy of our individual praise, for his name is set apart ('holy') because it is above every other name (103:1; Phil. 2:9-11). His throne is set in heaven (103:19) as he sits at the right hand of the Father. Christ is worthy of being praised by all 'his works' because he is the Creator, the one through whom all things came into being (103:22; John 1:3).

Concerning the redemptive work of Christ, as mediator of the covenant Christ not only faithfully fulfills the terms of the covenant (Luke 22:20; 1 Tim. 2:5; Heb. 3:1), but he also dispenses covenant blessings. In Mark 2:1-12 the power to forgive sins is demonstrated by the healing of the paralytic. The scribes doubt whether Jesus has the power to forgive sins, reasoning in their hearts, 'Who can forgive sins but God alone?' (Mark 2:7). To demonstrate his power to forgive sins Jesus heals the paralytic. Matthew 8:16-17 notes that Jesus cast out spirits with a word and healed all who were sick. Luke 4:40-41 mentions healing and the casting out of demons as a part of Jesus' work as the Christ (the Messiah). Christ is also the one 'who redeems your life from destruction' (103:4) and 'who satisfies your mouth with good things' (103:5). These refer to the full salvation that Christ has accomplished. He has come for deliverance (Matt. 2:15) and to give abundant, everlasting life (John 5:24, 10:10). Jesus offers food and drink that will fully satisfy (John 6:35, 4:13-14). Justice for the oppressed (103:6) and treating people with mercy (103:10) can also be demonstrated in the life of Jesus (Matt. 9:9-11; Mark 2:15-17). He is the one who dispenses covenant blessings to undeserving sinners. These blessings can be related to his work as priest and king. Although we experience those blessings now as God's people, the fullness of those blessings await the consummation. In the new heavens and the new earth our full salvation (spiritual and physical) will finally be ours. How can those who have experienced his covenant blessings not praise his name?

Psalm 93: The Lord Reigns – Divine Help in a Chaotic World
Psalm 93 is a hymn that focuses on the kingship of the LORD (Yahweh) in a world that seems so unstable. Instead of beginning with exhortations to praise God it sets forth Yahweh as king and the implications of his kingship for the world. Thus as we read or sing this psalm we are led to exalt the LORD who reigns over all.

The opening proclamation of Psalm 93 (the LORD reigns[19]) and the subject matter of the psalm is very similar to Psalms 94–99. Many group these psalms together as Yahweh kingship psalms (93–99),[20] which would remind God's people that Yahweh is on the throne and is in complete control of the universe.[21] Psalm 93 begins with a description of the LORD as king in terms of how he is dressed. Although God does not really have clothes, he is presented here in the manner in which a king would be dressed. Kings wear robes and the splendor of their power and might are displayed in their robes. Yahweh has a robe that no earthly king can match, for he is robed in majesty, a word that emphasizes God's glory.[22] Yahweh is also represented as having 'girded himself with strength'. This phrase means to be ready for action[23] and can refer to being ready for military battle (2 Sam. 22:40; Ps. 18:39), which fits the content of verses 3-4 of Psalm 93. Yahweh is presented as having a splendor and majesty that is greater than any other king, and he is ready and prepared to enter into battle on behalf of his people. No enemy can ultimately defeat those who have Yahweh as king.

The rest of the psalm gives further evidence of the superior majesty of Yahweh as it sets forth the results of his reign over the world. Yahweh is in complete charge of the universe, demonstrated in the fact that he has always been king and that the world is firmly established (vv. 1b-2). At the heart of the psalm is the declaration that Yahweh is mightier than the floods and the waters, which lift up their voice and make a great noise (vv. 3-4). Reading these words one might think of the ocean with its powerful, pounding waves. But there is something more going on in Psalm 93 than is at first apparent to us. It becomes apparent, however, if we put ourselves back into the world of the ancient Israelites. In the pagan beliefs of that day there was a battle among the gods for who would be king of the world. One of those gods was the sea god, whose name was Yam (the Hebrew word for sea).[24] Yam and the sea monsters battled with Baal for supremacy. We can find references to these ideas in many places of Scripture. For example, Psalm 89:9-10 states:

> You rule over the surging sea;
> when its waves mount up, you still them.
> You crushed Rahab, like one of the slain;
> with your strong arm you scattered your enemies.

Rahab can refer to the power and might of Egypt (Isa. 30:7). However, in Isaiah 51:9, Rahab is used in parallel with 'the dragon' (NASB), a reference to the chaos monster of pagan mythology. These ideas are not mentioned because there is any truth to them, but there is a war of ideas taking place. Yahweh is greater and more powerful than these false gods. He has defeated them. This battle is at the heart of Psalm 93:3-4. The torrential powers of the waters is a picture of chaotic forces unleashed in this world. The seas have lifted up their pounding waves. The forces of chaos have asserted their power to claim rule of the universe, but God is mightier than the sea. Thus the Israelites understood that in a world of instability, there is someone who provides permanence, and in a world of chaos, there is someone who is in control. The LORD, and no one else, is king. He has no rival. The LORD reigns!

Psalm 93 closes by reminding God's people of the benefits of having Yahweh as king, which should lead to further praise of God. Just as the world is firmly established, so also God's 'decrees/ testimonies' are established and sure. God has given his people the law to guide them in how to live their lives. This majestic God of splendor has also established his presence among his people, for verse 5 mentions the holiness of God's house, a reference to the temple as God's earthly throne and place of his presence.

Psalm 93 affirms that even though the world is a chaotic place and seems out of control at times, Yahweh is the king who is in control, who fights for his people, and who provides his presence and guidance in this world. Although in Psalm 93 the kingship of Yahweh is in view, partly as a response to the demise of the earthly king, the two sides of divine and human kingship come together in Jesus Christ.[25] He is the Son of David and he is also the Lord who rules the universe as king on behalf of his people (Phil. 2:11; Eph. 1:20-22). Jesus is the one who entered into the battle for us and defeated all our enemies. As our human representative Jesus could have prayed to the Lord to save him from the power of death and the evil one. However, in his death, burial, and resurrection he secured our victory over death so that now nothing can defeat us as his people (Col. 2:15). His presence, now manifested through the outpouring of the Spirit, empowers us to live for his glory and do battle with the enemy (Eph. 6:10-18). His word continues to give strength, encouragement, and direction. No matter what we are facing in life, our victory is secure in Jesus. One day he will come back and his kingship will be evident to everyone. All will bow before him and we will live in the glory of the victory he has accomplished for us.

Wisdom Psalms

Another type of psalm that falls under the category of Psalms of Orientation is the wisdom psalm. Although there is not a consensus on the number of criteria that distinguishes a wisdom psalm, or the number of psalms that fit this genre,[26] many scholars use the criteria of style and/or content to define a wisdom psalm. Stylistic characteristics include the formula 'blessed,' numerical sayings, 'better-than' sayings, an address of a teacher to a son, alphabetic structure, simple comparisons, and admonition.[27] The themes that are prominent in wisdom literature include the contrast between the righteous and the wicked, the two ways, preoccupation with the problem of retribution (the deed-consequence relationship), practical advice regarding conduct, and the fear of the Lord.[28] Wisdom has also been associated with creation[29] and torah (instruction).[30] The wisdom psalms in the category of Psalms of Orientation emphasize the order and blessings of life in creation (Ps. 19), the law (Pss. 19, 119), family (Pss. 127, 128), community (Ps. 133), and the contrast between the righteous and the wicked (Pss. 1, 49, 112).[31]

Psalm 19: The Glorious Effect of God's Revelation

One of the major problems of Psalm 19 is the unity of the psalm. The first part of the psalm deals with creation (vv. 1-6) and God is addressed as El. The second part of the psalm deals with the law (vv. 7-14) and God is addressed as the LORD (Yahweh). Although the relationship between these two parts of the psalm has been debated,[32] the unity of the psalm can be seen in the theme of God's revelation in creation and the law, which leads many to recognize this psalm as a wisdom psalm.[33]

The first part of Psalm 19 declares that creation testifies to the glory of God. There is a movement from the general description of the heavens, skies, and the earth in verses 1-4 to the specific focus of the sun in verses 5-6.[34] The verbs in verse 1 stress proclamation and the concepts in verses 2-4 emphasize information that comes from creation. This proclamation by creation never lets up but is continuous.[35] The testimony of creation is unusual in that it is silent,[36] but it goes out to all the earth[37] so that no one can escape it (v. 4a). The sun is set forth in verses 4b-6 as a glorious example of how creation declares the glory of God. It is constant as it rises each day, and it is universal in that nothing is hidden from its heat. The sun displays the glory of God in a powerful way in its bright heat, in its radiance that shines like the joy of the bridegroom,[38] and in its strength like a warrior who sets out on his course.[39]

The universal nature of God's revelation in creation has theological significance. God has not left himself without a witness. Even though he had a special relationship with Israel his glory is evident throughout the whole world. Paul develops the implications of God's universal revelation in creation in Romans 1:18-20, where instead of specifically mentioning the glory of God, he states how the wrath of God is revealed against unrighteousness.[40] Paul notes that God's invisible characteristics, especially his power and divine nature, can be seen from creation, so that people are without excuse before God. God's revelation in creation is general enough to give people the knowledge of God's power and glory leaving them without excuse, but it is not sufficient to show the way of salvation through faith (Romans 3:21-26). This means that even though Jesus Christ is identified as Creator (John 1:3), there is not enough knowledge in creation by itself to come to that conclusion. Further revelation is needed beyond what God has revealed in creation, which is developed in Psalm 19:7-14.

The transition from one part of the psalm to the other seems abrupt, marked by a change of subject matter and the use of the name the LORD (Yahweh). The characteristics of the law and its effects now come into view. The structured nature of verses 7-9 sets forth the comprehensive nature of the law for human life, and so parallels the sun in verse 6, which dominates the sky. The law itself can be life-imparting or scorching.[41]

The law is described with the following pattern: law synonym + Yahweh + adjective + participle + a noun affected.[42] The following chart shows the pattern:

Law synonym	Adjective	Participle + noun
Torah (law)	perfect	reviving the soul
Testimony	sure	making wise the simple
Precepts	right	rejoicing the heart
Commandment	pure	enlightening the eyes
Fear	clean	enduring forever
Rules	true	righteous altogether[43]

The law synonyms are all related to the covenant and focus on a particular aspect of the law. Torah in a broad sense refers to instruction. Testimony and Precepts are often synonymous with the covenant, the former stresses the witness character of the law in that it warns and instructs,[44] while the latter emphasizes the guidance of the law.[45] Commandment is a synonym for law,[46] and Rules, perhaps better translated 'Judgments,' is a term that describes what should take place in a particular case.[47] It is the term used for the case law of the covenant. The 'Fear of the LORD,' in parallel with other terms for the law, could refer to what God's revelation demands in the sense that it is the revealed way in which God is to be feared.[48]

The middle column lists a characteristic of the law. The first one is the most comprehensive and may serve as the basis for the rest.[49] The word 'perfect' stresses the sufficiency of the law.[50] The law is 'sure' in the sense that it is trustworthy and provides trustworthy guidance.[51] The law is 'right' in the sense that it is straight, not crooked or perverse.[52] The law is 'pure' (*bārāh*), a word that can mean clear, brilliant, radiant, and is often connected with the sun.[53] The law is 'clean', which stresses its ethical purity.[54] The faithfulness and accomplished certainty of the law comes out in the words 'true and righteous,' which brings the list to a close.

The effect of the law can be seen in the third column. The law revives life, bringing restoration and refreshment, gives wisdom to those who lack it, brings joy to the heart, enlightenment to the eyes – and it endures forever. It is obvious that the law is clearer and more powerful in its effects upon humanity than the revelation of God in creation. The benefit and value of the law is set forth in verses 10 and 11. The value and rewards connected to the law are better than those things that humans so desperately strive for: money and honey.[55] The perfection of the law brings to light the imperfections of the psalmist, so the psalm ends with an acknowledgement of sin and its power, a plea to be forgiven, and a desire to live in a way that is acceptable to God, the redeemer of his people.

Just as the law was central to the Mosaic covenant as God's word to his people, so Christ is central to the new covenant as God's final word to his people (Heb. 1:1). Christ inaugurates the new covenant. He not only teaches the word of God but is the Word of God (John 1:1) and the revelation of God (John 1:18). The Old Testament focuses on the law as the heart of the Mosaic covenant, whereas the New Testament focuses on Christ as the heart of the new covenant. This does not diminish the law, but the law must be read in light of Christ.[56] The words in the middle column that describe the character of the law also describe Christ. The word 'perfect' (tāmim) means whole, complete, without blemish. This term is used of the wholeness and completeness of the sacrificial offerings in that they are without blemish (Lev. 1:3). So Christ is without blemish and offers himself as such to God (Heb. 9:14; 1 Peter 1:19). He is perfect in the ultimate sense (Heb. 4:15). Christ is 'sure',[57] a concept that stresses faithful, which is used absolutely of Christ in 2 Timothy 2:13. Christ is also a faithful witness (Rev. 1:5), a faithful high priest (Heb. 2:17), and faithful over God's house as a son (Heb. 3:6). Christ is 'right' in the sense of righteous and upright.[58] The concept of a straight way is significant in Proverbs (LXX 20:11), is used in 2 Peter 2:15 of correct teaching, and has implications for Jesus' statement, 'I am the way, the truth, and the life' (John 14:6). He is the right way.

Christ is pure and clean (1 John 3:3) and has the power to make us clean (Matt. 8:2-3) by his word (John 15:3). Christ has the same effect as the law: he is the one who brings restoration (Acts 3:21), who is the true wisdom of God (1 Cor. 1:24; Col. 2:3), who is the source of true joy (John 15:11; Phil. 4:4), who enlightens the eyes (John 9:26, 39; 1 John 5:20), who endures forever (Heb. 13:8), and who is true (1 John 5:20; Rev. 3:7) and righteous (2 Tim. 4:8; 1 John 2:1). Christ is the fullness of God's revelation. He encompasses all that was revealed in the Old Testament in his work as covenant mediator, which includes his work as prophet in teaching God's people the law. For example, in the Sermon on the Mount in Matthew 5–7, Jesus explains the true meaning of the law.

Psalm 19 as a prayer of Jesus would extol the glory of God's revelation in creation and the law. On a different level, because he is the Creator, he would be delighting in his own creation (vv. 1-6), and because he is the final revelation, he would be magnifying his own word (vv. 7-11). As our *human* mediator he would pray to be kept from sin to maintain his innocence in order to accomplish his work as our Redeemer. He is the only one who can ultimately be declared innocent from hidden faults, and whose words are completely acceptable in the sight of God (vv. 12-14).

Paul quotes Psalm 19:4 [LXX 18:5] in Romans 10:18 in what appears to be an unusual way. Psalm 19:4 affirms the universality of God's revelation in creation, and Paul seems to quote it in affirming the universality of the preaching of the gospel. Some have argued that Paul really has the Gentiles in view in this passage,[59] or that the emphasis is on people in general, not just Israel,[60] to make a reference to the Gentiles in Romans 10:18 plausible: God did not leave himself without a witness to the Gentiles in the old covenant even though he had a special relationship with Israel. What is said concerning the universality of the heavenly bodies is now said about the spread of the gospel, which goes out to all the world.[61] Part of the point of referring to Psalm 19:4 could be to emphasize that all are without excuse before God because God's revelation is available to all. Now the 'word of Christ' (Romans 10:17) is made available to all. That Paul operates with a strong Christological hermeneutic can be seen earlier in Romans 10 where he virtually quotes Deuteronomy 30:11-15, and replaces what that passage says about the law with Christ.[62] Because Christ is the fullness of God's revelation what is said about the law (Romans 10:6-9) and about general revelation (Romans 10:18) can be said about him and the message of his gospel.

Psalm 49: The False Illusion of Wealth and the Cost of Redemption

Psalm 49 is a wisdom psalm.[63] The wisdom aspect is demonstrated in the theme of the prosperity of the wicked, as well as by the use of wisdom terminology (vv. 3-4, 10), and the appeal to all peoples (vv. 1-2). This psalm is part of the first group of psalms (42–49) that come from the 'sons of Korah', a Levitical family that became part of the singers and musicians whom David appointed to minister with song at the house of the LORD (1 Chron. 6:22, 31-32). The association of the sons of Korah with David continues the strong Davidic flavor in Book II that is also evident in Book I. The psalms of Korah that open Book II are laments that express a longing for restoration by God. Psalm 45 is a royal psalm that expresses hope, which leads to an emphasis that God is the refuge and security for the city of God (46–48) and the people of God, who will be redeemed from their trouble (49).[64]

Psalm 49 falls into three sections. It begins with an introduction (vv. 1-4), followed by two sections that reflect on the prosperity of the wicked, with each section ending with a similar refrain (vv. 12, 20). The subtle difference in the refrain relates to the point the psalmist is making concerning the prosperity of the wicked.[65]

Psalm 49 begins with a universal appeal to all peoples to pay heed to the wisdom expressed in the psalm. This wisdom is for all inhabitants of the world (v. 1) and for people of every social class (v. 2). Wisdom terminology permeates verses 3-4 as the psalmist promises to speak wisdom, give understanding, and solve a riddle.[66] The riddle has to do with the prosperity of the wicked, a prominent wisdom theme in light of the statements in the book of Proverbs that the wise will experience the blessings of wealth (10:22, 13:22) and the wicked will experience the judgment of God (3:24-25; 10:3, 27).[67]

The second section of the psalm (vv. 5-12) begins to solve the riddle by showing that wealth cannot deliver from death. A 'why' question is used to introduce what has been troubling the psalmist. He has been surrounded by the wicked who try to cheat him, who trust in their wealth, and who boast in their abundance. He has experienced 'days of evil' that have produced fear – not the healthy fear of the LORD but a deep-seated anxiety about the meaning and destiny of life that can derail a person's faith in God.[68] The question 'why should I fear?' is answered by showing that wealth cannot deliver from death. No amount of money can ever deliver a human life from death (v. 7). Although some may seek to perpetuate their memory by naming lands after themselves (v. 11),[69] everyone dies and leaves his wealth to others (v. 10). The point is driven home in the refrain (v. 12). Humans are like beasts in the sense that both die.[70] It does not matter how much wealth or fame someone has because none of that will remain. Even for the wealthy, death has the final word.

The final section of Psalm 49 argues the same point that the wealthy cannot take their wealth with them (v. 17), but the emphasis is on the false understanding that wealth produces in people. Wealth brings praise from others (v. 18) and gives a false security to people (v. 13), with the result that they have a distorted view of life. Those who do not think they need a (divine) shepherd will end up with a shepherd whose name is Death (v. 14).[71] The refrain of verse 20 drives home the point that a human being who does not understand the true meaning of wealth, life, and death is no different from the beasts, who also live within the horizon of this life. The psalmist answers the 'why' question of verse 5 with verse 16, 'Be not afraid when a man becomes rich.' The basis for this admonition is given in verse 15, which is a strong confession of faith and is the answer to the riddle: only God is able to ransom a life from death.[72] The final statement of verse 15 makes an allusion to the translation of Enoch (Gen. 5:24) and

Elijah (2 King 2:1, 9), who were taken into the presence of God apart from death.[73] Although some would deny that this verse is teaching life after death,[74] the examples of Enoch and Elijah would give God's people hope for life beyond death. Psalm 49 reinforces this hope by connecting the examples of Enoch and Elijah to the power of God to redeem from death. Death does not have the final word for those who trust in God.[75]

The message of Psalm 49 is still relevant for today, with the added knowledge of what Scripture specifically means when it says that only God can redeem a life (v. 15). The verb 'ransom, redeem' (pādāh) is used exclusively of the LORD in Deuteronomy as the one who ransomed Israel from Egypt. It is also used of the redemption of the firstborn through the payment of a price or the substitutionary death of an animal.[76] These regulations are given in the context of the Exodus from Egypt. Israel was God's firstborn (Exod. 4:21-23), and because Egypt would not let Israel's firstborn go, the Egyptians would lose their firstborn in the tenth plague. Thus Israel must redeem her firstborn. The payment of a price was enough for this redemption, but the redemption that Psalm 49 is talking about is a redemption from death. Only God could provide that redemption. God's plan of redemption (Eph. 1:3-14) is accomplished through God's own firstborn, Jesus Christ (Col. 1:15-20). God the Father provides for this redemption by sending his own Son to be the perfect ransom. No other price but the death of his Son, the perfect sacrifice, could redeem mankind (1 Peter 1:18-19). Jesus Christ in his life and death fully satisfied the justice of God so that sinners can be delivered (Gal. 3:13-14; Heb. 9:12). It is the work of Christ as our priest who offers himself as a sacrifice (Heb. 9:26, 10:11-14), combined with the person of Christ as God (John 1:1, 14; Romans 9:5) that makes our redemption possible. If Christ were not a human being, he could not be a priest. As priest he is able to sympathize with our struggles concerning the prosperity of the wicked, for he himself was poor while others lived in palaces (Matt. 8:20). He became poor that we might become rich (2 Cor. 8:9). He would have faced death with the confidence expressed in Psalm 49:15.

If Christ were not God, he could not provide the payment that is sufficient for our salvation. His resurrection seals our redemption (Romans 4:25) and assures us of a future life of victory in the presence of God (1 Cor. 15:20). God will one day 'take' us to himself (Luke 17:22-35; Acts 1:11). If a person trusts in his wealth he has a false sense of confidence and lacks understanding of the cost of salvation. He is no different from a beast that perishes because he lives only in the horizon of this life (2 Peter 2:12; Jude 10).

Psalms of Confidence

The final type of psalm that fits the category Psalms of Orientation are the psalms of confidence.[77] The dominant characteristics of these psalms are attitudes of trust and confidence.[78] The obstacles and difficulties of life are subordinated to the strong statements of confidence in God. These psalms also use striking metaphors to show an intimate awareness of God's presence.[79] Some examples of this type of psalm are 11, 16, 23, 27, 62, 91, 121, 125, and 131.[80]

Psalm 91: God's Promise of Ultimate Victory

This psalm contains some of the strongest affirmations of confidence in God's deliverance and protection in all of Scripture.[81] In fact, one wonders if this psalm does not promise too much. For example, it affirms that 'no evil shall be allowed to befall you, no plague come near your tent' (v. 10), 'a thousand may fall at your side, ten thousand at your right hand, but it [destruction] will not come near you' (v. 7), and 'with long life I will satisfy him' (v. 16).[82] Does God promise too much here? What happens when these promises are not fulfilled? Should early death through illness or the tragedies of life shake our confidence in God's power to protect?[83]

Psalm 91 is strategically placed in Book IV of the Psalms to reinforce the covenant promises of God. It is an answer to the concerns stated at the end of Book III related to the promises of the Davidic covenant (Ps. 89:49-51).[84] Psalm 90 is a psalm of Moses taking Israel back to her foundations and reminding her that God is the everlasting God. Psalm 91 uses titles of God that go back to the patriarchal period ('Most High' in Gen. 14:18-20 and 'Almighty' in Gen. 17:1, 28:3).[85] The concluding petitions of 90:13-17 are answered in 91:16 (seen in the use of the same two verbs 'satisfy' and 'show'). The connections between these two psalms, also seen in the rare word for 'dwelling' (*mā'ôn*) in 90:1 and 91:9, helps establish Israel in the power of the eternal God and the foundation of his covenant promises. Psalm 92 is the godly response of thanksgiving, followed by psalms that proclaim the reign of the LORD, Israel's king (93–100).86

The tremendous promises in 91:3-13 must be understood in light of the covenant that God made with his people, for they are a reflection of those covenant promises.87 The Mosaic covenant sets forth covenant blessings for God's people if they will obey him. It also sets forth covenant curses for disobedience, which could lead to loss of land in exile (Lev. 26; Deut. 27–28). There is clearly a close connection between the promises in Psalm 91 and the blessings and curses of the Mosaic covenant, as seen in the following comparison:

Mosaic covenant	*Psalm 91*
not afraid (Lev. 26:6)	verse 5
chase thousand/ten thousand (Lev. 26:7-8)	verse 7
God's dwelling (Lev. 26:11)	verse 9
beasts removed or let loose (Lev. 26:6, 22)	verse 13
pestilence (Lev. 26:5; Deut. 28:21)	verse 3
boils, diseases of Egypt (Deut. 28:34, 59)	verse 10

Psalm 91 is setting forth the blessings of the Mosaic covenant, the security that comes with those blessings, and the confidence that God will pour out those blessings. The structure of the Mosaic covenant makes the blessings and cursings of the covenant conditional on the response of God's people, as reflected in 91:9, 14. The reason Israel was sent into exile and lost her land is her disobedience, which brought on the covenant curse. Israel never experienced the fullness of covenant blessing. Part of the purpose of the Mosaic covenant was to show that Israel was not able to keep the terms of the covenant. It is clear in Isaiah 40–66 that Israel, the Servant, has failed in the mission God gave her and a different Servant is needed (Isa. 42:1-4, 19; 49:1-5; 50:4-9; and 52:13–53:12). Psalm 91 is a reminder to God's people of the fullness of covenant blessing that can be found in trusting God.

Where Israel failed to keep the terms of the covenant, Christ has succeeded so that as our representative he now offers to us the fullness of covenant blessing. Christ is the one who always responds in full faith and confidence in God. Such faith was demonstrated in the wilderness when Jesus was tempted by Satan with the words of this psalm to prove that he was the Son of God (Matt. 4:5-6). It is no accident that promises from Psalm 91 are used because the temptation was for Jesus to demonstrate the truth of this psalm in relationship to his identity. He was to prove that he was the Son of God by showing the truth of 91:11-12. But Jesus saw this temptation for what it was; it was not a demonstration of trust in God but a testing of God. He responded to this temptation with full confidence in God, the way he responded to every situation of his life (Heb. 5:7-8). He demonstrates for us what it is to live a life of trust in God. Because he lived a life full of faith and confidence in God he could pray Psalm 91 with the full confidence that God would answer his prayer. There is a change of person in Psalm 91 that makes this psalm interesting as a prayer of Jesus.[88] Verse 1 begins with the third person ('he who dwells'), and verse 2 switches to the first person ('I will say to the LORD'), which person then continues to speak to a third party in verses 3-13 ('he will deliver you'). There is general agreement that verses 14-16 are a divine oracle with God as the speaker, confirming what was stated in verses 3-13. As a prayer of Jesus, he would be the main speaker affirming his own stance of trust in God to deliver (vv. 2a, 9b), and he would then encourage others to have the same stance (91:3-8, 9a, 10-13). The psalm ends with a divine oracle of God (the Father) affirming that he will deliver Jesus, and all those who follow him in faith in fulfillment of the covenant blessings. In the context of the New Testament, Psalm 91:16 would refer to complete salvation and eternal life.

Christ's faithfulness ensures that we will experience the fullness of the covenant blessings reflected in Psalm 91. The main question is when will we experience the fullness of those blessings? If Christ in his first coming had brought the fullness of the kingdom we would now be experiencing full covenant blessings. However, Christ in his first coming inaugurated the kingdom through his death, burial, resurrection, and exaltation to glory.[89] He commissions his people to go out into all the world with the message of the good news of the gospel (Matt. 28:19-20), in fulfillment of the promise to Abraham of blessings to the nations (Gen. 12:1-3) through faith in Jesus Christ (Gal. 3:28). God's people have only received a down payment of what they will one day experience (Eph. 1:13-14), with the promise of persecution and suffering for the sake of Christ (John 15:18-25; 1 Peter 4:12-19). When Christ comes again in victory he will bring the fullness of the blessings of the kingdom, which God's people will experience in the new heavens and the new earth. The promises of Psalm 91 will be fulfilled for God's people at that point of victory.[90] In between the first and second comings of Christ, there may be hardship and the trials of life, but those who believe in Jesus Christ can live in full confidence of the promises in Psalm 91. Nothing can defeat the child of God. No disease, pestilence, or evil can ultimately harm the one who is in the secret place of protection (91:1), which for the believer is now 'in Christ' (Romans 8:1; Eph. 1:3-11). All our enemies will be defeated (91:8). The one who will trample the head of the serpent (Gen. 3:15) has come, and his followers will also trample the head of the serpent in victory (91:13; Romans 16:20).[91] Thus nothing can separate us from the love of Christ (Romans 8:31-39). Through the work of Christ our Mediator, who as king dispenses covenant blessings and wins our victory, we will be more than conquerors.

Psalm 46: Trusting in the Security of God's Presence

Psalm 91 is a psalm of confidence of an individual, as evidenced in the singular verb forms and pronouns, whereas Psalm 46 is a psalm of confidence of the community, as evidenced in the plural verb forms and pronouns.[92] The same security and confidence offered the individual in Psalm 91 is now affirmed by the community of God's people. The theme of confidence in God as a refuge dominates each section of the psalm,[93] reinforced by the refrain in verses 7 and 11. The basis of confidence is due to the presence of God and the effects of his presence.

Psalm 46 opens with a confessional statement declaring trust in God,[94] followed by a statement of the result of trusting God: we will not fear. Verses 2-3 describe a worst-case scenario of the dissolution of the world.[95] There are several ways the shaking of the earth and mountains, the falling of the mountains into the sea, and the roaring of the waters can be explained. Calvin takes it as hyperbolic language denoting the world being turned upside down.[96] It might describe an earthquake or some other natural disaster that would threaten God's people.[97] There may be allusions to the order established at creation where God set the boundaries of the waters in order for the dry land to appear, so making the earth habitable for humanity. Such boundaries were withdrawn in the flood as the waters covered the earth. Psalm 46 could be describing a 'moment of uncreation'.[98] In light of the ancient Near Eastern context, there may be allusions to the upheaval in the world caused by false gods of chaos (see Psalm 93).[99] The point of verses 1-3 is that God's people do not have to fear when the world seems unstable. The presence of God brings help even if the world is falling apart.

The instability of the world is further described in verse 6 in the raging of the nations and the moving of kingdoms, but such instability is contrasted with the peace and tranquility of the city of God (vv. 4-6). Even though the mountains and the kingdoms of the world may fall, the city of God will remain firm and stable.[100] The instability of the world and the rage of the nations has no effect on the city of God because of his presence there.[101] The city of God is holy because it is the place of his dwelling. His presence brings help, blessing, and peace. The picture of a river whose streams make glad God's city is a bold contrast to the roaring of the waters and the raging of the nations. Such a picture is a reminder of the Garden of Eden (Gen. 2:10) and is symbolic of the blessings that come with the presence of God.[102] A river flowing from the temple is picked up in Ezekiel 47 and Revelation 22 to describe the glorious blessings of God's presence. The place of God's dwelling is the center of the universe and the center of existence.

The power of God's presence is emphasized in the last section of Psalm 46. He has the power to bring an end to war by destroying the weapons of war. The two themes of the nations and the earth, prominent earlier in the psalm, come together in verse 10: God is exalted above both. Two sets of imperatives set the stage for verses 8-11. The first set in verse 8 is an invitation to see the power of God at work, and the second set in verse 10 calls on the nations to cease their rebellion and bow before God.[103] There is clearly an emphasis on the power of the LORD to defend his people against all foes. Yahweh is the divine warrior who fights for his people.[104] The name Yahweh of hosts, which occurs in the refrain (vv. 7, 11), refers to God as the leader of the heavenly armies.[105] This name is also associated with the ark as God's symbolic throne.[106] As king of the universe he is exalted above all and has the power to protect his people.

The confidence in God's protection comes from the power of his presence, which permeates Psalm 46. God is 'for us' (v. 1),[107] a present help in trouble (v. 1), in the midst of the city (v. 4), and 'with us' (vv. 7, 11). Although God is the king of the universe, he established his presence in the temple in Jerusalem. Yet it is clear in Psalm 46 that it is not the city itself that is the place of protection, but God and his presence.[108] God removed his presence from the temple in preparation for the destruction of the temple and the city in 587. Although the temple was rebuilt after the exile, God's people waited for the filling of the temple with the glory of God (Hag. 2:6-9). The manifestation of God's presence among his people comes into full reality in the incarnation of Jesus Christ. As God, Christ brings the reality of God's presence, and as king, he establishes the kingdom. As a member of the covenant community Christ can pray Psalm 46. He has the same confidence the community has in God, but he also understands that he is the one through whom God will work to fulfill the promises of Psalm 46. He also can declare 'know that I am God, I will be exalted among the nations.'

John picks up key concepts related to the tabernacle and temple and understands their reality to be manifested in Jesus Christ: 'the Word became flesh and dwelt among us, and we have seen his glory' (1:14). The verb 'dwelt' (skēnoō) is related to the noun used of the tabernacle (skēnē), and the glory connected with the temple (Exod. 40:34-38; 1 Kings 8:10-11) is now seen in Jesus Christ. Christ is the reality of the manifestation of God's presence with his people.[109] He is the true temple (John 2:18-22) because in him God is present with his people. It is not surprising that concepts from Psalm 46 are alluded to in the Gospels. He calms the raging waters with the rebuke of his voice and then demonstrates his power over the spiritual forces of wickedness (Ps. 46:2-3, 6; Mark 4:35–5:20; Luke 8:22-39). He comes preaching the kingdom of God (Mark 1:14-15), which is a spiritual kingdom that seems hidden, small, and insignificant, but will one day be manifested to all the world (the parables of the kingdom in Matt. 13 and 25:31-46). Rulers recognize Jesus in his ministry (Luke 7:1-10) and one day all kings will bow before him (Rev. 6:15-17, 19:16-21). He has come to establish peace between God and sinful humanity (Eph. 2:11-17), which will one day manifest itself in the ceasing of all wars. He brings the security and blessing of God's presence (Ps. 46:4-5). The great picture of a river flowing from the temple is fulfilled in him. He brings rivers of living waters that now flow from the new temple, the blessings and the power of the Spirit of God (John 7:37-39).[110] Not only is Jesus the temple, but now the church is the temple filled with God's presence (1 Cor. 3:16-17), as are individual believers (1 Cor. 6:19). Another temple building is not needed because we now have the presence of God, and in the new heavens and earth there will not be a temple because the full reality of God's presence will be manifested (Rev. 21:22). The city of God, the heavenly Jerusalem, is secure. No matter what upheavals take place in the world (Heb. 12:27-29),[111] God's kingdom and the new Jerusalem will one day be triumphant because Jesus is the divine warrior who will defeat all his foes. Martin Luther's great hymn 'A Mighty Fortress is our God' is based on Psalm 46, with clear connections to Christ as the one who defeats the enemy and establishes the kingdom.

Chapter 5

Indirect Messianic Psalms:
Psalms of Disorientation

Psalms of Disorientation deal with seasons of hurt, alienation, suffering, and death. Life seems chaotic and in painful disarray. The types of psalms that fall into this broad category are the lament psalms and the wisdom psalms, which state the struggles and the questions that arise when the wicked prosper and the righteous experience suffering.

The Lament Psalms
Psalms of lament express the language of suffering and are full of questions to God. They are the opposite of hymns, which express the language of praise and are full of joy.[1] There are more psalms of lament in the Psalms than there are hymns of praise to God, which demonstrates that life is full of trouble and sorrow.[2] However, the Psalter moves toward praise as it concludes with 'a fireworks of praise' (Psalms 146–150).[3]

There are three issues that surface in discussing the lament psalms: who is the one speaking (the 'I' of the individual laments), what situation is behind the lament, and who are the enemies?[4] Specific answers have been given to these questions. For example, the 'I' of the psalm has been identified as a personification of the nation itself,[5] or as the king as the representative of the people.[6] Some have tried to limit the situation of the laments to worship,[7] while others have focused on identifying the particular distress that has caused the lament, such as sickness[8] or some kind of judicial procedure where the psalmist is being falsely accused.[9] Those who identify the 'I' of these psalms with the king also tend to identify the enemies as national enemies.[10] The problem in trying to identify the situation or the particular enemy is that the psalms use metaphorical language to describe the problems the psalmist is facing. Such language loses some of its specific nature and allows it to apply to a variety of situations.[11]

The lament psalms contain several basic elements. They begin with an invocation addressed to God, many times followed by a plea for God to help.[12] The main part of the lament is the complaint, which arises out of some situation of distress. The psalmist might focus on his frustration with God, usually in the form of questions directed to God, or frustrations with his own thoughts and actions, or frustrations with the actions of others against him (the enemies).[13] Most laments move toward a statement of confidence that God has heard the complaint and that he will respond.[14] This assurance of being heard also leads to the praise of God so that many laments end with praise.[15] Not all of these elements will occur in every lament psalm, nor will they always occur in the same order.

The most numerous type of lament is the individual lament, characterized by an 'I' who is speaking.[16] The individual laments include 3–5, 9–10, 13–14, 22, 25, 39, 41, 42–43, 54–57, 69–71, 77, 86, 88, and 140–142. There are also community laments, which are very similar in their structure to individual laments. However, they are characterized by 'we' rather than 'I',[17] are a response to a communal disaster (such as war, drought, or famine),[18] and include a section where God's works in the past are recalled, contrasting them with what the community is currently experiencing.[19] They may culminate in an appeal to confirm the faithfulness of God.[20] The community laments have a setting in worship, perhaps connected to a fast.[21] They include 12, 44, 58, 60, 74, 79, 80, 83, and 85.

Psalm 79: The Taunt of the Nations – Where is Their God?

Psalm 79 is a community lament responding to a disaster that has occurred in Jerusalem, probably in connection to the destruction of the temple and the city by the Babylonians in 587BC. The complaint is laid out in verses 1-5, the petition to God in verses 6-12, and the concluding statement of confidence and praise of God in verse 13. There is a movement in the complaint from 'they' (vv. 1-3), to 'we' (v. 4), to 'you' (v. 5), which highlights the focus of the psalm on the nations, the people of God, and God. The first part of the petition has the same order of the nations (vv. 6-7), the people of God (v. 8), and God (v. 9),[22] leading to what some see as the climax and theological theme of the psalm: the assertion in verse 10a, 'Why should the nations say, "Where is their God?"'[23] The rest of the petition (vv. 10b-12) is an appeal for God to act on behalf of his people against the nations.

The complaint opens with a brief appeal to God, and then focuses on the crisis situation produced by the actions of the nations ('they'). The actions of the nations are horrible in themselves. The nations 'have defiled', 'have laid … in ruins', have given human bodies to the birds of the heavens, and have poured out blood like water. The actions of the enemy nations show no regard for human life. They leave dead bodies to be ravaged by birds and beasts,[24] and blood flows as freely as water. Not only are the actions of the nations horrible, but the focus of their actions also causes a sense of alarm and horror. They have acted against God's inheritance, God's holy temple, God's city of Jerusalem, God's servants, and God's faithful. The horrible consequences for God's people ('we') are laid out in verse 4. The enemy nations have no regard for God or his people with the result that God's people experience shame and ridicule. The appeal to God in verse 5 forms a transition to the petition to God for help, asking how long the LORD will be angry; in other words, how long will this situation continue? The mention in verse 5 of God's 'jealousy' in parallel with 'anger' not only explains why this disaster has occurred (God's judgment for the people's sin of going after false gods), but also gives hope that God will act on behalf of his people. God is zealous that Israel only has a relationship with him and there is hope that he will act against the nations to maintain that relationship.

The petition (vv. 6-12) calls upon God not only to act in judgment against the nations, but also to respond in mercy and forgiveness to his people. God's people have experienced his anger, and the first thing they request is that the nations would also experience God's anger because of what they have done to 'Jacob' (vv. 6-7). God does not have a relationship with the nations (v. 6), but he does have a long-standing covenant relationship with the patriarchs (Jacob). God is asked to protect his inheritance and act against the nations. The people of God ask for God's compassion and help in light of their sin. They know their need of deliverance and atonement (vv. 8-9). God is called upon to vindicate his people for the sake of his own glory (v. 9).

The connection between the low state of God's people and how it reflects on the character and power of God comes out in the question of verse 10a: 'Why should the nations say, "Where is their God?"' Israel's defeat makes it look like the sovereignty of God has failed.[25] The petition goes on to appeal to God to act in ways that would demonstrate the power of God and bring deliverance to God's people. God is called upon to avenge the blood of his servants (v. 10b) so that the nations and God's people would see that it is a serious thing to act against God's people. God is asked to demonstrate his power and preserve prisoners doomed to die (v. 11). God is also asked to turn back on the nations the taunts that God's people have experienced because those taunts are really against God (v. 12). God is the people's only hope of deliverance. The psalm ends, like most laments, with a statement of confident praise. Confidence is expressed in the statement that the people are still 'the sheep of your pasture' and that future generations will give praise to God's name. Although this disaster has struck God's people, they still have a future and a hope.

It is more difficult to connect a community lament to the person or work of Christ, but we get insight into his humanity as he experiences and expresses the questions, sufferings, and cries of those who lament. Psalm 79 contains two basic prayers: a prayer for judgment and a prayer for forgiveness that will lead to deliverance. Both prayers were dependent on God to act. As a member of the covenant community Jesus would have participated with the community in lamenting any disastrous community situation. He did lament over the stubbornness of Jerusalem in rejecting him (Matt. 23:37-38) and warned the people about what was going to happen to the temple and Jerusalem (Matt. 24:4-28). Psalm 79 laments what happened to Jerusalem and the temple because of the sins of the people. Although the sin is not mentioned in Psalm 79, it is clear in the historical context that the people had rejected the LORD and had pursued other gods. Jesus laments what is happening in Jerusalem and what will happen to Jerusalem because of the sins of the people in rejecting him. The sin in both places is in essence the same: a rejection of the LORD and his ways. The rejection of Jesus, from a human standpoint, leads to his crucifixion, which no doubt raises again the question 'Where is their God?' To many people such a horrible death was evidence that Jesus was not from God, but God's perspective was different. As Paul affirms: the word of the cross is foolishness to the Gentiles and a stumbling block to the Jews, but to those who are being saved it is the power of God (1 Cor. 1:18-25). The rejection of Jesus brings the judgment of God on the people and the city (AD70).

As part of the community Jesus could also pray for the sins of the community and pray that God would act in a way that would save the community, which is what his life and work was all about (here especially in its priestly and kingly role). He was the one sent by God to bring deliverance and salvation (Matt. 2:15). The forgiveness of sins comes through him. Jesus is now the focus of God's work of salvation. He has won the victory for his people in the resurrection, and now sits at the right hand of God in his exaltation. He is the one to whom the people of

God look for vindication and vengeance against the enemies of the gospel. As the church takes the good news of the gospel into all the world there will be opposition, trouble, and persecution (John 15:18-25). The martyrs cry out that the Lord would judge the wicked and avenge their blood (Rev. 6:10-11). They are told to wait a little longer because there will be more martyrs, but they understand that only in the judgment of God can the salvation of God's people become a reality (Rev. 16:6).[26] Christ will one day come in judgment against his enemies (Rev. 19:11-21) in order to vindicate his people. At that point the sheep of his pasture will be delivered to praise his name forever (Ps. 79:13).

Psalm 88: When God Does Not Answer

Psalm 88 is the lament of an individual who is in the midst of a very difficult situation. Although some connect the descriptions in the psalm with a terminal illness, like leprosy,[27] it is not necessary to limit the situation to an illness. The metaphorical language of the poetry is general enough to include other distressing situations.[28] Whatever situation is described, it is an extremely serious situation that does not show any hope for change. Even though most lament psalms have some movement toward confidence and praise, Psalm 88 is the only lament psalm that does not have any movement toward confidence or praise at the end. After the one glimmer of hope in the invocation at the beginning ('God of my salvation'), the psalm is full of darkness and ends in darkness (darkness is the last Hebrew word in the psalm). There is no response from God. The situation the psalmist is experiencing is not resolved. Truly we come face to face with the 'dark night of the soul' when God is absent and does not answer.

This psalm can be divided into three sections based on the assertions that the psalmist is crying out to God (1b, 9b, and 13). Three different words for 'crying out' are used with different times of the day mentioned (day and night [v. 1], every day [v. 9b], and in the morning [v. 13]), which demonstrates that the psalmist has exhausted every possible approach in seeking God.[29] Although the psalmist begins with a personal affirmation that God is the 'God of my salvation,' he quickly moves to an appeal to God to hear his prayer because the situation is so serious. The bitterness of the psalmist's experience is expressed in the phrase 'my soul is full of troubles' (v. 3). Usually the verb 'full' (*śāba'*) refers to being satisfied with what is good, but here the only thing the psalmist has enough of is trouble.[30] He has reached his limit and cannot take anymore. Through a series of lively phrases the nearness of death is described in verses 3b-5. He is already considered dead, a strong man without strength, like those who are forgotten. The real problem emerges at the end of verse 5, with explicit statements concerning God's active role in the situation in verses 6-8. Not only has God been silent in response to the psalmist's prayers, but he has been active in causing the distressing situation of the psalmist ('you have put me' in verse 6, 'your wrath lies heavy' and 'you overwhelm me' in verse 7, and then 'you have caused my companions to shun me' in verse 8). Not only has God abandoned the psalmist, but he has caused his companions to leave him as well. Although God has the power to act, he does not act, leaving the psalmist alone and forsaken by all.

The second statement of prayer (v. 9b) is followed by a series of rhetorical questions in verses 10-12, such as 'Do you work wonders for the dead?', 'Do the departed rise to praise you?', 'Is your steadfast love declared in the grave', and 'Are your wonders known in the darkness?' These questions expect a 'no' answer. The function and meaning of these questions has been debated. Some understand these questions as positive expressions of the psalmist's faith and hope,[31] but others see them negatively as calling God to account.[32] The fact that darkness permeates this psalm makes it hard to see these questions as positive expressions of faith. They are a method for the psalmist to use in asking God to act for him. But what do the questions mean? Are they evidence that there is no belief in life after death in the Old Testament? Do they demonstrate that God has no power in the realm of the dead? Other passages of Scripture affirm a belief in life after death in the Old Testament (see the discussion in Ps. 49 above) and that God has power in the realm of the dead (Amos 9:2).[33] The questions in verses 10-12 show the desperate nature of the situation and implore God to act before death takes over. They are a way for the psalmist to continue to appeal to God to act in his behalf.[34] The reason it is necessary for God to act before death comes is rooted in the earthly nature of the blessings of the covenant (see Deut. 28). The blessings of the covenant are a demonstration of God's favor and are manifested in a tangible way in the life of Israel.[35] The questions in verses 10-12 call on God to vindicate the psalmist now by acting in such a way that shows God's favor. Once death comes it will be too late for God to show his favor in this world and too late for the psalmist to offer the appropriate praise to God for his deliverance.

The third section also begins with a statement of prayer to God (v. 13) and is followed by questions and statements that are very similar to the rest of the psalm. Questions beginning with 'why' come in verse 14. Statements of being abandoned by friends come in verse 18. Death and God's wrath are mentioned in verses 15-16. What is distinct about the third section is the emphasis on God's role of rejecting the psalmist in not answering his prayer and the effect this has on the psalmist. The questions in verse 14 are personal questions. The pronouns 'my' and 'me' are used, which is different from the more objective questions in verses 10-12. God has rejected the psalmist so that he is afflicted, suffering the terrors of God, overwhelmed by God's wrath, and surrounded by God's dreadful assaults. The only thing the psalmist knows is darkness, which is the way the psalm ends.

What are we to do with such a dark, hopeless psalm? Psalm 88 reminds us that the believer may face dark situations of despair, situations that have no easy resolutions. There may be times when our prayers seem to rise no higher than the ceiling and we feel abandoned by God. The psalms do not avoid the tragic events of life and they give expression to the whole range of thoughts and emotions that are experienced in this world. Calvin calls the psalms 'An Anatomy of all the Parts of the Soul.'[36] Psalm 88 expresses the dark night of the soul of the believer. Sometimes we are quick to offer words of hope without hearing the cries of anguish. Psalm 88 gives legitimacy to expressing our deepest thoughts and emotions in prayer before God.[37] Just as the Israelites suffered affliction and cried out to God (Exod. 3:7), so the psalmist cries out to God in the midst of his affliction. Although Israel was delivered from Egypt, the psalmist feels there is no escape from his situation (88:8).

Yet darkness does not have the last word. Even though there are more lament psalms in the Psalter than hymns of praise or psalms of thanksgiving, there is a movement in the Psalter toward praise, as the Book of Psalms ends in a 'fireworks of praise.'[38] But one does not have to wait for the end of the Psalter, for Psalm 89 begins with a statement of praise. Although Psalm 89 struggles with the bleak situation of Israel in light of the promises of the Davidic covenant, it begins with the strong statement, 'I will sing of the steadfast love of the Lord forever.' Darkness gives way to the covenant loyalty of God (ḥesed).

Although it is legitimate for the believer to pray Psalm 88, ultimately Psalm 88 is not our prayer but the prayer of Jesus. Hebrews 5:7 states that 'Jesus offered up prayers and supplications, with loud cries and tears, to him who was able to save him from death.'[39] Psalm 88 fits the experience of Jesus as he struggled with the prospect of crucifixion in the Garden of Gethsemane.[40] Although the resurrection stands in the future, Jesus is overwhelmed by the darkness of the pit and the prospect of death on the cross. He is all alone, abandoned by everyone close to him (Mark 14:50; Luke 22:45, 54-62; 23:49). He not only faces the horror of the physical pain of being crucified, and so is counted as one who is already dead, he faces the horror of bearing the judgment of God against sin. Verse 7 is literally fulfilled in Jesus: 'your wrath lies heavy upon me.'[41] He was going to be abandoned by God, which is expressed in the questions of 88:14. Could not the rhetorical questions of 88:10-12 be similar to the experience of Jesus in Luke 22:44, where it describes Jesus being in agony and praying more earnestly, with his sweat becoming like great drops of blood? What was he praying? Luke 22:42 reports his prayer: 'Father, if you are willing, remove this cup from me. Nevertheless, not my will, but yours be done.' Jesus experienced the darkness and abandonment by God expressed in Psalm 88 as he hung on the cross suffering the judgment of God against sin. His human life ended in darkness, but only for a short time, for on the third day he burst from the grave conquering sin and death. Because Jesus experienced the dark night of the soul we are assured that darkness will not be the last word. Thus our prayer is not ultimately 'the darkness is my closest friend' (NIV) but 'Jesus, what a friend for sinners.'[42]

Psalms 109 and 137: The Curse of God's Judgment

The complaint portion of the lament may have a specific focus that allows for a further designation of the psalm. Some complaints focus on the distress caused by others and contain an element of curse.[43] Two psalms that have strong language of curse against the enemy are Psalms 109 and 137.[44] The former is an individual lament and the latter a community lament. It is beyond the scope of this book to give a full analysis of the imprecatory psalms,[45] but Psalms 109 and 137 will provide opportunity to deal with the curse element in the context of the Old Testament and in relationship to Christ.

Psalm 137 arises out of the experience of the community in exile in Babylon following the destruction of Jerusalem and the temple in 587 BC. Although the author may be looking back on that experience the memory is fresh and the historical situation is still unsettled.[46] Many divide the psalm into three sections (vv. 1-4, 5-6, and 7-9)[47] but it is possible to divide the psalm into two sections: the complaint (vv. 1-4) and the imprecation, which includes self-imprecation (vv. 5-6) and imprecation against the enemies (7-9). The complaint relates the grief of the community in exile and the taunting of the Babylonian captors. The self-curse emphasizes the importance of remembering Jerusalem. The curse against the enemies asks God to intervene to repay Edom and Babylon for what they did to Jerusalem. The curse against Babylon includes the following beatitude: 'Blessed shall he be who takes your little ones and dashes them against the rock!'

Psalm 109 is a lament of an individual who faces a situation of betrayal.[48] The complaint, which describes the situation, occurs in verses 1-5. The psalmist is under attack for no reason (v. 3). His acts of love and goodness have been responded to with acts of hatred and evil, including vicious lies. The curse against the enemy takes up a large section of the psalm (vv. 6-20), followed by a plea that God would help the psalmist in light of his deteriorating situation and for the sake of God's name (vv. 21-29). The psalm closes with a vow of thanksgiving (vv. 30-31), which promises to praise God when the psalmist is delivered. The lengthy curse section (vv. 6-10) asks God to repay the enemy for what he has done to the psalmist (vv. 16-19).[49] Not only are the actions and life of the enemy cursed (vv. 6-8), but also the lives of his wife and children (vv. 9-13), as well as the lives of his parents (vv. 14-15).

The problem of these psalms can be highlighted when they are compared with words of Jesus from the New Testament (Matt. 5:44). Jesus says we are to love our enemies, but 109:9 states, 'May his children be fatherless and his wife a widow!' Jesus says to bless those who curse you, but 137:9 states a blessing on the one who dashes the enemies' little ones against the rock. Jesus says to do good to those who hate you, but 109:11 states, 'May a creditor seize all that he has; may strangers plunder the fruits of his toil.' And finally, Jesus says to pray for those who persecute you (Matt. 5:44), but 109:6-7 states, 'Appoint a wicked man against him; let an accuser stand at his right hand ... let his prayer be counted as sin!' How should we respond to these psalms of cursing in light of Jesus' words? How can we reconcile these statements? Can we use these prayers today?

Although there are a variety of responses to the imprecatory psalms, our focus will be on the proper way to approach these psalms. Any view that sets up a dichotomy between the Old Testament and New Testament on this issue in order to question the legitimacy of these psalms is to be rejected.[50] The comparison between Psalms 109 and 137 and Jesus' statements in Matthew 5:44 is like comparing apples to oranges. Jesus is clearly speaking against personal revenge,[51] which the Old Testament is also against

(Lev. 19:18; Prov. 25:21-22 quoted by Paul in Romans 12:20). The Old Testament recognizes that vengeance belongs to God (Deut. 32:35; Ps. 94:1). David, the author of Psalm 109, was an example of not taking personal revenge in several instances of his life (1 Sam. 24 and 26; 2 Sam. 16:5-14). The Old Testament and the New Testament agree on the subject of personal revenge. It is also helpful to see that there is curse in the New Testament. Paul curses those who preach a different gospel (Gal. 1:8-9), the martyrs call for the avenging of their blood (Rev. 6:9-11), and Jesus utters curses against the Pharisees (Matt. 23:23-33). There is agreement between the Old Testament and New Testament in that both condemn personal revenge and both use curse, which means that there may be situations where these psalms of cursing are appropriate for today.

In order to see the contemporary relevance of the psalms of cursing, it is important to understand them in their Old Testament context. Both Psalms 137 and 109 arise out of great situations of distress. Psalm 137 originates from the Babylonian exile where the people have lost their most precious things: the city of Jerusalem, the temple, and sons and daughters (Ezek. 24:25). Their whole way of life has fallen apart, and they are being taunted by their captors. Psalm 109 arises out of a situation of great betrayal where the psalmist is mistreated, deceived, and lied about. Understanding the situation gives some insight into the response in these psalms and the difficulty some have today in understanding them. Those who have not lost that much have trouble with these psalms, but those who have been victimized and plundered understand the expressions of curse in these psalms. They express rage, anger, and intolerance for situations of injustice with a desire to see justice established again.[52] It is also possible that many have a shallow view of evil and wickedness, which may lead to a superficial view of prayer in light of the horrible events that happen in the world. These psalms do not avoid the hard situations of life and are a proper response to injustice.

Both psalms commit their situations into the hand of God. 137:7 calls on God to remember what Edom did on the day that

Jerusalem fell. The curses in these verses are to be carried out by God, or by the nation God brings to destroy Babylon. In Psalm 109 the psalmist almost breaks off in the middle of his description of how he is being mistreated with a statement of his response: 'but I – prayer' (v. 4).[53] This commitment of the situation to God also comes out in verses 26-27, where the desire is that it will become clear that God himself is the one who has intervened in bringing about the curses of verses 6-20. Both psalms call on God to intervene. The matter is left in God's hands with no intention for anyone other than God to bring about the desired outcome. Prayer in the face of injustice does have the calming effect of defusing a situation of justified anger and of reminding a person that God is in control and will ultimately take care of it.[54]

Both psalms call for the establishment of the righteousness of God's cause, not the cause of the person uttering the curse. In 137:5-6 there is self-imprecation if Jerusalem is forgotten. Jerusalem is important not just because it is the capital of the nation, but because it represents the purposes of God and the glory of his name. Here the cause of God is placed above the situation of the community in exile. They are not ultimately concerned about their situation but about the honor of God's name. The spokesman in verses 5-6 is even willing to offer a curse against his ability to play and praise again if Jerusalem is forgotten. The curse against Babylon is a call for God to deliver Israel and it recognizes what will happen when Babylon as a nation falls. Personal revenge is not the motivating factor of this psalm. In 109:21 the psalmist appeals for God to act 'for your name's sake.' Again it is the name and cause of God that is prominent. This is reinforced by the fact that this is a Davidic psalm. David as the king embodies the cause of God and represents the rule of God on the earth. For people to act against David is to act against the Lord's representative and anointed one.

Both psalms also relate to the covenant; in fact, covenant and cursing cannot be separated from each other because cursing is an integral part of covenants.[55] In the covenant with Abraham the curse protects the covenant servant and community, as exemplified in Genesis 12:3: 'I will bless those who bless you, and him who dishonors you I will curse.' Psalm 137:7-9 is an outworking of that principle. In the Mosaic covenant the curse is directed against the community of God's people or one of the community who breaks the covenant. This fits the situation in Psalm 109 because the one who has betrayed David is a member of his close associates, a member of the covenant community (v. 4a).[56] Twice in Psalm 109 the strong covenant word *ḥesed* is used (vv. 21, 26) in an appeal for God to show covenant loyalty by delivering the psalmist. The word is also used of the covenant breaker (v. 16) who did not show 'kindness' to the poor and needy. The curse aspect of the covenant expresses God's judgment on those outside the covenant community (Gen. 12:3) and on those inside the covenant community (Deut. 28).

The coming of Jesus Christ did not do away with covenant curse or the judgment of God. The Old Testament outlook was that when God came to save his people he would also destroy all their enemies. This would all take place on the Day of the Lord. The salvation of God's people would not take place without the destruction of God's enemies. This is reflected in the outlook of John the Baptist, who preached both salvation and judgment in Matthew 3:12, 'His winnowing fork is in his hand, and he will clear the threshing floor and gather his wheat into the barn, but the chaff he will burn with unquenchable fire.' Here John depicts judgment on the chaff and salvation to the wheat.

Yet John is thrown in prison and does not see judgment in the ministry of Jesus, so he sends messengers to Jesus to see if he is really the one or should they look for another (Matt. 11:2-6). Jesus answers with the evidence of salvation that has come in his ministry, and then closes with 'blessed is the one who is not offended at me.' Christ brings salvation, but the ultimate judgment is delayed. Thus in Luke 4 when Jesus is reading from Isaiah 61 he stops his reading with the phrase 'to proclaim the year of the Lord's favor' (Isa. 61:2; Luke 4:19) and does not read the very next phrase 'and the day of vengeance of our God.' The day of salvation has arrived, which culminates in the cross, burial, and resurrection. The day of judgment has been delayed, which will be carried out when Jesus comes again. In the meantime opportunity is given for the good news of the gospel to be taken throughout the world. As the gospel goes forth there is the real possibility of the conversion of God's enemies, not just condemnation or destruction. Both aspects are in view in the phrase of the Lord's prayer, 'thy kingdom come.' For God's kingdom to come may mean the destruction of God's enemies, but it may also mean the conversion of God's enemies through the preaching of the gospel.

David's experience of betrayal in Psalm 109 fits Jesus' experience of betrayal by close associates and members of the covenant community. As John 1:11 states, 'he came to his own and his own people did not receive him.' The description of deceit, lies, and hatred corresponds to the plotting of the scribes and Pharisees against Jesus (Matt. 26–27). Jesus does not take up his own cause but appeals to the Father in heaven to vindicate him even though he faced hardship (109:22-24), reproach (109:25) and death (109:26). Psalm 109 closes with a vow of thanksgiving looking forward to the day when Jesus could celebrate his deliverance from death (109:30-31).

Not only does Psalm 109 describe the experience of Jesus, but it also makes sense as a prayer of Jesus. It would be his appeal to God to deliver him from such bloodthirsty people and to save him from death. It would also be his words of curse against members of the covenant community who reject him. Such curses would especially apply to Judas, who betrayed Jesus into the hands of those who had him put to death. This is the use of 109:8 in Acts 1:21. The cursing in Psalm 109 is primarily directed against members of the covenant community who have broken the covenant or have fallen into apostasy. Covenant curse is reflected in the New Testament in situations where the gospel is at stake (Gal. 1:8-9), where members are warned against apostasy (Heb. 6:1-8; 10:26-31), or where church discipline has led to excommunication (Matt. 18:15-18; 1 Cor. 5:1, 9-13). The seriousness of breaking the covenant or falling into false teaching cannot be underestimated. As officers of the church carry out their responsibilities of governing the church, their desire is for reconciliation in church discipline, but they might become instruments of covenant curse if there is not repentance. This work is given to the church by Christ himself (Matt. 16:19; 1 Peter 5:1-4).[57]

The curses in Psalm 137 are primarily directed toward those outside the covenant community. The song speaks of the oppression of exile and the taunting of the nations. As a member of the covenant community it would not have been out of place for Jesus to pray this psalm, expressing his solidarity with the suffering of the community under foreign oppression (Rome). The self-imprecation in verses 4-6 would express his desire for the cause of God to triumph, even as he knew that the Jerusalem in Psalm 137 would not be focused anymore on the physical city but on the heavenly Jerusalem (Heb. 12:22-24; Rev. 21:1-4). Psalm 137 now applies to the new covenant community as they face persecution and oppression in taking the gospel into all the world. It also expresses the recognition that this world is not our final home and that we are living in a foreign land, not having reached our final destination. The curses of Psalm 137 could fit situations of persecution, and would be appropriate prayers in the face of extreme opposition. Any government or force that opposes the church stands in danger of the judgment of God.[58] Ultimately, Babylon becomes a symbol of any world power that opposes God and his people. When Babylon falls there is great rejoicing at the justice of the vengeance that has taken place (Rev. 19:1-3). The judgment against Babylon is led by none other than Jesus Christ, who in bringing victory and vindication to God's people destroys all the enemies of God's people.

Expressions of covenant curse are appropriate in the mouth of the covenant Lord. In his first coming he came in grace in order to announce that the great day of salvation had arrived and that he had come to deliver his people (Matt. 1:21; Luke 4:18-21). He prayed for those who were putting him to death (Luke 23:34) because he understood the magnitude of what they were doing in their ignorance and their rebellion against God. He abode by his own teaching in Matthew 5:38-44 and did not seek personal revenge. He did not come in his first coming as judge (John 12:47, 8:15). He set aside his own personal comfort so that the kingdom of God could be established through his death, burial, and resurrection. He now sits at the right hand of the Father as our king and the one to whom we pray for deliverance. Although God's people will experience, like Jesus, persecution and suffering, the goal is to live for the glory of Christ and his kingdom. We pray for the conversion of our enemies, but it is also legitimate that we pray for the destruction of those who violently oppose the kingdom of Christ. In this way it is appropriate for God's people today to use the psalms of imprecation, not for personal revenge, but as part of our prayer for the establishment of the cause of Christ. We need the imprecatory psalms to remind us how serious it is to reject Christ and how awful the nature of God's judgment will be. When Christ comes again as judge the psalms of cursing will be accomplished. Full covenant curse will be executed against all those who have rejected him. If we are living for the glory of Christ's kingdom we will long for the day when his kingdom will be fully established on earth as it is in heaven.

Psalm 51: A Prayer of Christ Our Priest

The complaint portion of a lament psalm might focus on the distress caused by sin, which leads to the confession of sin dominating the psalm. The trouble in the psalm is not external but is wholly internal as the psalmist struggles with his sinful self.[59] These psalms are called penitential psalms, and include 6, 38, 51, 102, 130, and 143.[60] Psalm 51 is probably the best-known penitential psalm[61] and is a good psalm to reflect on how a psalm of confession relates to Jesus Christ.

Psalm 51 is not an easy psalm to outline, perhaps due to the distress the psalmist was feeling over his sin.[62] What is clear in this psalm is the depth and pervasive character of sin, which is matched by the pleas of the psalmist for the mercy of God. The serious, heinous nature of sin comes out in a number of ways in this psalm.

First of all, the title of the psalm gives the setting of the psalm as David's adultery with Bathsheba, which also included the betrayal and murder of Uriah the Hittite, and no doubt a host of other sins related to the cover-up of these events.[63] This psalm fits such a grievous situation of sin and makes the urgency of the pleas for forgiveness understandable.

Second, all the major vocabulary for sin occurs in this psalm. The basic word for sin in the Old Testament is *ḥaṭṭā'* or its cognate *ḥaṭṭā't*. Both occur in Psalm 51 (2b, 3b, 4, 5, 9a, 13b). Sin is defined in the Old Testament in relationship to God and his word. It can have a broader usage in social and political contexts and can be translated as erring, fault, guilt, offense, or crime.[64] The first word the psalmist uses for his sin in Psalm 51 is *peša'* (vv. 1, 3a, 13a), which means 'willful, self-assertive defiance of God'.[65] This word for sin emphasizes rebellion, revolt, and disobedience to God. It is usually translated 'transgressions', although 'rebellious acts' might bring out the meaning a little better.[66] The other major word for sin is *'āwôn* (vv. 2a, 5a, 9b), which has a specific religious and ethical connotation, and is usually translated 'iniquity'. It is sometimes used as a summary word for all sins against God.[67] The repeated use of these different words for sin shows the depth and comprehensive nature of sin.[68]

Third, that there is no escape from sin is seen in the fact that David's sin is ever before him (v. 3b) and that sin was always a part of his human existence (v. 5). The statement 'in sin did my mother conceive me' is not a condemnation of the act of conception but is a recognition that sin is present from the very beginning.[69] He has never been 'sin free.' It follows that sin goes to the depths of our being and is not just a surface problem. This is seen in the emphasis in verse 6 on the 'inward being,' the inability of sacrifices to ultimately remove our problem of sin (v. 18), and the necessity of a broken spirit before God (v. 19). Psalm 51 should not be seen as a rejection of the sacrificial system, but as a recognition of the limitation of sacrifices. Without a broken spirit the sacrifices are not accepted by God.

Finally, the heinous and serious nature of sin is brought out in the statement in verse 4, 'Against you, you only, have I sinned.' This statement is not a denial that David had sinned against others, such as Bathsheba and Uriah, but it recognizes that sin ultimately has to do with God.[70] Sin is a theological category that can only be defined by the standard of God's law.[71] Even if no one else knows about our sin, God knows, and ultimately we must deal with God in terms of our sin.

The urgent pleas to God for forgiveness and restoration are evidence of the consequence of sin in David's life and the recognition that only God can take care of this problem. The opening plea for forgiveness (vv. 1-2) has four imperatives urging God to remove David's sin. The psalm begins with 'have mercy,' a cry for God's grace and favor. The three pleas that follow all call on God to take away the sin. The verb 'blot out' refers to vigorous action in wiping off or erasing something.[72] The verb 'wash' comes from the practice of washing clothes, which entailed beating the clothes and treading them in water to remove the dirt. The word 'cleanse' is used in ritual contexts to refer to the pronouncement that a person is clean from defilement and able to enter the worship of God again (Lev. 13:6, 24).[73] Such actions of God arise out of his covenant faithfulness (ḥesed) and abundant mercy.

The opening plea for forgiveness is followed by the prayer of confession (vv. 3-6), which is followed by further pleas for cleansing and restoration (vv. 7-15). Although there is overlap with some of the pleas in verses 1-2, the emphasis in this section is how such action by God would affect the psalmist. He desires to be 'clean,' which parallels 'whiter than snow' in verse 7. This emphasizes the effect of forgiveness. When our relationship with God is right we no longer feel dirty but clean. With forgiveness the broken relationship with God is restored so that joy and rejoicing return (vv. 8, 12). The psalmist also desires renewal, and recognizes that only God can bring this about. The verb 'create' (bārā', [v. 10]) is a strong verb that is reserved in the Old Testament for the creative activity of God alone. It refers to divine activity that brings forth something new[74] and expresses the psalmist's desire for inward renewal and change. This renewal goes to the depth of his being as he prays for a 'right spirit' (v. 10) and a 'willing spirit' (v. 12). The phrase 'right spirit' might better be translated 'steadfast spirit.'[75] Both of these expressions stress obedience. The 'steadfast spirit' would be a reliable spirit that would continue in obedience, and the 'willing spirit' would be a spirit that wants to obey God and not sin. Both of these come from God, who must renew the psalmist with a steadfast spirit and uphold the psalmist with a willing spirit. The emphasis on God's presence comes out in verse 11 where the presence of God and the Holy Spirit are parallel with each other. The concern in verse 11 is that the psalmist would not be removed from God's presence because of his sin but that renewal would bring God's presence through the Holy Spirit.[76] Sin removes us from God's presence and renewal restores God's presence. David also prays that God would deliver him from 'bloodguiltiness' (v. 14). This word is the plural word for 'blood' (literally 'bloods') and here probably refers to the guilt of David's sin[77] or the judgment of death resulting from sin.[78] To be delivered from guilt and the judgment of sin is a marvelous thing that will lead to rejoicing and praise (vv. 14b-15), and to teaching others the merciful ways of God (v. 13).

Psalm 51 shows a movement away from sin toward the presence and renewal of God. Sin is prominent at the beginning of the psalm through verse 9, but with the emphasis on renewal in verse 10 sin disappears and is replaced by God's presence. The name 'God' appears only once in verses 1-9, but five times in the second part of the psalm. God's presence is evidence of the grace that the psalmist has experienced. Sin has been removed, and it has been replaced by God himself.[79]

Psalm 51 ends with a plea for Jerusalem to experience the good grace of God so that proper sacrifices can be offered there. The psalmist is not just concerned about individual renewal, but corporate renewal so that the whole community could experience the wondrous grace of God.[80] Our relationship with God is not just a private matter but is always connected to a desire to see renewal come to God's people as a whole. When there is corporate renewal, proper worship takes place (v. 19).

The pervasive character of individual sin in Psalm 51 makes it difficult to relate this psalm to Christ, especially to understand it as a *prayer* of Christ. How can Jesus, who is without sin (Heb. 4:15), pray this psalm of confession? Jesus can pray Psalm 51 as our representative and priest before God. The priesthood of Christ is readily acknowledged to consist of the offering of sacrifices and the making of intercession on behalf of others (WSC 25). It is clear that Christ as our priest did not offer sacrifices but offered himself as our sacrifice to God (Heb. 9:12, 25-28), which is the basis for the forgiveness and removal of our sin. The intercession of Christ is normally discussed as his continuing work as our priest after he has gained access to God on our behalf. As our priest he pleads the merits of his sacrifice.[81] But it is also helpful to reflect on the intercession of Christ on our behalf before his resurrection and exaltation. In other words, it is helpful to reflect on the priesthood of Christ not just in his exaltation but in his humiliation. Hebrews 5:7 specifically mentions the prayers and supplications of Jesus during the days of his flesh. The prayer of Christ in John 17 includes prayers for those who will believe in the future. Jesus specifically tells Peter that even though he will deny his Savior, Jesus has prayed for Peter that his faith may not fail (Luke 22:32). The prayers of Jesus our priest must include prayers for our sins. The intercession of the priest in the Old Testament included the confession of the sins of the people. On the Day of Atonement the priest presented the live goat and confessed over it the transgressions of the people before releasing the goat into the wilderness (Lev. 16:21). Isaiah 53:12 brings together the bearing of sin by the Servant and his interceding for transgressors.[82] Although he was sinless, he became sin for us (2 Cor. 5:21). Because Jesus is our substitute and takes our place it is appropriate for him to confess our sins as he bears them in his sacrificial death. In being 'answerable for our guilt' Christ vicariously confessed and repented in our behalf.[83] Thus James Henry Thornwell can state:

> Jesus confesses the guilt of his brethren, adores the justice which dooms them to woe, and almost exacts from God as the condition of his own love that justice should not slacken . . . We come before God only in the name of our Priest who presents all of our worship before God's throne. Our prayers are not heard and received as ours, but as the prayers of Jesus; our praises are not accepted as ours but as the praises of Jesus. His intercession and atonement covers all defects and we are faultless and complete in Him.[84]

Jesus in Psalm 51 prays for us. He knows our sin because our sin has become his sin as he bears our sin on the cross. He pleads to God his Father for mercy and cleansing for us (Ps. 51:1-2). He understands the depth of our sin because he bears its heavy burden (Isa. 53:4). He knows that there is no escape from sin for us, because we are sinful from birth (Ps. 51:5), and thus there is no escape from sin for him. Since there is no good in us, he had to bear our sin even though he had no sin. He thus confessed our utter sinfulness.[85] He knew that sin had to be dealt with in relationship to God his Father (Ps. 51:4a) and that the judgment of God against sin was justified. He also knew that his perfect life and sacrifice would be the way that God 'might be just and the justifier of the one who has faith in Jesus' (Romans 3:26). Jesus understood the consequences of sin as he contemplated suffering on the cross (Luke 22:39-46), and he saw beyond the judgment of the cross to the joy of his accomplished work that brings a restored relationship with God (Heb. 12:2). As our sin-bearer he prayed for renewal and that God would not cast us away from his presence because of the sin he bore (Matt. 27:46). Jesus understood that his perfect sacrifice would remove the necessity of the sacrificial system, confirming that the sacrificial system of the Old Testament was not the final solution, but that through the sacrifice of himself we would be accepted. Christ brings the renewal that is not only spiritual, but will one day affect the whole world in the new heavens and earth, the heavenly Jerusalem.

Whenever we read Psalm 51 and contemplate our own sin, we can be thankful that Christ himself has confessed our sins and has taken our sins as his own as he hung on the cross. In his humanity he so identified with us that he bore the judgment of God that we deserve because of our sin. Praise be to God for the amazing, effective work of our high priest!

Psalm 26: An Affirmation of Integrity

The complaint portion of a lament psalm might focus on a situation of distress which leads to false accusations. The psalmist sometimes responds with assertions of innocence. These are called psalms of vindication and include 7, 15, 17, and 26.[86] The theme of Psalm 26 is the integrity of the psalmist in the midst of false accusations, which is then the basis for the plea of vindication and the certainty that the situation will turn out right for the psalmist. There is much discussion concerning the setting of Psalm 26. What kind of situation led to these assertions of integrity? Although it is identified as a psalm of David, very few modern commentators try to link this psalm to a particular situation in David's life.[87] Some take the psalm as the prayer of a falsely accused person who has fled to the temple to find asylum from his accusers and pursuers. At the temple he affirms his innocence and asks the LORD to judge his case and vindicate him (as in 1 Kings 8:31-32).[88] Others connect Psalm 26 to some kind of entrance liturgy at the temple, perhaps in connection with one of the major feasts, where the worshippers are met by priests and must affirm their integrity for entrance into the temple (see the question at the beginning of Psalm 15 and how it is answered in the rest of the psalm).[89] Although either of these settings are possible, it is hard to be certain because so much of the language of the psalms is general enough to be used in a number of situations.[90] It may just be the general prayer of a person who is unjustly accused and appeals to God for vindication.[91]

The theme of the integrity of the psalmist is basic to the structure of Psalm 26. The psalm is framed by the psalmist's assertion that he walks in integrity (vv. 1-3, 11-12). In the body of the psalm the psalmist affirms his integrity in relation to the wicked (vv. 4-5, 9-10) and in relation to worship (vv. 6-8). Thus many see a chiastic structure to Psalm 26, such as (A) walking in integrity (vv. 1-3), (B) relationship to the wicked (vv. 4-5), (C) relationship to worship (vv. 6-8), (B') relationship to the wicked (vv. 9-10), and (A') walking in integrity.[92]

The psalmist asserts his integrity by describing his way of life with the use of the verb 'walk,' which occurs in verses 1 and 3. He first asserts 'I have walked in my integrity' (v. 1) and then 'I have walked in your faithfulness' (v. 3). This is not a statement of perfection or sinlessness but is a description of the general tenor of the psalmist's life.[93] In the context of being falsely accused, it is a response to a specific charge that has been brought against the psalmist.[94] He proclaims his innocence of the charge by asserting the integrity of his life and his devotion to the LORD. The verb 'walk' connotes a whole life that is devoted to the LORD, which is emphasized in the rest of the psalm with the mentioning of heart and mind (v. 2), eyes (v. 3), hands (v. 6), and foot (v. 12). The integrity of the psalmist encompasses his whole being.[95] The emphasis on trusting in Yahweh and the movement from 'my integrity' (v. 1) to 'your faithfulness' (v. 3) also confirms that the psalmist is not claiming perfection. An attitude of trust looks away from oneself to God. Such an attitude is affirmed in verse 3 with the use of strong covenant terminology. The psalmist lives his life oriented toward God's 'steadfast love' (ḥesed) and thus walks in God's faithfulness ('emet). Both terms are covenant terms that emphasize covenant loyalty and enduring faithfulness.[96] God is the ultimate source of this kind of life.

Confidence in his own integrity is the context for the plea to the LORD to examine and vindicate the psalmist. The psalm begins with the plea 'vindicate me,' which can literally be read as 'judge me' (the use of šāphat). This is a request for a public recognition of the righteousness of the psalmist. The innocent will be judged and found to be 'not guilty' of the charge that has been brought against him.[97] Such confidence is seen in the request for God to examine the psalmist (v. 2), using terms that are used in the process of refining metal.[98] Such examination is more than an external perusal but goes to the inner recesses of the psalmist's life and denotes a complete openness to God.[99]

The psalmist further confirms his integrity by describing his relationship to the wicked (vv. 4-5 and 9-10).[100] He does not want to have anything to do with the wicked or with their evil devices. They are 'men of falsehood' (v. 4), a phrase that emphasizes a pursuit of vanity.[101] They are 'hypocrites' (v. 4), who conceal their real thoughts and motives. They are 'bloodthirsty men' (v. 9) whose hands are full of 'evil devices' and 'bribes' (v. 10). Such activities are directly opposed to the ways of the LORD. To keep from becoming entangled in such ways the psalmist dissociates himself from the community of the wicked (vv. 4-5). Instead of 'sitting' with the wicked he will walk with the LORD. Instead of being with the wicked in the 'assembly of evildoers' he will stand in the 'great assembly' to bless the LORD (v. 12). In confirmation of his integrity he asks God not to sweep him away with sinners (v. 9).

In contrast to being with the wicked, the psalmist expresses his desire to worship the LORD (vv. 6-8). He loves the temple of God where the glory of God dwells (v. 8). He confirms again his innocence (v. 6a) and the joy of giving thanks to God for his great deeds (v. 7). There is no dichotomy between the integrity of the psalmist and giving thanks to God for the great things God has done. Thanksgiving is a response to what God has done, which means the psalmist has nothing to boast about in himself. He boasts only in God.

Psalm 26 closes with the same concepts with which it began. Verse 11 reasserts the psalmist's desire to do what is right with the statement 'I shall walk in my integrity.' The plea for vindication in verse 1 is matched with the plea 'redeem me and be gracious to me' in verse 11. It becomes clear that the psalmist is not asserting his own sinlessness but that he looks to God for justification in light of the charge that has been brought against him.[102] The idea of trusting in the LORD so that the psalmist 'will not slip'[103] is picked up in verse 12 with the phrase 'my foot stands on level ground.' Both confidence in the LORD and assertions of his own integrity come together. The 'level ground' in the context of the psalm could refer to the temple, but it is also a metaphor for an upright life and moral integrity.[104] From beginning to end the psalmist asserts his integrity and looks to God to vindicate him.

It is not hard to see how the assertions of integrity in Psalm 26 relate to Jesus. His claims of being the Messiah (John 4:26; Luke 22:67) and the Son of God (Luke 22:70) were under attack as he was accused of false statements and blasphemy at his trial. Throughout John's Gospel Jesus affirms the truthfulness and integrity of his claims. His origin is from heaven (John 3:13). He is the light, and so has nothing to do with the evil deeds of darkness (John 2:19-21). There is no falsehood in him and his testimony is true (John 7:18; 8:14). Even though some do not believe, he tells the truth, which is reinforced with the rhetorical question 'Which one of you convicts me of sin?' (John 8:45-46). The hatred people had for Jesus was a fulfillment of the Scriptures: 'they hated me without cause' (John 15:25; Ps. 35:19). Jesus' integrity is affirmed by the witness of the Father (John 8:12-18). Jesus could pray the opening verses of Psalm 26, 'vindicate me ... for I have walked in my integrity.' He was put to the test (26:2) in the wilderness temptations and was tempted in all ways as we are, yet without sin (Heb. 4:15). His unwavering trust of the Father is seen in his submission to the Father's will in the garden of Gethsemane and his cry from the cross, 'Father, into your hands I commit my spirit' (Luke 23:46). His relationship with the wicked (26:4-5) can be seen in his denunciation of the hypocrisy of the scribes and Pharisees (Matt. 23). His zeal for worship and God's house (26:6-7) is demonstrated in the cleansing of the temple (John 2:16-22). Even though it appeared he was swept away with the wicked in his death (26:9), his prayer for redemption (26:11) and his full vindication (26:1) came on the third day when he was raised from the dead (Romans 1:4). Because of his faithfulness (Heb. 5:7-9) he ministers as our high priest in the heavenly tabernacle (Heb. 9:11-12) and sits at the right hand of God (Acts 2:33). To him judgment has been given (John 5:22; 2 Tim. 4:1).

The integrity of Jesus has implications for his life and his work as our high priest. The word for 'integrity' (*tōm*) in Psalm 26 is related to the word used for a sacrifice that was brought to God 'without blemish' (*tāmim*, Lev. 1:3). Christ offered himself 'without blemish' to God as our sacrifice and through his blood secured 'eternal redemption' (Heb. 9:12-14). The nature of Christ's life as sinless and the effectiveness of his sacrificial death shows that when he prayed Psalm 26 it was not just a prayer that responded to a false accusation in one area of life, but included his whole life. Christ's prayer of Psalm 26 is an assertion of a life of perfection and it is by his sinless life and perfect death that we are accepted by God.

Psalm 73: The Prosperity of the Wicked – From Crisis to Faith

Earlier it was noted that a major theme of the wisdom psalms is the contrast between the way and destiny of the righteous and the wicked.[105] However, sometimes that contrast seems to break down when the wicked prosper and the righteous suffer. Wisdom psalms which express the struggles and questions of the righteous when the wicked prosper fit the broad category of Psalms of Disorientation.[106]

Although there has been much discussion of the genre of Psalm 73,[107] it clearly demonstrates wisdom characteristics and themes. The psalm focuses on the problem of the prosperity of the wicked and the intense struggle this caused for the psalmist's own faith and trust in God. The intent of the psalm is to teach God's people the true end of the wicked and the blessings of the presence of God. The instructional nature of the psalm and the reflective, first person style to convey the message are characteristics of wisdom.[108] In fact, there are many parallels between Psalm 73 and Ecclesiastes.[109]

The movement from a crisis of faith because of the prosperity of the wicked to the affirmation of the true end of the wicked and the reality of the presence of God is seen in the structure of Psalm 73. The problem is laid out in verses 1-12, the turning point comes in verses 13-17, and the solution is set forth in verses 18-28.[110] Each of these sections begins with the Hebrew particle 'ak, which strikes a note of certainty and can be translated 'truly'.[111] The movement from crisis to faith can be seen in the different perceptions of the psalmist toward himself and the wicked in verses 1-12 as compared with verses 18-28. In verses 1-12 he recounts his own plight (vv. 1-3) and the prosperity of the wicked (vv. 4-12), but in verses 18-28 he recounts the plight of the wicked (vv. 18-20) and his own prosperity, or blessings (vv. 21-28). There is a complete reversal of how the psalmist views his own situation and the situation of the wicked.[112] The reason for this change is given in verses 13-17.

In setting out the problem the psalmist begins with a confessional statement that God is good to Israel, who are defined further as those who are pure in heart (v. 1). But the certainty of this statement is called into question in the contrasting phrase 'but as for me' at the beginning of verse 2. The psalmist nearly slipped, no doubt calling into question the confession that God is good to the pure in heart, when he saw the prosperity of the wicked and became envious of their life (v. 3). He describes their prosperity in verses 4-12. They live a life of ease and experience little trouble in this life, even appearing to be free from the normal frustrations and miseries of life (vv. 4-5). Such ease makes them self-reliant and arrogant,[113] wearing pride like a necklace for all to see, and commonly committing acts of violence (v. 6). The prosperity of the wicked leads to arrogant speech which rails even against heaven itself (vv. 7-8). They question whether God is aware of their boasts because nothing happens to them in their arrogant attitudes (v. 11). In other words, they do not see the judgment of God against their activities, but are at ease and increase in wealth (v. 12). Thus the wicked are living in open defiance against God and are not experiencing any bad consequences because of their wicked actions.

The turning point for the psalmist is described in verses 13-17, but this section begins with the crisis of faith the psalmist is experiencing. The prosperity of the wicked causes the psalmist to question the benefit of a life lived in honor of God (v. 13). One would expect that the pure in heart would be blessed by God and the wicked would experience the consequences of their evil deeds, but because this is not happening the psalmist questions the benefit of living a life in honor of God. This disjunction between the psalmist's experience of the prosperity of the wicked and what he expected to happen to the wicked leads to an intense inner turmoil. The psalmist is unable to solve this problem in his own understanding and his attempts to do so become wearisome (v. 16). He is extremely plagued by this problem (v. 14) and recognizes that an affirmation of such a view of the wicked could negatively impact the people of God (v. 15).[114] The change of perspective toward the wicked comes when the psalmist enters the temple and then perceives the true end of the wicked.[115] The mirage of experience and observations, as well as mere outward appearance, is broken. The destiny of the wicked is clear because their final outcome is seen in relationship to the judgment of God.[116]

The new outlook of the psalmist is demonstrated in the rest of Psalm 73. There is a movement from 'I' and 'they' to 'God.'[117] God is only mentioned three times in verses 1-17, once in the opening confession (v. 1), once by the wicked themselves in questioning whether God knows (v. 11), and once in the phrase 'sanctuary of God' (v. 17). But the word 'God' permeates the rest of the psalm as the psalmist addresses God directly (you), and refers explicitly to God six times. Instead of being dominated by experience the psalmist now has a God-centered perspective. From this perspective the plight of the wicked is addressed again (vv. 18-20) and their true end is stated (this section also begins with the affirmation 'truly'). In the first part of the psalm the psalmist was on slippery ground and the wicked were secure, but now the wicked are on slippery ground and the psalmist is secure.[118] The wicked are here today and gone tomorrow, suddenly swept away. From this new outlook the psalmist comments on his previous struggle (vv. 21-22). He confesses his brutish stupidity and then emphasizes the renewed sense of God's presence (vv. 23-28). The only thing that matters is a relationship with God, which is the greatest desire of his heart (v. 25). The transforming nature of the presence of God is seen in verse 28. The psalmist is now secure in God as his refuge and is able to proclaim the works of God. He also affirms the opening confession of God's goodness (v. 1), which is now defined as being near to God.[119] God's presence is with the psalmist in this life, and then 'you will receive me to glory' (v. 24). Although this last phrase is greatly debated, the presence of God certainly outlasts death itself.[120] In contrast to the end of the wicked, the psalmist is confident of his end, the glorious presence of God.[121]

There are several ways that Psalm 73 might relate to Christ. If one sees the 'I' that speaks this psalm as Christ, then it describes his struggle with the goodness of God in light of the seeming triumph of the wicked over him in his death. The struggle in Gethsemane included the prospect that he was going to be delivered over to the judgment of wicked hands (Acts 2:23) to experience the judgment of God against sin on the cross. It seems the wicked have triumphed in mocking his kingship (Luke 23:36-38) and in getting rid of him in his death. Their pride, arrogance, and violence is demonstrated in how they treated the Son of God with apparent impunity (Luke 24:18-25). The struggle of Jesus, from his human nature, to avoid the coming ordeal at the hands of the wicked on the cross can be related to the statements of the psalmist in 73:2 where he almost stumbled. Jesus faced this temptation, but did not fail or slip. In the garden he became aware of the presence of God to sustain him through the cross, perhaps in the angel that came to strengthen him (Luke 22:43). He was able to see beyond the appearance of the triumph of the wicked to the glory he would receive in the power of the resurrection and his place at the right hand of the Father.

Psalm 73 is also relevant for believers who struggle with the prosperity of the wicked and the seeming futility of living a pure life before God. It seems at times that the wicked get their way without any hint of the justice or judgment of God. At such times it is appropriate to look to the place of God's presence where Christ is our refuge and strength. As our high priest he continues to pray for us when we struggle with the apparent ease and arrogance of the wicked. As our prophet he continues to instruct us through his word so that we can see through the false appearances of this world and understand the true end of the wicked. As our king he reigns and we can be assured he will accomplish his purposes in this world and in our lives. In the giving of the Spirit at Pentecost we are empowered by his presence to face the challenges of this life, and in Christ's resurrection we see more clearly our victory and that one day we will be received into glory. With exuberance we proclaim his works and we confess that truly God is good to the pure in heart.

Chapter 6

Indirect Messianic Psalms:
Psalms of New Orientation

The third broad category of psalms is the psalms of New Orientation. They express thanksgiving for the faithfulness and deliverance of God through a difficult time of crisis and despair so that joy and blessing are a part of life again.[1] God has been faithful to bring a person through the difficulty of life, and the person responds with thanksgiving. The two types of psalms that fit this category are the psalms of thanksgiving and the psalms of remembrance.[2]

Psalms of Thanksgiving

The psalms of thanksgiving can be understood in relationship to the hymn and the lament. The hymn praises God in general terms for who he is and what he has done, but the psalms of thanksgiving praise God for a specific action of God on behalf of the psalmist.[3] The laments anticipate God's deliverance but the psalms of thanksgiving celebrate a deliverance that has already occurred. The psalms of thanksgiving are psalms of answered prayer.[4] Many times the psalms of thanksgiving will include in them references to the difficult situation that the psalmist was facing. The psalmist is full of thanksgiving because God has brought him through that difficult situation. This offering of thanks often takes place in the temple, is accompanied by a sacrifice of thanksgiving, and sometimes is in response to a vow that was made when an individual was in trouble. The structure of a psalm of thanksgiving centers on God's deliverance. It usually begins with a statement of the intention of the psalmist to give thanks and a brief reason why the thanksgiving is being offered. The main section is the narration of the psalmist's experience of trouble and God's deliverance. The conclusion usually includes further testimony to God's graciousness.[5] Psalms of thanksgiving can be individual expressions of thanksgiving (18, 30, 32, 34, 92, 116, 118, and 138)[6] or the community's expression of thanksgiving (65, 67, 75, 107, and 124).[7] The community psalms of thanksgiving have the same basic structure as the individual psalms of thanksgiving, with communal elements added, such as plural pronouns, or an address to Israel, or clear indicators that the first person singular pronouns refer to Israel.[8]

Psalm 32: How to Spell Relief – Forgiveness

Psalm 32 has traditionally been associated with the penitential psalms (6, 32, 38, 51, 102, 130), but the focus of the psalm goes beyond the confession of sin to the results of the confession of sin: forgiveness, joy, and thanksgiving. It is not a lament over sin but is a thanksgiving for the forgiveness of sin. The experience of the psalmist in being silent about his sin (vv. 3-4) is told for the purpose of showing the difference between silence and confession. The psalmist, however, has come through the situation and is on the other side of it, full of joy for the forgiveness of sin. Although it is an individual psalm of thanksgiving,[9] the experience of the psalmist is recounted for the benefit of the community of God's people. The strong wisdom element in the psalm, noted by the two-fold use of 'blessed' (vv. 1-2) and the instructional component of verses 8-11, does not call into question the thanksgiving nature of the psalm, but emphasizes that the experience of the psalmist is instructional for the community.

The movement of Psalm 32 reinforces the message of thanksgiving for the forgiveness of sin. It begins with the proclamation of blessedness for those whose sins are forgiven (vv. 1-2), announcing the conclusion at the beginning of the psalm.[10] Then the experience of the psalmist shows the negative consequences in his life when he avoided his sin, with forgiveness coming only when he confessed his sin (vv. 3-5). The turning point of the psalm comes in verse 6 ('therefore') where the psalmist exhorts others to pray to God to experience the same kind of deliverance. In case there is any doubt or resistance to the psalmist's exhortation, there is instruction that includes admonishment to follow the way that leads to trusting in the Lord (vv. 8-10). The psalm ends with a final call for the righteous to rejoice in the Lord (v. 11).[11] There are three different words for sin used in verses 1-2. They are repeated in verse 5 where confession and forgiveness occur. Following the 'therefore' of verse 6, where the exhortation to others begins, none of the words for sin occurs again,[12] which reinforces the message of the joy of forgiveness. God really does remove sin.

Psalm 32 opens with a joyful exclamation of the forgiveness of sin. The word 'blessed' is also the word that begins Psalm 1. Part of the 'way' of the righteous (1:6, 32:6), and the blessing and prosperity of the righteous represented in the simile of the tree (1:3), includes the forgiveness of sin.[13] The use of three different words for sin and three different actions of God in relationship to that sin not only shows the pervasive character of sin in the life of the psalmist, but also the complete removal of sin by the action of God.[14] God takes away the burden of rebellion (1a), he covers up our deviations from his law so that they are no longer visible (1b), and he does not charge our iniquity or deviations against us (2a).[15] True blessedness consists in having every kind of sin removed in forgiveness.

The blessedness of forgiveness is contrasted with the negative consequences when there is no forgiveness because a person is silent about his sin and refuses to acknowledge it. The psalmist speaks from his own experience (vv. 3-5) and recounts both physical and spiritual consequences when sin is avoided. Although the wasting away of the bones could be a metaphorical reference to the weakness of spiritual life,[16] it is hard to avoid the conclusion that sin has physical consequences as well.[17] The effects of sin are felt deeply in the wasting away of the bones, the drying up of strength, and the constant groaning. Ultimately such effects come from the heavy hand of God's judgment in his disapproval of sin. A person whose sin is not forgiven is miserable. Relief comes when the psalmist no longer is silent, but confesses his sin and receives forgiveness (v. 5).

The tremendous relief that comes from forgiveness leads the psalmist to exhort others to pray to God. When those who are godly or faithful find themselves in great need, they should pray to God who will protect and preserve them. Although forgiveness is certainly included in this exhortation, it also includes any kind of trouble from which God is able to deliver.[18] God can bring the same kind of relief by surrounding a person with 'shouts of deliverance' (v. 7). To ensure that people get the point the psalmist instructs them further (vv. 8-10). He admonishes them not to be like the horse or mule which have no understanding and must be led around with bit and bridle. To continue in that way is to experience the sorrows of the wicked (v. 10). The only way to be protected by God's covenant faithfulness is to trust in God. Those who are forgiven are righteous and upright, and have every reason to rejoice and shout for joy (v. 11).

Psalm 32 is another psalm that is difficult at first to see as a prayer of Jesus because he did not need forgiveness for his own sins. However, if Psalm 51 can be a prayer of Jesus as our representative, so can Psalm 32. Jesus can affirm the blessedness of forgiveness because he knows that it is his work on the cross as our priest that is the basis of the forgiveness of sin. The burden of sin can be lifted off the sinner (the word 'forgiven' [nāśā'] means to 'bear away' or 'lift off') because Jesus himself bore the weight of sin. Sin is covered because of his shed blood. Sin is not charged against a person because Jesus has paid the penalty for that sin (vv. 1-2). Jesus as our sin bearer felt the full impact of the negative consequences of sin on the cross, including all the emotional, spiritual, and physical ramifications of what suffering on the cross and bearing the judgment of God for our sin entailed. The psalmist tried to avoid sin by keeping silent about it and suffered the consequences in his life until he came to confess his transgressions to the Lord (vv. 3-5). Jesus' silence does not relate to covering up his own sin, because he was sinless, but relates to his willingness to endure the punishment for the sins of others without affirming his own righteousness, or without calling on the hosts of heaven to deliver him as a way to avoid the cross.[19] As our representative he confesses our sins so we can receive forgiveness.

The turning point in verse 6 exhorts others to pray to God to be delivered. Jesus himself experienced the power of God's deliverance when he was raised from the dead on the third day. He experienced deliverance from the rush of great waters, the preservation from trouble, and the shouts of deliverance that come from the mighty power of God (vv. 6-7). Although there is some debate concerning who is speaking in verses 8-9,[20] these verses make sense as the instruction of Jesus to his people because he is in a unique position to exhort us to submit ourselves to God's way. He is our faithful high priest who is able to sympathize with our weaknesses (Heb. 4:15). The one who trusted in God and was delivered now exhorts God's people to be glad and rejoice. He was able to see beyond the suffering of the cross to the joy that lay beyond ('who for the joy set before him endured the cross,' Heb. 12:2), for he knew that the day of the forgiveness of sin lay on the other side of his work on the cross. He rejoices in his finished work that brings the forgiveness of our sin, and we who have experienced the relief of the forgiveness of sin should also rejoice in what he has done for us.

Psalm 107: Thanksgiving for God's Covenant Faithfulness

Thanksgiving for God's steadfast love or covenant faithfulness (*ḥesed*) is the dominant theme of Psalm 107. Most agree that 107:1-32 is a song of thanksgiving,[21] but there is debate on the relationship of verses 33-43 to the rest of the psalm, and how these verses should be characterized. There are elements of both hymn and wisdom in verses 33-43, so that Anderson calls these verses a wisdom hymn.[22] VanGemeren designates the whole psalm as a thanksgiving wisdom psalm concluding with hymnic praise to the LORD.[23]

Songs of thanksgiving many times recount the experience from which the thanksgiving arises. Psalm 107 does this in a couple of ways. It is the first psalm in the Fifth Book of the Psalter (Psalms 107–150) and seems related to psalms that have come before. It may be a response to Psalm 89:49, ' LORD, where is your steadfast love (*ḥesed*) of old, which by your faithfulness you swore to David?' Psalm 89 closes Book III and laments the condition of the monarchy and the promises of the Davidic covenant. Psalm 107 is at least a partial demonstration of God's steadfast love. It is also a response to 106:47, 'Save us, O LORD our God, and gather us from among the nations, that we may give thanks to your holy name.' Psalm 107 is the thanksgiving response to the answer to the prayer of God's people being brought back from exile.[24] But not only is there general thanksgiving for God's deliverance, Psalm 107 goes on to demonstrate a variety of situations in which God acted in a mighty way to deliver his people and bring them back to the land. The structure of verses 1-32 reinforces the element of thanksgiving by calling on different groups to give thanks to God for what he has done (vv. 4-9, 10-16, 17-22, and 23-32).[25] In each stanza the report of the cry to the LORD and deliverance (vv. 6, 13, 19, 28) and the summons to give thanks (vv. 8, 15, 21, 31) are identical.[26] Thus each stanza contains an exhortation to thank the LORD for his steadfast love (*ḥesed*), which reinforces the opening exhortation in verse 1. Thus thanksgiving and God's covenant faithfulness permeate verses 1-32.

Those who are exhorted to give thanks are identified as the redeemed who have been gathered from the lands (vv. 2-3).[27] The four different situations from which God delivered his people to bring them back to the land are wandering lost without a permanent place to live (vv. 4-9), sitting in the darkness of prison (vv. 10-16), suffering the affliction of illness (vv. 17-22), and facing perils at sea (vv. 23-32). These are not only specific situations in which God has acted, but they also may act as 'open paradigms' for ways we can expect God to act in similar situations.[28] In each of the summons to give thanks (vv. 8, 15, 21, 31), the acts of God's deliverance are called 'wondrous works', a demonstration of his mighty power to save.

In the second part of Psalm 107, verses 33-43, the basic structure related to the four groups who were delivered is gone so that the strong exhortation to give thanks recedes into the background. There is a more meditative tone that reflects on the ways of God and his providence.[29] The point is that God has the power to change things. He can work in any situation to deliver his people and bring about his purposes. This is great news to the righteous and brings silence to the wicked. The wise will attend to God's ways and will meditate on the steadfast love (*ḥesed*) of the LORD. Such meditation will affect believers, as Calvin comments:

> The joy mentioned arises from this that there is nothing more calculated to increase our faith than the knowledge of the providence of God because without it we would be harassed with doubts and fears being uncertain whether this world is governed by chance. The knowledge of God's providence brings a calm state of mind.[30]

Psalm 107 is a community psalm of thanksgiving that exhorts the redeemed to give thanks for the covenant faithfulness of God who is able to deliver from any trouble. As a part of that covenant community Jesus would have participated in the giving of thanks to God for his deliverance and provision. Jesus himself experienced things similar to the exiles. He experienced hunger in the wilderness (Matt. 4:1-4) and did not have a permanent place to lay his head (Matt. 8:20). He suffered the affliction of being taken into custody and rudely treated (Matt. 27:27-30). From his human nature he can give thanks as one redeemed from the gates of death (107:18). He experienced great changes brought about by God (107:33-38) because he was a person in great need who was raised up by God (107:41). From his birth to his death and resurrection he experienced the covenant faithfulness of God. Yet Jesus was more than just a human being. He himself had the power to deliver and it is interesting that the things Psalm 107 relate about God are the very things that Jesus accomplished in his ministry. He fed the hungry in the wilderness (Mark 6:30-44; 8:1-10). He liberated those bound by demonic powers (Mark 12:21-28; Luke 4:16-21). He healed and forgave the sick (Mark 2:1-12). He stilled the storms at sea (Matt. 8:23-27; Mark 4:35-41). In Jesus Christ the steadfast love of God is manifested.[31] Those who have been delivered by the work of Christ are now exhorted to give thanks to God for his steadfast love. Christ is able to deliver his people from any situation of trouble.

Psalms of Remembrance

In the psalms of thanksgiving God is praised for how he has responded in a specific situation to a specific request. Other psalms, called psalms of remembrance,[32] recount the mighty acts of God in Israel's history. The purpose of these psalms was to allow Israel to confess its faith in God and to teach people the meaning of their history, which should lead to the praise of God for what he has done. These psalms also lay a foundation for hope that God would act in a similar way for God's people in the present and the future.[33] Psalms of this type are united by content rather than form,[34] and include 78, 105, 106, 135, and 136.

Psalm 105: God's Covenant Faithfulness on Full Display

This psalm brings together two major elements that establish the major theme of God's faithfulness. There is an historical review of God's providential preservation and deliverance of his people throughout her early history. God's faithfulness is rooted in his covenant promises. There is also an exhortation for God's people to praise him for his wonderful covenant faithfulness.[35] Although the psalm ends with the familiar 'Hallelujah' ('Praise the LORD' in the ESV), the psalm moves toward the purpose of God's actions for his people in history (v. 45): that they might gratefully live in obedience to the law.

The first section of Psalm 105 (vv. 1-11)36 brings together praise and remembering. God's people are summoned to praise God in verses 1-6 through a series of imperatives: give thanks, call, make known, sing, sing praises, tell, glory, seek (two different verbs), and remember. The focus of praise is the character of the LORD, which is displayed in his mighty deeds. The intensity of the summons to praise is matched by the greatness of the deeds of the LORD. When God's people remember his wondrous works, miracles, and judgments (v. 5), the only appropriate response is praise. The summons to praise (vv. 1-6) is followed by the ground of praise (vv. 7-11): God remembers his covenant promises to Abraham. God's covenant is the heart around which the whole psalm turns and it frames the historical review (vv. 7-11 and 42). Thus the historical review of God's wonderful deeds in history is grounded in his covenant promises. The exhortation to praise God at the beginning of the psalm is also rooted in God's faithfulness to his covenant promises. The particular promise of the Abrahamic covenant that Psalm 105 revolves around is the promise of the land of Canaan, as stated in verse 11. For God to fulfill this promise encompasses two truths brought together in verse 7. God chose Israel as his people (v. 7a) to give them the land and God is able to give them the land because he is the sovereign God of the nations (v. 7b).[37]

The historical review can be divided into three sections: Canaan to Egypt (vv. 12-23), in Egypt (vv. 24-36), and from Egypt back to Canaan (vv. 37-45). The emphasis in each section is God's faithfulness to preserve and deliver his people so that the promise of land will be fulfilled. The patriarchs are the focus in verses 12-15. Although they were few in number and only sojourners on the land, God protected them from oppression, even rebuking kings on their account (perhaps a reference to Gen. 12, 20, and 26). The patriarchs are called 'anointed ones' and 'prophets' (v. 15). These terms stress their special relationship with God. Abraham is called a prophet in his role of praying for Abimelech's household (Gen. 20:7). The patriarchs were prophets in the sense that they received covenant revelation.[38] The term 'anointed' becomes prominent later in Israel's history and may be used here in a secondary sense of one called by God and equipped for a certain task.[39] Joseph is the focus of verses 16-23. God's sovereignty is demonstrated in the famine that God sent and in how God worked in the difficult circumstances of Joseph's life to take him from prison to the position of leader of the nation. Joseph was also the instrument through which Jacob and his sons came to Egypt.

The period of Israel's sojourn in Egypt is described in verses 24-36. The emphasis is on what God did for his people in making them fruitful, stronger than their foes, and in delivering them from Egypt through the plagues. God is the one who is active in this section. His sovereignty is the basis for his covenant faithfulness because he has the power to do as he has promised.[40] The exodus from Egypt and the journey toward the land of Canaan is described in verses 37-45. The emphasis is on the provision of God for his people (silver and gold, the pillar of cloud and fire, food and water). God's actions are again connected to the Abrahamic promises (v. 42) and the promise of land is fulfilled in verse 44.

Part of the intent behind God's actions in giving Israel the land is that they would live faithful lives in obedience to God's law (v. 45). Our response to God's faithfulness is gratefully to submit our lives to him in praise and obedience. God remembers his covenant and acts on our behalf. We remember what God has done for us and we give him praise and offer our lives to him. This message was relevant for God's people all throughout the Old Testament. David used a part of this psalm to celebrate the bringing of the ark to Jerusalem (1 Chron. 16) when the land was secure (1 Chron. 14:17; 2 Sam. 7:1). The loss of land and exile were momentous events in Israel. The placement of Psalm 105 near the end of Book IV of the Psalter (90–106) gives it relevance for the exilic community.[41] The patriarchs were few in number and did not have full possession of the land, but God rebuked kings on their account. So he can do for Israel in exile. Joseph was oppressed and humiliated before he was exalted. God can bring Israel through her humiliation to the establishment of the kingdom again. God acted in a mighty way to subdue Egypt and bring Israel out of her bondage. So God can act again in a mighty way in a new exodus out of Babylon. God provided for his people everything they needed in the wilderness on the way to the land of Canaan. So God can provide everything the exiles need in the journey back to their land. The promise of land is not dead. God will faithfully fulfill his promises.[42]

The same message of God's faithfulness to his covenant promises would have been relevant to Jesus Christ as the one who came to fulfill those covenant promises. Jesus was a part of the covenant community summoned to praise God for his covenant faithfulness. He too would remember all that God had done for his people and would be encouraged that God would not abandon him. The patriarchs were few in number and lived as sojourners on the land. Jesus had no place to call home (Luke 9:58) and stood alone, abandoned by his disciples, at his hour of need (Matt. 26:56). The life of Joseph in its broad outlines is the same path that Jesus' life traveled. His path went from the humiliation of the cross to exaltation to the highest position (Phil. 2:5-11). God did not abandon Joseph and God would not abandon him. The power of God to deliver his people from Egypt would be displayed again in his power to deliver them from the bondage of Satan through the resurrection of Jesus from the dead. God provided for his Servant everything he needed and demonstrated once again his faithfulness to the covenant promises. All the promises are Yes and Amen in Jesus Christ (2 Cor. 1:20).

The same message of God's faithfulness to his covenant promises is relevant to the church, but even more so as we have seen the wondrous works that God has accomplished for us in Jesus Christ. We are in a similar position to the patriarchs. The promise of the inheritance of land still awaits us in the future in the new heavens and new earth. We may be few in number and not yet in full possession of our inheritance, but God will preserve and protect his people. He is sovereignly working out his purposes in the church just as he did in the difficult days of Joseph's humiliation.

Our goal is to be faithful even unto death for there is a crown of life awaiting us (Rev. 2:10). Our humiliation will lead to exaltation at the coming of our king. God has the power to multiply his people in difficult circumstances as he did in Egypt, even making us stronger than our foes. We affirm the power of God to deliver his people as he did in the exodus. We have experienced the power of God to deliver us in the regenerating work of the Holy Spirit. We look forward to the day when God will once again display his power for all the world to see. We will then experience the fullness of all that God has in store for us. Until then, God will preserve and provide all that his people need. Our response is to praise him and to offer our lives to him in humble obedience for his covenant faithfulness.

Psalm 106: Israel's Covenant Faithlessness on Full Display

Psalm 106 also gives an historical review of Israel's history. It differs from Psalm 105 in several respects. The history that is reviewed is different. Psalm 105 focuses on the covenant with Abraham and the promise of land. The historical review begins with the patriarchs, focuses on the exodus event, mentions briefly the wilderness period, but ends with possession of the land. Psalm 106 begins with Egypt and the crossing of the Red Sea, focuses on the wilderness experience of Israel, and then briefly reviews their history in the land. The focus on different periods of Israel's history relates to the different emphasis in each psalm. Psalm 105 emphasizes the mighty acts of deliverance by God for his people. Psalm 106 emphasizes the rebellion of God's people. The history of God's people was a history of covenant faithlessness and disobedience. This history has implications for the present community of God's people. Psalm 106 sets before Israel how they are to respond in their present difficulties and it gives them hope because they see how God has been faithful and gracious to his people in the past.

Psalm 106 is structured in such a way that everything in the psalm is related to the appeal for God to save his people out of exile that they may give thanks to his holy name (v. 47). The psalm is framed by 'Praise the LORD' (Hallelujah). Past problems and present difficulties are set within the framework of praise. There follows at the beginning of the psalm an exhortation for God's people to give thanks to the LORD for his goodness and steadfast love (covenant loyalty), which will be on display in the historical review that follows. Verse 2 utters a rhetorical question that expects the answer 'no one.'[43] No one can utter the mighty deeds of the LORD or declare all his praise. The gracious deeds of God and the unfathomable depths of the praise he deserves will become evident in the historical review of Israel's rebellion. Praise offered by human beings is inadequate to express God's praiseworthiness.[44] Verse 3 then offers a blessing on those who observe justice and do righteousness at all times. This expresses the ideal of covenant faithfulness to be lived out by God's people (Deut. 33:21; Micah 6:8; Deut. 6:25), which will be so clearly lacking in the history of Israel. However, the psalmist has confidence that God will again deliver his people, who are called 'chosen ones' and 'your inheritance' (v. 5). These terms should remind Israel of her privileged covenant position. The psalmist also calls on God to remember him when showing favor to the people so that he can participate in the blessing, joy, and glory of God's salvation (vv. 4-5). The well-being of the individual is found only in the well-being of the nation.[45] This individual appeal sets the stage for the corporate appeal for deliverance in verse 47.[46]

The history of the faithlessness of Israel begins in verse 6 with a statement of confession, 'both we and our fathers have sinned.'[47] The historical review is not just informational but shows the covenant solidarity between the exilic generation and the earlier generations of God's people.[48] They share the common problem of covenant faithlessness. Each section of historical review highlights an aspect of covenant faithlessness, which is many times contrasted with acts of covenant faithfulness, either by God or by a member of the covenant community. Covenant faithlessness started already in Egypt at the Red Sea (vv. 7-12) where Israel did not consider and did not remember the great deeds of the LORD. They did not have the wisdom[49] to connect the character of the God they worshiped to their problem at the Red Sea. Instead they rebelled. God demonstrated his power and faithfulness by leading them across the Red Sea and destroying their enemies. Rebellion gave way to faith and praise (v. 12). But their faith did not last long for they soon forgot the character of God and became impatient (vv. 13-15).[50] Their desire for meat took precedence over the plan and timing of God and they tested him in the wilderness. God provided meat but he sent along with it judgment to remind them of his sovereignty.

Covenant faithlessness is also displayed in the people's jealousy toward God's ordained leaders (vv. 16-18), idolatry (vv. 19-23 and 28-31), and unbelief in the power of God to give them the promised land (vv. 24-27). The heinousness of the idolatry is seen not only in that they forgot the great things that God had done for them, but that they exchanged the glory of the God who had delivered them for an idol that could do nothing (v. 20). Instead of a strong covenant bond of faithfulness to the LORD, they yoked themselves to Baal of Peor, the idol of the Midianites (v. 28). Their propensity toward unbelief and idolatry continues after they take the land of Canaan (vv. 34-39). They disobeyed the command to destroy the nations in the land. Instead of being a separate people they mixed with the Canaanites and learnt to follow their wicked ways, including infant sacrifice (v. 37). They became unclean and defiled the land (vv. 38-39).

God did not leave himself without a witness to his people during their rebellion. His judgments against their sin (vv. 15, 17-18, 26-27) should have been testimony to his holy character and a warning that covenant faithlessness brings covenant judgment. Moses 'stood in the breach' before God (v. 23) on behalf of the people when God wanted to destroy them. Moses' intercession turned away God's wrath from his people. Phinehas also intervened when the plague of God's judgment broke out, and was an instrument to bring to an end the anger of God and the plague (v. 30). Over and over again God demonstrated his covenant loyalty through his covenant patience. When his people were in distress and called out to him, he remembered his covenant and delivered them (vv. 43, 45). God's covenant faithfulness in the light of so much covenant faithlessness on the part of his people is the basis of the appeal for God once again to deliver his people by gathering them from the nations.

The cry for help in 106:47 is answered in Psalm 107, a psalm of thanksgiving that gives thanks to God for gathering his people from the lands. Psalm 106 ends Book IV and Psalm 107 begins Book V. Both Books demonstrate the concerns of the exilic and postexilic communities related to restoration and kingship (see ch. 1). Even after the return from exile restoration was a struggle (see Ezra and Nehemiah). God's people continued in covenant faithlessness and sin (see the confession of sin in Neh. 9). Kingship was never a reality after the exile and Israel was never fully independent as a nation, even down to the days of Christ. The full deliverance that Psalm 106 longs for is not begun until Jesus Christ.

There are a number of ways to contemplate the meaning of Psalm 106 in relationship to Jesus Christ. As a member of the covenant community the history of Israel was his history. Although he himself was not a sinner, he identified himself with the community of God's people and their sinful history. But the problem of sin was not confined to the history of Israel, as Paul makes clear in Romans 1 (Romans 1:23 uses Ps. 106:20). The power of the gospel is for both Jews and Greeks because all have sinned (Romans 1:16, 3:23). Jesus came to deliver from the power of sin and to enable people to live lives of covenant faithfulness.

Psalm 106 lays out a history of covenant disobedience followed by covenant judgment and curse. Part of the purpose of the law was to show the sinfulness of humanity and the inability of human beings to keep its righteous standard.[51] Israel had the opportunity to keep the law and live (Lev. 18:5), but failed, and so lost the land and fell under covenant curse (Deut. 28). Phinehas was an example in one situation of what Israel was called to do: be obedient to God and live. His act of intervention on behalf of the nation stopped the plague and that act was 'counted to him as righteousness' (Ps. 106:31).[52] Those are the same words that are used of Abraham, who believed God and it was 'counted to him as righteousness' (Gen. 15:6). If only Israel could keep the law then covenant blessing would be poured out upon them (Deut. 27), but the whole history of Israel stands as a testimony that no one is able fully to keep the law, which is why faith is the way of salvation. Even the covenant mediator Moses, whose intercession turned away the wrath of God from Israel (106:23), was kept from the land of Canaan because of his sin (106:32-33). The history of Israel is a microcosm of the history of mankind, as Paul notes in Romans 1–3.[53] Salvation must be by grace through faith, as the example of Abraham shows (Romans 4:13-25). The only one who could fulfill 106:3 and whose whole life of good deeds could be credited to him as righteousness is Jesus Christ. Through faith in his works we are saved. Even though he knew no sin, he bore the covenant curse on behalf of his people (Gal. 3:10-14). Jesus is the ultimate example of the covenant faithfulness of God who delivers his faithless people.

It is interesting to reflect on Psalm 106 as a prayer of Christ. His recital of the history of rebellion and his identification with the sinful covenant community would have been a part of his priestly work of the confession of our sins (see Ps. 51). The recital of the mighty acts of God would have given encouragement to Jesus, according to his human nature, that his Father was the faithful, covenant-keeping God and would not fail him. The prayer in 106:4-5 brings together favor for the psalmist and God's deliverance of his people – 'help me when you save them.' These two come together powerfully in Jesus. The people of God are saved because God helps Jesus. The power of death is conquered on the third day, the day of resurrection. The powerful results are expressed in 106:5 because Jesus does see the blessings of God fall upon his people. The blessing of 106:3 is offered by Jesus for his people who have been transformed by his power to live a life that reflects his character. Our works are counted as righteous only because of what Jesus has done for us. For the present we still struggle with the old nature,[54] but a day is coming when we will do righteousness and observe justice for all times. For now we look to the power of the Spirit to help us keep the law,[55] confessing our sins when we fail. As the community of believers we give thanks to the Lord because we have seen his covenant faithfulness demonstrated in Jesus. Even though we have been faithless, he has delivered us fully and completely – 'and let all the people say, "Amen!"'

Chapter 7

The Royal Psalms

The monarchy, along with the prophets and the priesthood, was one of the main institutions in Israel.[1] The importance of kingship can be seen in the promise to Abraham that kings would come forth from him (Gen. 17:6), in the law regulating how a king should conduct himself (Deut. 17:14-20), and in the amount of history devoted to the rise of kingship and to the reigns of kings in the historical books. The high point of kingship is reached in David and the early part of Solomon's reign. The theological foundation for the dynasty of David is established in the promises of God to David in the Davidic covenant (2 Sam. 7). There is little wonder that ideas associated with the king and his reign have such a prominent place in the Psalms, much more so than concepts associated with either the prophets or the priesthood.[2] At the heart of the theology of the psalms is the idea of kingship, concerning both the human king and God as king. James Mays argues that the organizing metaphor for the theology of the psalms is the concept 'the LORD reigns.' He sees all the functions and topics of the psalms fitting into the pattern of the active sovereignty of God, who has chosen a people, a king, and a place through which to display his rule of righteousness and justice through the law.[3] Not only is kingship important for the present reality of Israel's existence, but at the heart of the vision of Israel's future are ideas associated with the reign of the king.[4] The loss of kingship in the Babylonian exile puts a strain on the promises of God to David concerning descendants to sit on the throne. The royal psalms keep alive the hope that the Davidic dynasty would rise again.[5]

The royal psalms are defined on the basis of content rather than any particular structure.[6] Although there is not complete agreement on which psalms fit this category, the following psalms are commonly considered royal psalms: 2, 18, 20, 21, 45, 72, 89, 101, 110, 132, and 144.[7] The common thread in the royal psalms is kingship.[8] Many royal psalms refer specifically to 'the king' (2, 18, 20, 21, 45, 72, 89), or sometimes to the king as the 'anointed' (2, 18, 20, 45, 89, 132).[9] If the king is not specifically mentioned, other concepts and activities related to the king are described, such as his conquests or his reign in righteousness and in justice. Although there is much discussion concerning the origin and setting of the royal psalms, the psalms themselves reflect situations related to the activities of the king, such as coronation (2, 110), a royal wedding (45), issues related to war (18, 20, 144),[10] ruling in righteousness and justice (72, 101), and the promises related to the Davidic covenant (89, 132).

The Royal Psalms, the Historical King, and the Messiah

One of the main issues in the royal psalms is the relationship of the psalm to the historical king or the historical situation. This issue is particularly pertinent to royal psalms that are also considered directly Messianic (especially 2 and 110). The problem centers on statements in these psalms that go beyond any historical situation of Israel's history; for example, 2:8 states that God would make the ends of the earth the inheritance of the king, who is the anointed one (the messiah).[11] Nowhere in Israel's history did a king's rule extend over the ends of the earth. And so the question arises as to how the tensions between such statements of universal rule and the historical reality of the kings of Israel are to be handled. It is helpful to lay out the various answers to this question as a backdrop to the discussion of the royal psalms.

One approach is that the language of 2:8 is typical of the language of the royal court in the ANE, where hyperbole is used to describe the reign of a monarch even though that language is not historically accurate.[12] This explanation does not recognize the difference between the gods of the nations and the God of Israel, who is the Creator and ruler of the world. Because the king of Israel is a representative of the LORD (Yahweh), statements of universal rule are not just hyperbole, but are rooted in the historical possibility of Yahweh's universal rule coming to earth. The kingdoms of David and Solomon were significant empires in their own day and offered historical hope for a more expanded kingdom,[13] which is fulfilled in Christ. Thus statements of hyperbole in the psalms are true in relationship to Christ, but this connection requires a divine author who gives unity to revelation and its progression in history.

A second answer to this question so focuses on the function and meaning of a psalm in its historical context that it denies any future, Messianic meaning until later developments in history. Because God is the universal God the jurisdiction of his earthly king could be stated in world-wide terms, but this was only an ideal. After the end of the monarchy, during the exile, radical rethinking took place concerning kingship. Messianic and eschatological concepts became attached to the concept of the 'anointed one.' In the case of Psalm 2, the original meaning is not explicitly Messianic, but it came to be understood as Messianic due to the developments of later history.[14] This view is commendable for stressing the historical context for the meaning of a psalm and for seeing the significance of the changes in Israel's history, which might affect the development of the meaning of a psalm. However, there is a tendency among some to draw a dichotomy between the original meaning of the psalm and the later Messianic, eschatological meaning that came to be associated with the psalm (see ch. 2 for further discussion of this problem).[15]

One is not sure if the later Messianic meaning is always a proper development of the original meaning, or only just one possibility among many others.[16]

Another way to handle the tension between universal statements, such as 2:8, and the historical reality of the kings of Israel is through typology. A type is a person, event, or institution that serves as an example or pattern for later events, persons, or institutions. In other words, God works a certain way in the Old Testament (the type) that is foundational for the way he will work in the fulfillment in the New Testament (the antitype). Typology is rooted in a view of history that is under God's sovereign control so that what happens in the Old Testament anticipates the events of the New Testament fulfillment (hence the importance of the divine author).[17] The relationship between type and antitype is not an arbitrary relationship. It is dependent on the meaning of a text in its Old Testament setting and the development of history in the progress of revelation for understanding the fulfillment of the antitype.[18] There is not a dichotomy between the original, historical meaning of a text and the later meaning, but a development of the original meaning in light of historical changes, like the exile, and further revelation.[19] The Davidic kingdom is seen as a type of Christ's kingdom. Statements that do not fit the historical situation related to the monarchy in the Old Testament are seen as a type of Christ's universal kingdom. Thus the 'ideal' kingdom of God in the kingdom of Israel is best seen from the perspective of the development of God's promise through David's lineage to the coming of the Messiah.[20] Calvin argues that the temporal kingdom of David was a shadow and earnest of the eternal kingdom established by Christ.[21] Although Calvin is very careful not to jump too soon to Christ and the New Testament in interpreting the Old Testament and the Psalms (see ch. 1), in Psalm 2 he quickly makes connections to Christ and the New Testament.

The final approach in understanding the universal statements in the Psalms in comparison with the actual historical situation of the monarchy is to see such statements as directly messianic, or directly prophetic, of Christ. In this view Psalm 2 does not refer to an actual historical king but refers directly to the future, coming Messiah, Jesus Christ. Several reasons are given for this view. Because some statements of the psalms, such as the universal nature of his reign and the trust people are to place in the king, cannot apply to any earthly king, they must apply to Christ.[22] The way the New Testament handles Psalm 16 and the affirmation that David is a prophet in the New Testament (Acts 2:29-32) is seen as evidence that David prophesied concerning the coming of Christ directly.[23] If one accepts at face value the statements of Peter in Acts 2:29-32 concerning David and Psalm 16, then the possibility of this view must be affirmed. However, whether a psalm or statements in a psalm are a direct prediction of Christ must be worked out in light of the peculiarities of each psalm.

The Royal Psalms and the Davidic Covenant

The best way to approach a royal psalm is to understand how the psalm fits into the historical setting of the monarchy, especially its relationship to the concepts of the Davidic covenant. The key promises of the Davidic covenant include a descendant (seed) of David who will build the LORD's house, a father-son relationship between the LORD and the descendant, an enduring house or dynasty, and an enduring kingdom (2 Sam. 7:12-16). These ideas reflect a royal grant covenant where a great king bestows blessings on a lesser king for loyalty to the greater king. These blessings include the right of an enduring dynasty, protection from enemies, and the establishment of a father-son relationship. The lesser king is designated 'son,' as well as 'servant.'[24] These ideas are reflected in the covenant relationship between Ahaz and the king of Assyria. Ahaz calls himself a son and a servant of the king of Assyria (2 Kings 16:7). Thus, any Davidic king could be called 'son of God' and could expect the blessing and protection that is included in the Davidic covenant.[25] What is quite remarkable in some of the royal psalms is how close a relationship there is between the king and God. What is said about God is affirmed about the king. Although the king is never considered divine, the parallels between the actions of the king and the actions of God make it possible to speak of the king in ways where his actions are seen to be God's actions. Such parallels are especially evident in Psalms 45, 89, and 110. This solves a problem in Psalm 45 and prepares one for statements concerning Christ, whose actions really are divine actions.

The royal psalms discussed in this chapter have a significant place in the structure of the Psalter. The early ideals connected to the Davidic king (Ps. 2, 45, 72) give way to the crisis of the monarchy in the exile (Ps. 89). But God has not forgotten his promises to David. A king will arise to defeat all his enemies (Ps. 110) and establish the reign of God in Zion (Ps. 132). This king will also be victorious in the final eschatological battle (Ps. 144).[26] All these royal psalms speak of some aspect of the kingship of Christ. Psalm 2 speaks of the close relationship of the king to God. The king is the Son who will rule the nations. Psalm 45 relates the marriage of the king, which would be a significant event for the kingdom, and has implications for the relationship between Christ and his bride, the church. Psalm 72 presents the righteous reign of the king and the results of that reign for the people. Psalm 89 laments the judgment from God on the king and calls on God to remember his promises to David. Psalm 110 celebrates the victory of the king over his enemies. Psalm 132 affirms the faithfulness of God to his covenant promises in the establishment of the reign of the king in Zion. And finally, Psalm 144 speaks of the final victory of the king. Most of these psalms have a typological relationship to Christ (Pss. 2, 45, 72, 89, 132, and 144). The concept of 'Son' in Psalm 2 is best understood in the sense of 'fuller meaning' because the meaning of 'Son' in Psalm 2 is expanded to include the deity of Christ in the Gospels.[27] Psalm 110 is the only psalm in our analysis that is understood as a direct prediction of Christ because of the unique combination of kingly and priestly roles in one person.

Psalm 2: The Establishment of God's Reign Through His Anointed

Although the basic structure of Psalm 2 is fairly straightforward, there is debate about its historical setting. Some try to find a situation that would fit the description of the nations rebelling in verse 1, but that approach has not been too successful.[28] Others connect the concepts in Psalm 2 to the coronation of the king, or some festival celebrating the coronation of the king,[29] but the accounts of a king's coronation in the Old Testament are few, and the ones that are described vary in the details.[30] Although it is possible that Psalm 2 is connected to the coronation ceremony of a king, it is preferable to read it in light of the covenant with David in 2 Samuel 7, where the greatness of David's name and kingdom are affirmed, the concept 'son' is given to those who follow in the Davidic line of kingship,[31] and God's choice of David and his line matches up to 'his anointed' as God's chosen representative (Ps. 2:2).[32] Thus, the affirmations of Psalm 2 could be related to any Davidic king who would follow God in obedience. Such obedience would bring the consolidation of his kingdom like David's kingdom and put him in a position to ask for the nations as his inheritance (Ps. 2:8).

The promises of the Davidic covenant were not fulfilled in any Davidic king of the Old Testament. Their history was a history of rebellion against God, which led to the end of the monarchy, the destruction of the temple, and the Babylonian exile. But the hope of the promises to David were kept alive. It is possible that the placement of the royal psalms in Books I–III of the Psalter relate to kingship and the Davidic hope (see ch. 1). Psalms 1–2 serve as introductory psalms to the Psalter influencing how the psalms are to be read. Psalm 1 stresses the blessed life of an *individual* who meditates on God's torah, while Psalm 2 introduces the covenant promises of Davidic kingship in relationship to the community of the nations, with the reminder that God reigns through his king.[33] This is a confirmation of the Davidic promises even though it looks like the Davidic covenant is in jeopardy later in the Psalter (Ps. 89). God will establish his reign through his king.

The structure of Psalm 2 supports the basic message of the psalm that God will establish his reign through his anointed king. The first section (vv. 1-3) describes the rebellion of the nations against the rule of God and his anointed king. It is clear that whatever the nations do to throw off the rule of God will not succeed. The opening question of the psalm may express astonishment at the futile efforts of the nations.[34] Their plotting will be in vain. No matter how ferocious, or violent, or determined people are to throw off God's rule, they will not succeed. God's response is given in the second section (vv. 4-6). He laughs at their feeble attempts, derides them for their feeble efforts, and speaks in wrathful judgment toward them. The one enthroned in heaven is secure and cannot be overthrown. Not only is God in heaven secure, but so is the king that he has installed. The 'I' of 'I have installed' is emphatic in Hebrew, emphasizing God's action to establish his rule through his king.[35]

In the third section (vv. 7-9) the anointed king himself speaks, setting forth the decree of the Lord, which defines his relationship with God: 'you are my son, today I have begotten you.' This language reflects the language of the Davidic covenant (2 Sam. 7:14), which reinforces the promises God made to David and to his line.[36] At the heart of God's promise is the special relationship of sonship, which is not a physical or mythological relationship, as in Egypt,[37] but is a legal relationship, described by many as adoption.[38] The king is declared to be son of God[39] and as son he represents the covenant relationship between God and the people of Israel. Israel was God's son in Egypt, even his firstborn (Exod. 4:22), and became a kingdom at Mt. Sinai, with God dwelling in their midst through the tabernacle as king. Yahweh led them forth to battle (Num. 10:35-36) and defeated their enemies.[40] The king, as God's representative, also leads the people into battle as Yahweh fights for his people. As the representative of the Creator and Ruler of the nations, the king's inheritance included the rule of the nations (v. 8). Because the terms son and firstborn (Ps. 89:27) could be used of both the king and the people, the king represented the people as well. The destiny of the king was important for Israel, as other royal psalms will show. For the king to rule the nations (v. 9) would mean that God's people would also rule the nations. It is because of this special relationship between the king and God that the victory of the king is assured: he will one day rule the world.

The last section of Psalm 2 (vv. 10-12) is a warning to the nations to submit to the rule of God's anointed king. In light of the decree of Yahweh they should act wisely and be willing to submit to Yahweh's rule through this king. For those who refuse there are deadly consequences, but those who submit will receive great blessing (v. 12). Even in the face of opposition the triumph of God's rule through his king is assured.

The concepts of Psalm 2 could relate to any Davidic king in light of the promises of the Davidic covenant. However, those promises were never fulfilled in any Davidic king, and with the destruction of the monarchy and the exile to Babylon the fulfillment of those promises looked bleak. However, the hope of those promises was kept alive and they are clearly applied to Jesus Christ, who is the Davidic king through whom God will rule the world. The opposition of nations and rulers against God and against his anointed (Messiah or Christ) is connected to the opposition of Herod, Pontius Pilate, the Gentiles, and the people of Israel against Jesus, who is called the one anointed by God (Acts 4:27). Psalm 2 also has implications in Acts 4 concerning the opposition that Peter and John, and the early church, were facing from the Jewish leaders who tried to hinder them from speaking in the name of Jesus.[41] The early church displayed the same confidence expressed in 2:1-6. They did not back down from the threats and plots against God's anointed king. Instead, they ask for boldness to continue to speak in Jesus' name, which God grants through a demonstration of his power (Acts 4:31) and the success of their preaching (Acts 4:32-37). Even in the midst of opposition God is establishing his rule through the proclamation of the name of his king.

The Gospels also affirm that Jesus is God's anointed king. Jesus came preaching that the kingdom of God is near, which demanded the response of repentance.[42] The admonition to the rulers to be wise and submit to his rule applies to all those who hear his message. He is declared to be the Son of God at several key events of his ministry. There may be an allusion to Psalm 2 at Jesus' baptism (Matt. 3:17; Mark 1:9-11; Luke 3:21-22) and transfiguration (Matt. 17:1-8; Mark 9:2-8), where a voice from heaven affirms, 'This is my beloved Son, with whom I am well pleased.' Paul specifically quotes from 2:7 to affirm the resurrection of Jesus (Acts 13:30-33). The people at Jesus' baptism may not have understood the full meaning of the declaration of sonship,[43] but there are indications at his baptism that sonship goes beyond what is said about the human Davidic king in the Old Testament. Although Jesus begins his public ministry by identifying himself with sinners who need cleansing as part of his fulfillment of the law, he himself does not need cleansing (Matt. 3:11-14). Instead of the anointing oil, which is symbolic of the Spirit, the presence of the Spirit himself is seen in the dove coming on Jesus (3:16). At the beginning of his public ministry Jesus is openly declared to be the anointed one (the Christ)[44] and is equipped, according to his human nature, with the gifts of the Spirit for his ministry.[45] This is his public coronation day as king and son. But the nature of his kingship is hinted at in the allusion to Isaiah 42:1-4 ('in whom I am well pleased'), connecting Jesus to the servant of Isaiah, who combines Messianic authority and suffering servanthood.[46] At the transfiguration the declaration 'this is my Son' comes as Peter wants to make three tabernacles, one for Jesus, one for Moses, and one for Elijah.[47] But Jesus is not on the same level as Moses and Elijah. He stands out from them and is the one to be obeyed ('hear him'). Jesus is the authoritative Son, affirmed by Moses and Elijah, who represents the law and the prophets.

Yet Jesus was not the kind of son or king the people desired. His sonship and kingship is ridiculed and called into question due to his suffering (Matt. 27:40-43), but he is vindicated in his resurrection where his victory over sin and death is demonstrated and proclaimed (Acts 13:38). As Paul confirms in Romans 1:4, Jesus is 'declared to be the Son of God with power ... by the resurrection from the dead.'[48] What is said about Jesus and what he accomplishes is more than any human king could accomplish. The uniqueness of his birth sets him apart as Son of God (Luke 1:35). The demons recognize the power of the Son over them (Matt. 8:28; Mark 3:11), he is worshipped as Son of God by his disciples (Matt. 14:33), and the unusual events surrounding his death bring an affirmation from the centurion at the foot of the cross that Jesus is the Son (Matt. 27:54; Mark 15:39). The Gospel of John was written that people might believe that Jesus is the Son of God and through that belief come to experience true life. He can bestow such abundant life because he is God, who will raise the dead (John 5:25). He is accused of blasphemy because he calls himself Son of God (John 10:36). In response to Jesus' previous knowledge of him Nathanael brings together sonship and kingship in his exclamation, 'you are the Son of God! You are the king of Israel' (John 1:49). That Jesus is Son in ways that go beyond a human sonship is affirmed in Hebrews 1:5, where Psalm 2:7 is cited to demonstrate his superiority to angels. He sits at the right hand of the Majesty on high and has inherited a more excellent name than the angels (Heb. 1:4). Although Jesus fulfills the original destiny of humanity in becoming a little lower than the angels (Ps. 8:4-6; Heb. 2:6-8), he is also superior to the angels and more than a mere human in his deity.

Although some see a dichotomy between the Old Testament picture of a king who will possess the nations and dash them in pieces like pottery and the suffering of Christ on the cross,[49] one cannot understand the total picture of Jesus' kingship by limiting it to his ministry of suffering in his first coming. Even in his first coming there are glimpses of his authority, as seen in his casting out demons and his response to the Gentile and Jewish rulers during his trial. Even now the church proclaims the good news of the reign of Christ to the nations who are becoming a part of his inheritance. We are sent by the one who has been given *all* authority in heaven and on earth (Matt. 28:19-20). Even now he is reigning from the right hand of the Father by virtue of his resurrection and ascension, so that even now everything is under his feet (Eph. 1:20-23). But the full disclosure to the world of his rule will become clear when he comes again. Thus it is not surprising to see 2:9 alluded to in Revelation 19:15, where he comes as the almighty king who will strike down the nations and rule them with the rod of iron. He will receive the nations as his inheritance and his kingdom will extend to the ends of the earth. Not only are all those who trust in him blessed so that they will not perish, but they will also reign with him. The very words spoken of the Davidic king in 2:9, and the words used to describe the rule of Jesus, the king of kings (Rev. 19:15), are also used to describe those who are faithful to him to the end. Following Christ to victory they will be given authority over the nations and will rule them with a rod of iron (Rev. 2:26-27). In Christ they will fulfill their true destiny of dominion over creation (Gen. 1:26-28) and over everything that opposes God.

The concept 'son' in the Old Testament refers to the human king who is brought into a covenant relationship with Yahweh as his representative. It could refer to any Israelite king. As applied to Jesus it also includes the idea of deity. Some understand Psalm 2 as a direct prediction of Christ because David is presented as a prophet and the psalm is applied directly to Christ in the New Testament.[50] Although a possibility, this view makes it difficult to make sense of the psalm in its Old Testament context. Others understand Psalm 2 in a typological relationship with Jesus Christ. Calvin understands the temporal kingdom of David as a type of the kingdom of Christ.[51] Van Groningen understands the concept 'son' in a typological way. Although the son-king is not divine, he does represent deity and deity expresses itself through the human king. The human king is a symbol through which Yahweh is present. As a symbol he serves as a type that will come to full reality in the future.[52] Typology is an appropriate way to approach Psalm 2 because typology deals with persons, like David, or institutions, like kingship.

It is also fruitful, however, to explore the implications of fuller meaning in relationship to the concept 'son.' Fuller meaning usually focuses more on the meaning of concepts. There may be a development of the meaning of son between the use of son in Psalm 2 and its meaning in relationship to Jesus. The king was the son of God, representative of the people, who was to be obedient to God so that God would give the people victory over their enemies. A glimpse of such a king is seen in David and the early years of Solomon's reign, but the failure of the human kings pointed the way to a different kind of son. It is no coincidence that the texts proclaiming a son who will bring in universal righteousness (Isa. 9:6-7; 11:1-10) comes after king Ahaz rejects the way of trusting in Yahweh (Isa. 7). Just as later in Isaiah a different servant is needed, so here a different son is needed to accomplish God's purposes, a son who is 'Wonderful Counselor, Mighty God, Everlasting Father, Prince of Peace' (Isa. 9:6). Many of the psalms in Books I–III of the Psalter are connected with David, and may have been composed by him or with his kingship in view, which would be the meaning of the psalm in its historical context. With the failure of the monarchy David's kingship becomes an ideal looking forward to a king who will rule in righteousness, a son who will possess the ends of the earth. The royal psalms within the completed Psalter reflect this longing and the references to the king take on more of an eschatological focus within the final context of the Psalter. When the fullness of revelation comes in Jesus Christ the full meaning of son is revealed, a son who fulfills all that son means in the Old Testament, and a son who is more than a human king.

Psalm 45: The Marriage Celebration of the King

Psalm 45 is full of the pageantry that would surround a wedding for the king, which would truly be a national and religious event in the life of the nation.[53] Thus it would appear that this psalm is rooted in a particular, historical royal wedding. The composition of the psalm is addressed to the king (v. 1) and the structure of the psalm revolves around the presentation of the bridegroom and the bride. After the introduction of verse 1, there is the praise of the bridegroom king (vv. 2-9), the presentation of the bride (vv. 10-16), and the future blessings that will come from this royal union (vv. 16-17). The king is praised for his physical demeanor, which includes gracious speech (v. 2),[54] his military victory for the cause of truth (vv. 3-5), and the splendor of the wedding event (vv. 8-9). The bride is instructed on how to relate to her husband king (vv. 10-12) and is then brought to the king in all her beauty with her attendants (vv. 13-15). The instructions to the bride include an admonition to forget her own people (which may mean she is a foreign bride), a brief statement to encourage proper respect for the king, and the blessings she will experience because of her position as bride. Those blessings include relationships with the richest of the people of the earth, as represented in the people of Tyre.[55] The future blessings of this royal union (vv. 16-17) include sons who will be in high positions, the praise of the nations, and the perpetual memory of the name of the king in future generations. Thus it appears that Psalm 45 was composed for a royal wedding of one of the kings of Israel.[56]

The difficulty in understanding Psalm 45 as a reference to a king of Israel comes in verses 6 and 7, where the king seems to be addressed as God (Elohim): 'Your throne, O God, is forever and ever.' This statement comes in the middle of celebrating the victories of the king without any indication of a change of subject or person addressed. The king is exhorted in verse 4 to ride out victoriously for the cause of righteousness, and in verse 7 is the statement, 'you have loved righteousness.' The military victory of the king over his enemies is presented in verse 5. If the psalm is a royal wedding song of the king, and the context of these verses is talking about the king, how does one explain the direct address to God in verse 6a?

This problem is handled a number of different ways. One approach is to translate verse 6a in a way that eliminates the problem. Kraus translates the phrase as 'your throne, O divine one,' and recognizes the possibility that *'elohim* might be applied to the Davidic king in the sense that the king is the son of God by adoption and that some Old Testament statements move the king close to the LORD (Yahweh), such as 2 Samuel 14:17.[57] However, Kraus recognizes that nowhere else in the Old Testament is *'elohim* used of the king and that the deification of the earthly king goes against the basic faith of Israel. Others take *'elohim* as a reference to the throne of the king and not the king himself; for example, the NEB translates the phrase, 'your throne is like God's throne, eternal' and the RSV, 'your divine throne.'[58] Mitchell Dahood, followed by Craigie, takes the noun phrase 'your throne' and makes it into a verb phrase, 'has enthroned you,' resulting in the translation, 'the eternal and everlasting God has enthroned you.' Although Craigie notes that this translation is not without difficulty, he believes it makes the best sense in the context of the psalm because it is the king that is in view.[59]

Most of the above translations of 45:6 try to avoid the problem of addressing the king with the term *'elohim*. However, the best translation of this verse is 'your throne, O God, is forever and ever.'[60] This translation is in line with all the ancient versions[61] and is followed by the NASB, KJV, NKJV, NIV and ESV. But how does one explain this translation in the context of Psalm 45? Some argue that it is appropriate to apply the term *'elohim* to the human king because elsewhere in Scripture earthly authorities are called *'elohim* as God's representatives on earth (Exod. 21:6; 22:7; Ps. 138:1). In this view the king is so closely identified with *'elohim* that he can be called *'elohim*.[62] This identification is explained in a number of ways. The king is seen as the perfect realization of the close relationship between God and the king,[63] or he is presented as a divinely chosen and gifted person (but not divine by nature),[64] or he is presented as the messianic royal agent who reflects the promise of 2 Samuel 7:13 and so is addressed as *'elohim*.[65] Most who apply *'elohim* to the human king go on to say that verse 7 makes it clear that the human king is subordinate to *'elohim*.[66]

Those who try to retranslate 45:6, or who apply the term *'elohim* to the Davidic king, tend to deny that Psalm 45 had any Messianic meaning in its original, historical context. Delitzsch comments that the Prophetically Messianic sense is not the original meaning of the psalm.[67] Craigie states that the Messianic meaning is a secondary meaning but not the meaning in the original context.[68] Van Groningen notes that Psalm 45 does not predict the coming of the Messiah.[69] If the original meaning of the psalm is not Messianic, then the Messianic meaning must have developed later. Delitzsch believes the Messianic meaning is very old and that the author of the psalm is warranted in regarding the king as Messianic in light of the Davidic promises.[70] Many see a reinterpretation of the meaning of the psalm in light of the exile when the promises to David were reinterpreted and hopes were pushed into the future. The community began to look for a Messiah, a future descendant of David, who would establish a kingdom that would never fail. Many of the psalms, like Psalm 45, were reinterpreted with this Messianic understanding.[71]

Others argue that the original meaning of 45:6-7 is Messianic and that these verses refer to the Messiah, Jesus Christ. Calvin understands the psalm to be about Solomon and his kingdom in its historical context, but believes the psalm typically refers to Christ because the eternal duration of the kingdom is emphasized and the term Elohim is used (which can only apply to Christ).[72] Others take the psalm as a direct prediction of Christ, the Messiah, because none of the historical marriages of any king fit the psalm and things are said in the psalm that transcend any earthly king.[73] Harman argues that there is a sudden introduction of a Messianic element into Psalm 45 as the psalmist sees the glory of the Davidic ruler typifying the kingly rule of the Messiah, and so addresses the Messiah directly. Such a sudden Messianic element introduced into a text is paralleled, he believes, in Isaiah 9:6-7.[74]

There is much to commend the view that 45:6-7 is a direct prediction of Christ, but it tends to separate 45:6 from the historical context. Even typology is built on the fact that the type has meaning to the original historical audience. If Elohim in verse 6 is a direct prediction of Christ, then what is the meaning in the historical context? On the other hand, there are problems with the view that does not see any Messianic meaning in the original context; such a view alleges a difference between the original, nonmessianic meaning of the psalm, and the later Messianic meaning. Wilson argues that there is ambiguity in Psalm 45 related to who is in view in the military actions that are described. Is God acting or is the king acting, or both?[75] The throne of the king is not his throne, it is God's throne (1 Chron. 29:23). The king leads the people in military battle, but Yahweh is the one who fights for his people and wins the victory. In light of the fact that God stands behind the king, it would not be out of place to address God in the context of speaking about the king. Such could be the case in verse 6, with verse 7 making the transition back to the king in the phrase 'God, your God, has anointed you.' This meaning in context is also the basis for the Messianic meaning, which is a development of the original meaning.[76] The coming of Christ, a king who is both God and man, allows 45:6 to be legitimately applied to him, as in Hebrews 1:6-7.

If 45:6 ultimately refers to Christ, how do we understand the rest of the psalm in relationship to Christ? The best approach is a typological approach that sees the event of the royal wedding of the king as a type of the relationship between Christ the king and his bride, the church. The covenant of marriage is a concept used in Scripture to refer to the relationship between God and Israel (Hosea 1–3), and the relationship between Christ and his people (Eph. 5:22-33). In answer to a question from the disciples of John the Baptist concerning why the disciples of Jesus do not fast (Matt. 9:14-17), Jesus compares himself to a bridegroom and states that it is inappropriate for the wedding guests to mourn while the bridegroom is present. The healing ministry of Jesus (Matt. 9–10) is evidence that the salvation of the kingdom has come in him. How can someone fast in light of that good news? However, when the bridegroom is taken away, a reference to his coming death, then his disciples will fast.[77] Jesus inaugurated the salvation of the kingdom at his first coming, but the fullness of the kingdom will not arrive until he comes again. Until then the invitation goes out for people to receive this good news of the kingdom. Jesus uses the parable of the royal marriage (Matt. 22:1-14) to emphasize the necessity of accepting the invitation to the wedding feast and to come wearing the proper robe given by the king.[78] The wedding feast is the messianic kingdom and the robe is symbolic of the proper attitude toward the king.[79]

The book of Revelation uses the feast of the marriage supper of the Lamb to describe the uniting of Christ with his bride at the end of history (Rev. 19:6-8). There is great rejoicing as the bride is presented clothed with linen bright and pure, symbolic of the righteous deeds of the saints. Christ has provided everything that the bride needs by sanctifying her, cleansing her with the washing of water with the word, and by presenting the church to himself without spot or wrinkle (Eph. 5:26-27). Thus there is great rejoicing and all glory is given to the Lord who has made everything possible. It is appropriate to contemplate the meaning of the royal wedding of Psalm 45 in light of these wedding concepts.

The beauty and pageantry of a wedding is displayed in Matthew 22:1-14 and Revelation 19:6-8 in the preparation of the feast, the invitation of guests, and the emphasis on garments and robes. Revelation 19:6-8 especially emphasizes the multitude of guests and the great joy of the occasion. The coming of the king and the kingdom, whether in its initial manifestation in the first coming of Christ (as in Matt. 9:14-17 and 22:1-14), or in its fullness in the second coming of Christ (Rev. 19:6-8), generates tremendous joy and celebration. At the wedding feast there is the presentation of the bridegroom king and the bride. The king is praised for his beauty and his gracious speech. It is interesting that although Saul and David are praised for their physical appearance (1 Sam. 9:2; 17:43), physical appearance was not the *basis* for the choice of David (1 Sam. 16:7). The gracious speech of the king brings out an inner quality of character that comes from the blessing of God (Ps. 45:2). Luke 2:40, 52 states that Jesus grew strong physically, but he also grew in favor (the word for grace) with God and man and increased in wisdom. It was not the outward beauty of Christ that draws us to him. In fact, because of his suffering 'he had no beauty that we should desire him' (Isa. 53:2). Our joy in Christ our king is found in his work of grace for us. There is no doubt that when he comes again it will be a beautiful sight for his bride. Revelation 19:11-16 presents Christ as the king riding forth in the cause of truth and righteousness (Ps. 45:3-4) finally to defeat all his enemies.

The bride is also presented in all her beauty. She is instructed to be loyal to the king and to submit to his authority. Paul develops these ideas in relationship to the mystery of the oneness of marriage and the relationship of Christ to the church. Christ is head of the church and the church submits to Christ. Christ loves the church sacrificially and prepares to present her without spot or wrinkle (Eph. 5:22-27). In Revelation 19:6-8 the bride is presented, having made herself ready, being clothed with fine linen, which is identified with the righteous deeds of the saints. Here the bride's responsibility to make herself ready is emphasized. In Ephesians 5 it is Christ who presents the bride by cleansing her. The fact that the bride in Psalm 45 is a foreigner (v. 10) fits in with the Old Testament idea that it is God's purpose to bless the nations and that the church is made up of Gentiles as well as Jews (Eph. 2:11-22). The result of this union produces sons who reign (Ps. 45:16; Rev. 3:21), the praise of the nations (Ps. 45:17; Rev. 21:26), and a name that endures forever (Ps. 45:17; Phil. 2:9-10). What a glorious day it will be when the bridegroom king comes. Are you preparing yourself as his bride to meet him?

Psalm 72: The Blessings of the Reign of a Righteous King

Psalm 72 is a prayer for the king asking that God bring about his rule on the earth through the reign of the king.[80] This psalm begins with the title 'for Solomon'[81] and ends with a doxology that closes Book II of the Psalter, followed by the postscript 'the prayers of David ... are ended.'[82] It is likely this psalm was composed by David for Solomon, with the father praying that the reign of his son would reflect the justice of God and the blessings that flow forth from such a righteous reign.[83] Although the structure of Psalm 72 is difficult,[84] the content of the psalm focuses on the effects of the righteous reign of the king, especially on the poor and on creation. The righteous reign of the king produces an abundance of material blessings. Some divide the psalm into three sections, each beginning with a petition for the king (1-7, 8-14, 15-19).[85] It is possible to see a chiastic structure to the psalm which also revolves around three requests:[86]

A First request (vv. 1b-c)	God give the king justice
B Reason of request (vv. 2-4)	justice for the poor/ prosperity for the people
C Consequence (vv. 5-7)	fear of Yahweh/prosperity for the righteous
D Second Request (v. 8)	God give the king international rule
C¹ Consequence (vv. 9-11)	kings and nations serve the king
B¹ Reason (vv. 12-14)	deliverance of the poor from oppression
A¹ Third Request (vv. 15-17)	God give the king long life; summary of the main ideas of the psalm

The first request is that God would grant the king the justice and righteousness that belongs to God (vv. 1b-c).[87] Justice and righteousness are characteristics of God's reign and should be a part of the king's reign as he is to enact God's rule through his reign.[88] The second request is that God would extend the reign of the king over the whole earth, with the consequence that kings and nations would serve him (vv. 9-11). The third request is that God would grant the king long life. A king who reigns in righteousness will consolidate his empire as a basis on which to influence the world. A long life for such a king would be a blessing to those under his charge. And so prayer is to be made for the king continually (v. 15).

The first request is followed by the reason for the request (vv. 2-4) and the consequence of the request (vv. 5-7). The reason for granting justice to the king is two-fold. A righteous king delivers the poor (vv. 2, 4) and allows for prosperity and wholeness to come to the people. Even the mountains, which are usually barren, bring forth fertility for the people.[89] The word used to refer to this prosperity is *šālōm* (peace), which stresses wholeness in the political, economic, social, and spiritual dimensions of life.[90] Thus the king is the instrument of God's blessing for his people (v. 6), which will result in people fearing the LORD.[91] A proper ruler inspires the proper reverence and worship of God.[92]

The second request, which is for dominion over the earth (v. 8), is followed by the consequence that all the kings will bow down before him and all the nations will serve him (vv. 9-11). Then comes the reason for the request of universal dominion: the poor will be delivered (vv. 12-14). Deliverance and redemption come to the poor and needy throughout the world.

The third request, which is for long life (v. 15), is followed by statements that call for blessing to fall on the production of creation (v. 16) and on the people themselves (v. 17b). Such a king is worthy of a long life and a name that endures forever (vv. 15, 17a).

Although the doxology (vv. 18-19) may be outside of the structure of this psalm, the placement of the doxology at the end of this psalm is a reminder that God himself is the one who accomplishes these things and that the whole earth should be filled with his glory.[93]

Although some take this psalm as a direct prophecy of the reign of Christ,[94] it is better to take the reign of the king in Psalm 72 as a type of the reign of Christ because the psalm clearly reflects the historical reality of Solomon's reign.[95] The title of the psalm connects the psalm to Solomon, and the imagery and language of the peaceful and prosperous reign of the king also has allusions to Solomon's reign. Solomon prayed for wisdom to judge the people with justice (1 Kings 3:11), and justice is given priority in Psalm 72.[96] This psalm is itself a prayer for the king that his reign would bring blessing. Thus the verses in this psalm were originally petitions for the king. Some of the petitions have specific connections to Solomon. The effects of wisdom and justice are emphasized in 1 Kings 3–4 in the well-ordered administration of his kingdom (4:1-19), the deliverance of the living child to the right prostitute mother (3:16-28), and the great material blessings that God's people experienced under Solomon (4:20). He not only ruled over the extended boundaries of the promised land (3:21), with 72:8 being a poetic paraphrase of the land promise in Exodus 23:31,[97] but his influence extended to the people of all nations and the kings of the earth (4:34), who brought gifts to Solomon (1 Kings 10:24-25). A clear example of this is the coming of the Queen of Sheba to Jerusalem because of the reports she had heard about the wisdom of Solomon and the prosperity of the land (1 Kings 10:7). She brought much gold (1 Kings 10:2), which is also reflected in the petitions of 72:10 and 15. Thus Solomon's fame spread to the ends of the earth and through the account given to us in 1 Kings his fame has continued as long as the sun (Ps. 72:17). It is apparent that these prayers for Solomon were answered by God.

It is also apparent that Psalm 72 is not ultimately fulfilled in Solomon. God had promised Solomon that his days would be lengthened (1 Kings 3:14; Ps. 72:15) if he would be obedient and walk in God's ways, but Solomon later in life turned away from the Lord (1 Kings 11). Thus the great kingdom was divided after his death. This prayer for Solomon, or for any Davidic king, takes on added significance in the exilic and postexilic periods when the monarchy is no longer in existence. Psalm 72 becomes a prayer for a future Davidic king who will arise to fulfill these petitions. The use of 72:8 in Zechariah 9:10 reinforces the eschatological and Messianic connections of Psalm 72.[98] Christ is the fulfillment of the hopes and prayers in Psalm 72, so that in him the petitions become a reality.

The statements in Psalm 72 must be understood in light of the first and second comings of Christ. Now that the righteous king has come and won the victory on the cross, we do not pray for him as much as we pray for the full coming of his righteous kingdom ('your kingdom come'). Christ does possess the justice and righteousness of God (the first request of 72:1; see also Matt. 27:19 and John 5:30) because he is God incarnate. The gospel of Christ is good news to the poor because he delivers from oppression (Matt. 11:5) and brings forth the blessings of creation in material abundance. It is interesting that just before the feeding of the five thousand in John 6 Jesus is on a mountain (Ps. 72:3, 16; John 6:3), and after the multitudes are fed the people come to try and make Jesus king (John 6:15). Do they recognize the connection between material blessing and the coming reign of the righteous king? One day this righteous king will come again (Rev. 19:11) and make all things new, ending pain, sorrow, and death (Rev. 21:4-5) and bringing the fullness of life (Rev. 22:1-5). The consequence will be that nations and kings will honor and serve this king (Rev. 21:24-26). This will fulfill the second request of 72:8. The third request of 72:15 looks forward to the continuing reign of this righteous king. Christ's name will endure forever, for he is eternal, and through him the glorious name of God will be blessed forever and the whole earth will be filled with the glory of God's presence (Ps. 72:19). What a day that will be when we see the return of our glorious king!

Psalm 89: The Tribulations of the King

Psalm 89 is made up of three sections: a hymn to Yahweh for his faithfulness (vv. 1-18), a review of the oracle that established the Davidic covenant and its promises (vv. 19-37), and a lament over the apparent failure of the promises to David in light of the condition of the monarchy (vv. 38-51). The psalm closes with a doxology (v. 52) that marks the end of Book III of the Psalter (Pss. 73–89). Although these three sections are distinct and are clearly set off from each other[99] they have strong thematic connections with each other. The key words of the psalm are 'steadfast love' (ḥesed) and 'faithfulness' ('ĕmûnāh), each occurring seven times in the psalm and in all three sections of the psalm.[100] The hymn praises God's faithfulness, with an emphasis on God's power in creation, and the oracle shows how the faithfulness of God is the foundation for the promises of the Davidic covenant. The lament then questions the existence of this faithfulness because the present situation of the covenant community gives no evidence that the promises of God to David were being fulfilled.[101]

Psalm 89 opens with the psalmist expressing his desire to sing and make known the steadfast love[102] and faithfulness of Yahweh. Verses 2 and 3 mention the two things that are going to be developed in the first two sections of the psalm: God's

139

steadfast love and faithfulness established in the heavens and God's covenant with David.[103] The hymn goes on to show how the heavens and the heavenly hosts praise the power of God who rules over his creation, a rule that exemplifies God's steadfast love and faithfulness (vv. 5, 14). In the oracle (vv. 19-37), the key terms 'steadfast love' and 'faithfulness' are also prominent in God's covenant with David (verses 24, 28, and 33 use 'steadfast love' and verses 24 and 33 use 'faithfulness').

The promises of David take on the same character of enduring stability as the creation, for the same God who rules over creation has made an oath to his servant David (v. 3) to establish his throne (v. 29). What is true of Yahweh (the LORD) in verse 1 and is built into the heavens in verse 2, is now displayed in David as Yahweh's representative in verse 24. In fact, what is remarkable about the hymn and the oracle is how much overlap there is between what is said about Yahweh in the hymn and what is said about David in the oracle.[104] Yahweh is presented as the head of the heavenly assembly in 89:6-7, and as head of the heavenly assembly he is called the Most High (*'elyôn*) in Psalm 82:6. Yahweh will make David the firstborn, the highest (*'elyôn*) of the kings of the earth (v. 27). It is clear from the parallel with 'highest' that the term 'firstborn' does not refer to one who is literally born first, but to one who has all the privileges and blessings that come with having the highest place.[105] As Yahweh is the Most High of the heavenly assembly, so David is the highest of the kings of the earth and will defeat all his enemies (vv. 22-23). Yahweh rules the raging sea and scatters his enemies (vv. 9-10) displaying the strength of his hand (v. 13). Yahweh will also place David's hand on the sea and his right hand on the rivers (v. 25).[106] David, as Yahweh's representative, also rules the sea. Yahweh exalts the horn of his people (v. 17) and Yahweh will exalt the horn of David in Yahweh's name (v. 24), a promise to exalt the kingdom of David over his enemies.[107] Such a close relationship between Yahweh and the Davidic king was expressed in Psalm 2:7 and is exemplified in 89:26 in the cry of David, 'You are my Father.' The heavenly rule of Yahweh, the Creator of the heavens and the earth, is manifested on the earth through the reign of David. The promises to David in verses 20-28 are extended to his descendants in verses 29-37,[108] which are a reflection of the promises in 2 Samuel 7. David's throne will last 'as long as the sun' (v. 36).

The strong statements in the first two sections of the psalm concerning God's steadfast love and faithfulness, his powerful rule in the heavens, his promises to David and his descendants to establish a throne, his oath to fulfill the promises, and his affirmations that he will not violate the covenant and will not lie to David, make the lament all the more jarring to the reader. Verses 38-45 describe a situation that is the exact opposite of the promises in the first two sections of the psalm. Instead of being the highest of the kings of the earth with an enduring throne, the throne and the crown are cast down to the dust (vv. 39, 44). Instead of David's right hand ruling the sea and rivers, the right hand of the enemy is exalted (v. 42). Instead of the horn of David being exalted in victory, the kingdom experiences the humility of defeat (vv. 43-44). The incongruity between the promises of God to David and the current situation of the kingdom has an explanation that goes back to the Davidic covenant itself, and is expressed in verses 31-33. God will punish transgression with the rod, which explains the situation in verses 38-45, for the psalmist recognizes that God is full of wrath against the anointed (v. 38). The strong statements of rejecting the king and renouncing the covenant (vv. 38-39) relate to the punishment of the Davidic kings who have not obeyed God. Thus the problem is not the steadfast love and faithfulness of God, but the problem is the unfaithfulness of the anointed king. The questions in verses 46-51 are a cry for God to fulfill his covenant promise of commitment to the Davidic line and to demonstrate his steadfast love of old which he swore to David (v. 49). The psalmist is calling for God to move beyond discipline and wrath (v. 46) and to show again his favor to the Davidic line.

The questions of Psalm 89 were never answered in the postexilic period. The desire for the fulfillment of the promises to David remained only a hope. But the hope did not die. The very structure of the Psalter keeps that hope alive. Even though the days of the glory of David's kingdom are past, and the confidence of God's rule through his anointed (Psalm 2) has come to naught, and the righteous rule of the righteous king (Psalm 72) is nowhere to be seen, the questions of Psalm 89 call for God to act. Psalm 89 closes Book III and reflects the situation and desires of the postexilic community in their longing for a king.[109] This longing is answered in several ways. The structure of Books IV and V give God's people hope. Book 4 opens with Psalm 90, a psalm of Moses taking the community back to the foundation of their faith. Psalm 91 is one of the strongest psalms of confidence in the Psalter. Psalms 93–100 are classified as Yahweh kingship psalms reminding God's people that Yahweh remains king even if there is not a king that sits on the throne.[110] Psalm 101, another royal psalm, shows the commitment of the Davidic king to meet the ideals of the Davidic covenant. It is a message of the king's repentance and determination to follow the royal standard so that a cessation of chastisement will take place, paving the way for the possibility of restoration. Psalm 101 may answer the questions of Psalm 89, setting the stage for Psalm 110.[111]

The hope expressed in Psalm 89 does not come to full fruition until the coming of Jesus Christ, the seed of David. There are many ways that Psalm 89 can relate to Christ. The main things that were set forth concerning Yahweh and the king can also be said of Christ. As David is the firstborn, the highest of the kings of the earth, so Christ is the firstborn over all creation, the one through whom all things were created (Col. 1:15). Christ has the highest place in creation and is the ruler of the kings of the earth (Luke 1:32; Rev. 1:5). Christ displays his power over creation by ruling the sea (Mark 4:39). Christ fulfills the promises of the Davidic covenant because his throne will endure forever (Luke 1:31-33). In Christ God demonstrates his steadfast love and faithfulness (John 1:14; 14:6). Even the struggle of Psalm 89 relates to the work of Christ, for he did come as a king who was rejected and suffered humiliation. Much of what is said about the king in verses 38-44 relate to Christ. He was cast off and rejected. The full wrath of God was against Christ, not for his own disobedience, but for the disobedience of his people. He was the scorn of those around him and the right hand of his enemies seemed to triumph over him. In the structure of the Psalter Psalm 89 shows the temporary rejection and suffering of the Messiah, but the hope for a Messiah will reappear in the later royal psalms.[112]

Psalm 110: The Triumph of the King-Priest

There are many difficulties surrounding the interpretation of this psalm. There is no consensus on the structure or the setting. There are problems related to the translation of the Hebrew at certain points, what specific clauses in the psalm actually mean, and the identification of the speaker and to whom he is speaking. The relationship of the king to the priesthood and the implications of the priesthood of Melchizedek are also much discussed. There does seem to be general agreement that Psalm 110 is a royal song.[113] Many of the details of the psalm are interpreted in light of the proposed setting of the psalm, so our approach will be to set forth the major views on the setting to see how that influences interpretation of the details of the psalm.[114]

It is helpful to analyze the structure of the psalm before reviewing its setting. The general approach is to see two divine oracles in the psalm, giving it a two-part structure, with each section beginning with an oracle.[115] The first section is verses 1-3, which begins with the divine oracle, 'sit at my right hand.' The second section is verses 4-7, which begins with the divine oracle 'you are a priest.' Each of these oracles is developed in a similar fashion, as can be seen from the following chart:[116]

	No 1	*No 2 vv 4-7*
Oracle	sit at my right hand	you are a priest
Elaboration	until I make enemies a footstool	the order of Melchizedek
Explanation	scepter from Zion rule over enemies, willing response	Lord at right hand victory over enemies confident response

The main settings for Psalm 110 are a royal coronation, a real military battle, or the literary context that focuses on an eschatological meaning for the psalm.[117] The royal coronation view has been termed the 'most popular setting'[118] and is based on the fact that verses 1 and 4 seem to deal with the enthronement of a king at the city of Jerusalem.[119] In this view the date would most likely be before the fall of the monarchy.[120] In this coronation ceremony a speaker utters the oracle of the LORD to 'my Lord.' The speaker is a prophet or an official at the sanctuary who speaks the oracle of the LORD to the king ('my Lord').[121] The oracle 'sit at my right hand' is a call for the enthronement of the king at the place of honor, with the assurance that all his enemies will be defeated.[122] In the explanation of the oracle, the scepter from Zion (v. 2) is a symbol of power sent out by the LORD to extend the power and influence of the king,[123] with the result that the king rules over his enemies.[124] Verse 3 is difficult and is understood differently by those who argue for a royal coronation setting. Kraus takes verse 3a as a reference to the nobility surrounding the king on the day of enthronement. Verse 3b alludes to the wondrous birth of the king by using mysterious images. The king is begotten in the heavenly sphere and has a heavenly divine origin.[125] Allen, on the other hand, takes verse 3 to refer to the people of the king volunteering freely on the day of battle, materializing mysteriously like the God-given dew on the mountains at daybreak.[126]

The royal coronation view also understands the second oracle, 'you are a priest,' as addressed to the king. The office of priest is now conveyed to the king, who inherits it from the Jebusite predecessors in Jerusalem.[127] Thus David can engage in priestly activities, such as wearing the priestly garments, blessing the people, interceding for the cultic assembly in prayer, and presiding over the rites (2 Sam. 6:14; 24:17). The combination of king and priest in one person is in line with the Melchizedek priesthood.[128] Verses 5-6 address the LORD (Yahweh) as 'the Lord' (Adonai) and describe his activities on behalf of the king to defeat all his enemies. Although the king is an instrument in God's hands, Yahweh is the real power behind the throne and the one who accomplishes the things in verses 5-6.[129] Verse 7 reverts back to a description of the king, who stops to drink from the stream beside the road. This refers to a rite of drinking from the Gihon spring as a part of the enthronement ceremony (1 Kings 1:38), a sacramental means of receiving divine resources for the task. The king is empowered for his task and will be victorious.[130]

Another setting for Psalm 110 is a real military battle. Kaiser does not specifically identify the battle but calls it a 'decisive battle' that David won.[131] Delitzsch identifies the conflict with David's triumph over Ammon.[132] Others relate the psalm to David's conquest of Jerusalem.[133] The military language of the psalm and the emphasis on victory over enemies give support to a military context. On this view the speaker in verse 1, who utters the oracle of the LORD, is David himself. He speaks about one whom he calls 'my lord.'[134] The Lord about whom David speaks is invited to take his place at the right hand, which is the place of highest honor and comes with the promise of complete victory over the enemies.[135] The scepter from Zion (v. 2) goes back to the promise made to Judah in Genesis 49:10 and is a symbol of the authority to rule.[136] Verse 3a refers to the 'entirely cheerful readiness' of the covenant people to volunteer for the army of God and to go forth into battle.[137] These willing volunteers are 'arrayed in holy majesty,' which may be a reference to the holy garments of the priests now worn by the army.[138] The last phrase of verse 3 emphasizes that the volunteers are youth. They are likened to the dew at dawn, which is a picture of the sudden appearance and the vigor of the volunteers.[139]

The difficulty of situating the second oracle, 'you are a priest according to the order of Melchizedek,' into any historical period of Israel's history has led many to argue for a direct Messianic reference. Although in a restricted sense the king could perform some priestly duties, there were limits placed on what the king could do in the sanctuary (2 Chron. 26:16-21). To consider a king in Israel a priest forever is believed to be contrary to the biblical evidence and Israelite practice.[140] The priesthood of Melchizedek is a type of the priesthood of Christ: both are kings as well as priests, and both have their priesthood directly from God, not through the Levitical order.[141] Christ's priesthood is greater than the Melchizedek type because of what it accomplishes for God's people. Delitzsch appeals to Zechariah 6:12-13, which also unites the offices of king and priest into one person, for justification of understanding the fulfillment of Psalm 110 in the eschatological future.[142]

The rest of the psalm refers to the successful work of the Messiah, the priest-king, over his enemies. There is not agreement whether the phrase 'the Lord is at your right hand' is addressed to the Messiah himself[143] or to the LORD (Yahweh),[144] but either way the LORD acts through the priest-king to execute judgment and to conquer all enemies. Verse 7 probably refers to the priest-king who stops at a brook to refresh himself on his pursuit of the enemy, leading to complete victory.[145]

The final view of the setting of Psalm 110 stresses the literary context of Psalm 110 within the final form of the Psalter. Building on Gerald Wilson's work concerning the importance of the placement of the royal psalms in Books I–III,[146] Kim wants to show the importance of the placement of the royal psalms in Books IV and V of the Psalter.[147] Although Psalm 110 may have originated during the monarchy,[148] it is placed in the literary context of the postexilic situation (Ps. 107 is a psalm of thanksgiving for return from exile). By showing connections between Psalm 110 and prophetic texts (Zech. 9–14, Joel 3–4, and Ezek. 34–48), Kim offers a new genre designation of Psalm 110 as eschatological. The final editors of the Psalter had an eschatological purpose, which is highlighted by the placement of the royal psalms. The royal psalms show the progress of the fulfillment of the Davidic covenant. The eschatological nature of Psalm 110 has implications for how the psalm is to be understood and will bridge the gap between the original meaning of the psalm and its use by the New Testament.[149]

The central message of Psalm 110 in this view is the Messiah's eschatological warfare against the enemies and their defeat on the Day of Yahweh. The speaker in the first oracle is identified by the superscription as David. David receives the oracle and speaks directly of the eschatological Messiah, identified as David's Lord.[150] To sit at the right hand refers to the Messiah's heavenly session. On the coming eschatological Day Yahweh will make the Messiah's enemies his footstool (v. 1). The ruling of this king from Zion, the place of Yahweh's eschatological presence, is a realization of the promise in Psalms 2:8 and 72:8.[151] On this day of eschatological battle the people come willingly (v. 3a) to the place of battle. The phrase 'on the holy mountains,' identified with Zion, is the place where the Messiah gathers the people for eschatological warfare. The 'dew' of the mountain is a figure for the people of the Messiah and a metaphor for God's blessing on the young men of the army.[152]

The second oracle refers directly to the Messiah and describes his priestly office, which differs from Aaron's, but is like Melchizedek's priesthood. The kingly and priestly office are brought together in one person. The scene changes back to the eschatological battlefield in verses 5-6 where the subject is Yahweh but the person addressed is the Messiah. The Lord on the Messiah's right hand will shatter kings on the day of wrath. An abrupt change of subject is introduced in verse 7, for it is not easy to view Yahweh as drinking from the stream. This is the action of the king Messiah as Yahweh's representative. Thus there is a close correlation in verses 5-7 between the actions of Yahweh and the actions of the Messiah. The water imagery in verse 7 may refer to life-giving waters, as found in Ezekiel 47. The Messiah may be drinking from the life-giving waters in the eschatological temple, where this water was thought to have originated. Verse 7 ends with the triumphant posture of the Messiah after his victory.[153]

A comparison of these three views shows how the different settings of Psalm 110 have an effect on the interpretation of the psalm; however, there is a lot of overlap between them. The superscription ('A Psalm of David') and the content of Psalm 110 tie the psalm to Jerusalem, where the Melchizedek tradition of combining king and priest in one person had historical roots (Gen. 14:18-20). Thus the psalm may have been composed to celebrate the capture of Jerusalem by David and may have been used by succeeding kings in some kind of enthronement ceremony.[154] The problem with connecting Psalm 110 to such an historical situation is that the combination of king and priest in one person was not the way things operated in Israel. Therefore, there is a disconnection between the psalm's presentation of king and priest in one person and the way things actually operated in Israel. Perhaps it is possible to view king David as inheriting the Jebusite kingship when he captured Jerusalem, but the union of king and priest together in one person was not passed down to his descendants. Plus, there is little evidence that David himself fully acted as a priest.

It is better to see Psalm 110 as a direct prediction of the Messiah by David himself. The first oracle is introduced by a phrase common in the prophets (the LORD says), a formula of prophetic revelation signifying a divine utterance.[155] David utters a prophecy of the coming Messiah who will combine in his person the office of king and priest. The historical account of Melchizedek and Abraham (Gen. 14:18-20), and the ties of Melchizedek to Jerusalem, may have been the basis for this revelation about the future Messiah. Zechariah 6:12-13 later picks up this concept. The placement of Psalm 110 in Book V of the Psalter is significant. It shows the progress of the Davidic covenant with the promise of world-wide conquest actualized. This promise was given to the anointed one at the time of his installation in Psalm 2, was prayed for in Psalm 72, was temporarily hindered in Psalm 89, but is actualized in Psalm 110.[156]

The meaning of Psalm 110 refers directly to Christ, which is the way the New Testament handles the psalm. Jesus himself refers to verse 1 as having been spoken by David through the Holy Spirit. He uses the verse to reveal the new identity of the Messiah as the Son of God, as well as the Son of David (Matt. 22:41-46; Mark 12:35-37).[157] The first oracle refers to Christ's kingship as he now sits enthroned at the right hand of God the Father (Acts 2:34-35), seated above all authorities and powers (Eph. 1:20-21). Christ now reigns from that place of honor until all his enemies are under his feet (1 Cor. 15:25). Those who have been called by Christ the King come willingly to enter into the spiritual battle that now rages (Ps. 110:3a; Eph. 6:10-18). Wherever the gospel goes forth God calls forth his people, sometimes suddenly and unexpectedly (Ps. 110:3b). We go forth as kings and priests clothed in garments that are not defiled (Rev. 3:4). It is interesting that when Jesus comes again the armies of heaven will follow him clothed in white linen (Rev. 19:14).

The second oracle is also picked up in the New Testament, especially the book of Hebrews, to refer to the priesthood of Christ. The priesthood of Christ is not in the line of Aaron (Jesus is of the line of Judah), but his priesthood is of a higher order, 'according to the power of an endless life' (Heb. 7:16), bringing a better hope than the Levitical priesthood. Jesus' priesthood is different, because Jesus himself is different from the normal priests (Heb. 7:26-28). He has an unchangeable priesthood that provides a full and complete salvation (Heb. 7:24-25). Psalm 110:5-6 connects this priesthood with the conquest of enemies, which is a reminder that Jesus' work as our priest cannot be separated from the defeat of all his enemies. His priestly work on the cross was to win the victory over sin, death, and the devil, and his continuing intercession as our priest helps us to fight this spiritual battle. In the confidence of his complete victory (Ps. 110:7) is the security of our victory.[158]

Psalm 132: The Fulfillment of the Davidic Promises – Kingship, Temple, Zion

Psalm 132 is a royal psalm that focuses on God's promises to David concerning the continuance of one of his descendants on the throne 'forever' (v. 12). These promises are foundational for God to act on behalf of the 'anointed' one (vv. 10, 17). There is also a strong emphasis in Psalm 132 on Jerusalem as God's dwelling place, which makes it a place of rest.[159] These two basic concepts are interwoven into the fabric of Psalm 132. Although there are a variety of different types of materials in this psalm,[160] there is a basic structure that highlights the parallels between David's concern to establish a dwelling place for the LORD (v. 5) and the LORD's covenant promises to David concerning his descendants (vv. 11-12). The first section (vv. 1-10) is a prayer on behalf of the Davidic king based on the oath that David swore not to have rest himself until a proper dwelling place for the ark is found. The second half (vv. 11-18) is an answer to that prayer based on the oath that the LORD swore concerning the descendants of David.[161]

The first part of Psalm 132 is a prayer for the Davidic king with verses 1 and 10 framing the unit and containing the actual petitions. The first verse asks the LORD to 'remember' all the hardships that David endured in finding a proper place for the ark, the LORD's dwelling place. Verses 2-5 give the oath that David made concerning his desire to find a place for the ark. He would not rest until a proper dwelling place was found for the LORD's ark. Verses 6-9 show the fulfillment of David's vow in bringing the ark to the proper place of rest, which is recorded in the historical account in 2 Samuel 6. The section ends with another petition for the Davidic king 'for the sake of your servant David.' Thus continuing prayer is made for the 'anointed' king (v. 10) based on David's efforts on behalf of the ark.

The significance of the ark cannot be overlooked in this part of the psalm. The ark was the LORD's 'dwelling place' (vv. 5, 7) where he manifested his presence and power. It is called his 'footstool' (v. 7) because God was enthroned above the cherubim. The ark represented the rule of God on earth.[162] It is called the 'ark of your might' (v. 8) because it represents the power of the LORD who led the people forth in battle, defeating all their enemies. Thus verse 8, 'Arise O LORD,' recalls Numbers 10:35, but in the context of Psalm 132 it is also a call for the LORD to manifest his presence as God's people come to worship at the ark (v. 7). There is an emphasis on finding the right place for the ark (vv. 5, 13, 17), a concern of Deuteronomy 12:5, as the 'resting place' for God (v. 8). This alludes to Numbers 10:33 and recalls the promises of God to bless his people with security from all their enemies in the land of Canaan (Joshua 21:43-45). Thus 132:9 is the proper response of the priests and the people to the reminder of God's rest and security.

For the sake of David and on behalf of his efforts related to the ark, two petitions are made for the Davidic king. The first is 'remember' (v. 1), which is a call for the LORD to act in accordance with his covenant promises. To remember is much more than just bringing something to mind, for it stresses action. In Exodus 2:24 God remembered his covenant and delivered his people out of Egypt. Here God is to remember the efforts of David for the ark so that he will take action on behalf of the Davidic king. The petition of verse 1 is stated negatively in verse 10 as the prayer is made that God would not reject the 'anointed' king.[163]

This prayer is answered in verses 11-18 by stating the oath that the LORD made to David that one of his descendants would sit on the throne (vv. 11-12). Just as David had made an oath to the LORD, so the LORD had made an oath to David. Just as David was concerned with the throne of the LORD, the ark, so the LORD was concerned with the throne of David.[164] Verses 13-18 show God's commitment to keep his oath by using the same concepts in verses 1-10 and reminding the people that the LORD was behind the activity of David described in the first part of the psalm. David had sought out a place for the ark and that location was the very site that God had chosen for his dwelling place (vv. 13-14). Zion was God's desired dwelling place.[165] From God's resting place he would pour out on his people abundant blessing so that they could live in security (v. 15). The exhortation to the priests and the people in verse 9 is affirmed in verse 16. The prayer of verses 1-10 is answered in verses 17-18.[166] God promises that once again the strength (the horn) of David would be restored and his dynasty would not be extinguished; rather, it would shine like a lamp.[167] Proof of this will be seen in the crown being restored and the enemies being clothed with shame. God will answer the prayer of his people and he will be faithful to his covenant promises.

Although there is debate about the historical setting and date of Psalm 132,[168] the psalm became part of the 'Songs of Ascent'

(120–134). It may also take on special significance in relation to the Davidic covenant and the outworking of God's royal promises in the context of Book V of the Psalter. The Songs of Ascent were probably songs sung by pilgrims on their way to the festivals in Jerusalem. This group of psalms has several characteristics that tie them together, such as frequent references to Zion and Jerusalem, exhortations to the people as a group, and concerns with issues of daily life juxtaposed with national concerns. Most of these songs are brief, except for Psalm 132. Its length may be an indication of its importance. In the context of the Songs of Ascent it gives the rationale for making the pilgrimage to Jerusalem: Zion is God's dwelling place and the site of the Davidic throne.[169] In the context of Book V, which expresses the concerns of the postexilic community related to the king, Psalm 132 uses the term for messiah twice ('anointed,' vv. 10, 17). In the original historical context this term would have referred to the Davidic king and it could be a call for the restoration of the Davidic dynasty in the postexilic period.[170] But it is also likely that the psalm is hoping for the eschatological Messiah. In the literary context of the Psalter Psalm 132 demonstrates that the rejection of the Messiah in Psalm 89 is not final. 89:39 laments the defilement of the crown of the 'anointed' one, but 132:18 affirms that the crown of the 'anointed' will shine. In 89:42 the enemies have triumphed over the king, but in 132:18 the enemies are defeated and humiliated.[171] Thus Psalm 132 gives hope to God's people that the promises related to the Davidic covenant will be fulfilled. A king will come, a horn will sprout for David.

Psalm 132 is fulfilled in Christ as he is the descendant of David, the son who will sit on the throne forever. He is the horn who sprouted for David (see also Ezek. 29:21, Luke 1:69).[172] Christ is the fulfillment of the prayer in 132:1-10, for God remembered his covenant promises 'for the sake of David' and he did not reject the 'anointed' one. If Psalm 89 refers to the humiliation of the anointed, it is tempting to see Psalm 132 as the psalm of triumph after the humiliation, with associations of resurrection (132:8) and ascension (132:8, 14). In other words, Psalm 132 describes the fulfillment of the Davidic promises related to kingship, temple, and Zion through the ministry of Christ as he sits at the right hand of the Father. The earthly ark as the resting place and dwelling of God was a copy of the heavenly reality (Heb. 8:1-6). Christ came as the one who fulfilled the temple concept of God dwelling with his people: the Word became flesh and tabernacled among us (John 1:14). He is Immanuel, God with us (Matt. 1:23), and offers to his people true rest (Matt. 11:28). He does not carry out his ministry at the earthly tabernacle, but at the heavenly tabernacle where God dwells. Having defeated his enemies on the cross, he now sits on the throne of God reigning until all enemies are under his feet (1 Cor. 15:25). He has chosen Zion, and we as God's people have come to Mt. Zion, the city of the living God, the heavenly Jerusalem (Heb. 12:22). From Zion Christ pours out his blessings of salvation on his covenant people. The saints shout for joy (Ps. 132:16) as they await the final triumph and the full security and rest that Christ will bring at his second coming. There will be no temple in the new Jerusalem come down out of heaven. The dwelling place of God will be with his people and the kingdom rule of Christ will be fully manifested (Rev. 21:2-5, 22). The lamp (Ps. 132:17) will be the Lamb whose glory will shine brightly (Rev. 21:23). God's people will experience true security and rest (Rev. 21:4). Thanks be to God that he has remembered his covenant promises to David.

Psalm 144: The Final Eschatological Victory

A word that many use to characterize Psalm 144 is mixture. It is seen as a mixture of different elements.[173] The first eleven verses seem to be spoken by a king (v. 10) and are an appeal for God to deliver him from the hand of foreigners (v. 11). Verses 12-15 are communal (spoken in first person plural) and are a prayer for God's people to experience covenant blessings.[174] The psalm ends with a doxology recounting the blessings of the people whose God is the LORD. The distinct nature of Psalm 144 as a mixture of elements can be explained through its connection with Psalm 18 and its placement in the Psalter.[175] The first eleven verses are a re-use of Psalm 18, except the royal thanksgiving for deliverance accomplished in Psalm 18 is now a call for God to deliver once again. The warfare imagery in Psalm 18 is moved forward in Psalm 144 showing the urgency of the situation. Although the original setting may have been a plea of the king before a battle,[176] the placement of the psalm in Book V reflects the concerns of the postexilic community concerning foreigners (v. 11). Psalm 144 is placed in the final Davidic collection of the Psalter (138–145), keeping alive the hopes of the post-exilic community for a Davidic king. Thus the psalm looks forward and expresses the hope of victory and blessing through him. This future hope is an eschatological one as the journey to the end of the Psalter brings God's people to the final eschatological battle (reflected also in 149:5-9).[177] The final victory of God's people will result in an outpouring of eschatological blessings (144:12-15) and the participation of all creation in the praise of God (150).

Psalm 144 is a request that God would give the king victory so that[178] covenant blessing could be experienced by God's people once again. The first part of the psalm is the request for deliverance (vv. 1-11), which is based on a number of different elements. The psalm opens with praise of the LORD who has the ability to give victory in battle. It is the LORD who trains the king for battle and who subdues peoples under him. Confidence in the LORD is expressed in six affirmations of trust that show his power to deliver (rock, steadfast love, fortress, stronghold, deliverer, shield). God, because of his covenant loyalty (steadfast love), provides strength and security for the king in battle. Ultimately it is not the power of the army or great military strategy that brings victory, but the power of the LORD.

The need of the king for God's help is expressed in verses 3-4, which allude to Psalm 8:4: 'what is man that you regard him?' In Psalm 8 the question raises the insignificance of man within the vastness of God's creation, with the affirmation of the high place in creation for human beings (8:5-8). In Psalm 144 the frailty of man is affirmed ('like a breath') emphasizing the need for God to deliver soon.[179] It is possible that verse 4 is a statement on the fleeting nature of the deceitful enemy (v. 8). The psalmist requests for God to demonstrate his power in a theophany, similar to the demonstration of his presence at Mt. Sinai (vv. 5-8).[180] The powerful presence of the LORD will have no trouble defeating this enemy. Before the final request for deliverance (v. 11) the psalmist celebrates the past victories that God gave to the kings, especially King David. Victory will lead to a new song of praise to God (v. 9).

Victory in battle will also lead to an outpouring of covenant blessings (vv. 12-15). These verses are a reflection of the blessings laid out in Deuteronomy 28:1-14. These blessings focus on fruitfulness and abundance in every aspect of life, including healthy sons and daughters, a full harvest, a prolific flock, and peace and security in the streets of the towns and cities. When God defeats their enemies these covenant blessings will be experienced by God's people. Their privileged position of blessing is brought about through their covenant relationship with the LORD.[181] The psalm ends with a doxology reminding God's people of this blessing (v. 15).

The placement of Psalm 144, a Davidic psalm, in Book V keeps the promises of the Davidic covenant alive for God's people. A collection of Davidic psalms frames Book V (108–110, 138–145), with the latter collection coming just before the closing psalms of praise (146–150). There are also connections between Psalms 2 and 144 in the theme of the rebellion of the people and in the closing of each psalm with a doxology. What was inaugurated in Psalm 2 is now coming to a close in the final defeat of God's enemies.[182] This eschatological hope is something for which God's people today still wait: the coming of our king in the clouds of heaven to bring a final defeat to the forces of evil. The frailty of the human nature of our king was seen in his humiliation and death, which fits the plea for God to rescue and deliver him from the deceitful enemies (vv. 3-4, 11).[183] The initial victory has been won because our king was delivered from the power of death leading to a new song of victory (v. 9). Although our king reigns now at God's right hand and God's people experience spiritual and some temporal blessings now, the full outpouring of blessings that Psalm 144 speaks about will not take place until the final victory. Our king will return in full battle array coming in power from heaven in the full glory of deity to defeat all his enemies and bestow on his people full covenant blessing (Rev. 19:11-21). The abundant fruitfulness of eschatological blessings will be theirs to enjoy to the full in the new heavens and earth. This abundant blessing of final victory will lead God's people to full and abundant praise of their king (Pss. 146–150) as all creation joins in the chorus. We are blessed to have a king who is the LORD!

Chapter 8

Direct Messianic Psalms

The following psalms have traditionally been considered Messianic psalms: 2, 8, 16, 22, 40, 45, 68, 69, 72, 89, 109, 110, 118, and 132.[1] They speak more directly of the Messiah and his work and are used in the New Testament in this way. Several of these *pgs 67* psalms have been examined already. Psalm 109 was covered as *–97* an imprecatory psalm (see Chapter 5) and the royal psalms of the group were analyzed in the last chapter (2, 45, 72, 89, 110, and 132). In this chapter the following psalms will be examined: 8, 16, 22, 40, 68, and 118. The specific element in each psalm that has led to the Messianic connection will be pointed out, but it will also become evident how the whole psalm is important for understanding the Messiah, so that other parts of each psalm also relate to Christ.

Psalm 8: The Crowning Glory of God's Creation
Psalm 8 is a hymn that contemplates the role of human beings in this world in light of the majesty of God in creation.[2] Many hymns begin with exhortations to praise God, followed by reasons as to why people should praise him (see the discussion of hymn

in Chapter 4). Psalm 8 accomplishes the same thing in a slightly different way. It focuses our attention on the excellency of God's name by beginning and ending with the same acclamation. Thus the psalm begins with God and ends with God. The point is that the role of human beings within this world cannot be understood apart from a correct understanding of God. As Calvin writes near the beginning of the *Institutes*, 'It is certain that man never achieves a clear knowledge of himself unless he has first looked upon God's face.'[3] Every false view of who we are as human beings and our role in this world is due in part to a faulty understanding of God.

Following the opening acclamation of the excellency of God's name Psalm 8 breaks down into two parts. The first part continues to focus on God (vv. 1b-2). The second part reflects on the role of human beings in this great and vast world in light of the glory and majesty of God in creation (vv. 3-8).[4] Because understanding God is necessary in order to understand the role of human beings in this world, it is helpful to see what verses 1-2 say about God.

The Psalm begins with the name LORD (Yahweh). This name takes on special significance in relationship to the Exodus from Egypt, where Yahweh displays his faithfulness to his covenant promises in delivering his people from the bondage of Egypt. He delivers his people by defeating the Egyptian gods through the plagues. In Exodus 15 Yahweh is celebrated as a divine warrior who fights for his people. The name Yahweh is also prominent in the covenant promises to David in 2 Samuel 7. Thus the name Yahweh is associated with covenant faithfulness and the deliverance of his people in the fulfillment of his covenant promises. It is this name that is declared to be excellent or magnificent in all the earth. This term is a royal attribute reflecting his victories (Exod. 15:6), his might in judgment (Ps. 76:4), his law (Isa. 42:21), and his rule over creation.[5] God's name is superior to all other names for he is the only true and living God. There is no other name that is greater because there is no other god that can match the awesome power and majesty of God. These ideas also set God apart from creation so that he cannot be identified with it. Thus Scripture denies any form of pantheism that would confuse the distinction between God and creation, which inevitably leads to moral relativism and the denial of the difference between human beings, made in God's image, and the animals.

The name LORD (Yahweh) is followed by the name Lord (Adonai), a name which stresses God's ability to govern. Yahweh is the Lord of creation and the universal ruler,[6] ideas which are reflected in verse 2. The power of Yahweh is seen in the contrast in verse 2 between the enemies of God and the children.[7] Through the mouth of children God has established strength. The power of God is seen in that he can work to defeat his enemies through the weakness of children.[8]

The second part of the psalm also sets forth the power of God in creation by setting the vastness of the heavens and the stars next to the statement that this world is the work of God's fingers. The heavens are magnificent, yet they were shaped and fashioned by the fingers of God, which underscores the greatness of God.[9] By contrast human beings seem so insignificant, which leads to the rhetorical question: what is man? Why would God pay any attention to human beings?

The answer to this question has far-reaching implications concerning issues of morality, human dignity, and the relationship between people and animals. If humans are the product of evolutionary chance, then there is no basis for ethics or treating each other with respect. We are in essence no different from the animal world. But Scripture represents human beings as the crowning glory of God's creation with a special place in the created world.

Human beings are defined, first of all, in relationship to 'God' (v. 5). The Hebrew term is Elohim, which is the general term for God in the Old Testament. The high place of humans within God's creation is seen in that their place in creation is a little lower than Elohim.[10] This view is supported by the next phrase in verse 5, which uses royal terminology: 'you have crowned him with glory and honor.' It is very significant that Psalm 8 first of all stresses God's role as king over his creation in verses 1-2. Now royal terms are also used of human beings in verse 5. Glory and honor are the marks of a king, applied to God (Ps. 29:1, 104:1), and now applied to mankind.[11]

The reign of human beings within God's creation is demonstrated in our dominion over the animal world (vv. 6-8). As stewards of God's creation we should endeavor to take care of God's creation. Yet human beings are not on the same level as the animals. Similar ideas are expressed in Genesis 1:26-28, where human beings are made in the image of God and are given dominion over God's creation, including the animal world.

Psalm 8 is concerned about the proper role of human beings within God's creation. The fact that the Psalm begins and ends with God, and that the ideas of Genesis 1:26-28 are reflected in the Psalm, explains why Psalm 8 does not touch on the failure of human beings faithfully to carry out their proper role in creation. Such failure becomes evident in the fall in Genesis 3, and is evident today in our own lives and the events of the world.[12] Such failure raises the question of how we can live according to God's purposes for us in this fallen world. Several things can be said about this question in the Old Testament context, but ultimately the answer will be found in Jesus Christ.

Although Psalm 8 sets forth the proper role of humanity within creation without an emphasis on the failure of humans to live out that role, the surrounding psalms reflect the problems of living in a fallen world. The prayers surrounding Psalm 8 are prayers for deliverance in the face of the wicked who are causing trouble (see Pss. 3–7, 9–10). Psalm 2 highlights the turmoil of the nations as they try to throw off the rule of God. In this context Psalm 8 sets forth the proper role of human beings in this world in relationship to God as a reminder of why they were created.

The royal terminology in Psalm 8, which is a reflection of Genesis 1:26-28, sets forth the hope of what human beings can become. The context of Psalm 8 in Book I of the Psalter (Pss. 1–41) is also important. Book I has a strong Davidic emphasis because most of the psalms are attributed to David. This emphasis highlights the idea of the king. Psalm 2 explicitly focuses on the king who will bring in the reign of righteousness. In Psalm 2 this king is given dominion over the nations.[13] The reign of this king over the nations would bring about the establishment of the proper role of humanity within creation.

Jesus Christ is the fulfillment of the hopes expressed in Psalm 8. The use of Psalm 8 in Hebrews 2 is what has led many to identify this psalm as a Messianic psalm, but other parts of the psalm are also important in showing forth Christ. He is the Creator (John 1) and his name is superior to all other names (Phil. 2:9-10). He demonstrates his power through weakness. Jesus himself quotes from 8:2 in Matthew 21:16. The chief priests and scribes are indignant with Jesus. He had cleansed the temple by driving out the money changers. He then healed the blind and the lame that came to him in the temple. Also, children had picked up the cry of the multitude in the triumphal entry of Jesus into Jerusalem and began to proclaim in the temple, 'Hosanna to the Son of David.' This made the leaders angry, and in response Jesus quotes 8:2. The Septuagint, which Jesus quotes, has 'perfected praise' instead of 'established strength'.[14] In the context of Psalm 8 this praise would include the magnificence of God's name and glory. Not only is it appropriate to proclaim that Jesus is the Son of David, but he is also deserving of the praise reserved for the LORD. The quote from Psalm 8 also sets out the contrast between the children and the enemies of God. The chief priests and scribes clearly fall into the latter category because of their opposition to God.[15] It is no surprise that there follow in Matthew parables dealing with the rejection of Jesus by the leadership of Israel (Matt. 21:28-46; 22:1-14).

Not only is Jesus deserving of the praise due to the LORD, but he also can utter the words of Psalm 8 in praise to the LORD. Hebrews 2:6-8 quotes Psalm 8:4-6 in reference to the work of Jesus in his humanity. It is very interesting that what Psalm 8 says about human beings is applied directly to Jesus Christ: Jesus is made a little lower than the angels, Jesus is crowned with glory and honor, and the dominion given to human beings over creation is not yet complete according to God's original design, but we see

Jesus in his suffering and death (Heb. 2:8-9).[16] The purposes of God for human beings in this world are fulfilled in Christ. We find our true humanity and identity in him. Jesus has come to restore through his suffering and death God's original purpose for us that was marred by sin. Through Jesus we are restored to our kingly role of dominion over creation. Hebrews 2:5 views this dominion as eschatological because it speaks of the world to come. This eschatological restoration of human rule is accomplished already in Jesus who represents all redeemed humanity in achieving this dominion.[17] This dominion will include victory over death (1 Cor. 15:27-28) and will be established in its fullness when Jesus comes again, when our true destiny as human beings will be restored in the new heavens and earth.

Psalm 16: Confidence Beyond the Grave

Psalm 16 is recognized as a psalm of confidence because trust in the LORD dominates it.[18] There is no general structure to psalms of confidence but the tone of these psalms is full of affirmations of trust and confidence in the LORD (see Chapter 4). Psalm 16 opens with a brief prayer and statement of faith (vv. 1-2), followed by a contrast between the godly and the ungodly (vv. 3-4). David expresses confidence in God for his present situation (vv. 5-8) and for his future (vv. 9-11). The psalm climaxes in strong statements of confidence in the LORD that extend even beyond the grave.[19] The last verses of Psalm 16 are used in the New Testament to refer to the resurrection of Jesus (Acts 2:22-32; 13:35-37) and are the basis for understanding this psalm as a direct Messianic psalm.

Psalm 16 opens with a prayer to God to preserve David because he has taken refuge in God. The word 'preserve' and the word 'refuge' both stress protection. David prays for God to preserve him because he has sought God for protection.[20] He has confidence in God's ability to protect, which is demonstrated in his statement of faith in verse 2: 'You are my Lord; I have no good apart from you.'[21] This declaration demonstrates confident allegiance in God and recognizes that the good that the psalmist has experienced comes only from God.[22]

The meaning of verses 3-4 is greatly debated, with much of the debate focused on the nouns *q̆dôšîm* and *'addîr* in verse 3. Some understand the first noun as referring to pagan gods and emend the second noun to read 'mighty ones' instead of 'excellent ones.'[23] In this view verse 3 refers to someone who is a worshiper of false gods.[24] Such false allegiance would stand in contrast to the true confession in verse 1. Others understand *q̆dôšîm* as referring to the saints, who are the excellent ones (*'addîr*) in whom the psalmist delights.[25] With either view there is a contrast stated in verse 4b between the psalmist and the idol worshippers. If verse 3 refers to idol worshippers, then the psalmist states in verse 4 that those who worship idols experience sorrows that multiply, and he will not participate in their worship. If verse 3 refers to the saints, then a stronger contrast is set up between the delight found in fellowship with them versus the sorrows of those who are idol worshippers. Either way a person should have no confidence in idols.

In contrast to the idols, David has great confidence in the LORD. The terminology of verses 5-6 is related to the inheritance of land. Each family was given a portion of land as their inheritance, which represented sustenance, provision, and life. David expresses the beauty and goodness of his inheritance (v. 6), which includes the land but ultimately is found in the LORD himself.[26] David affirms that the LORD is his portion and his cup.[27] In other words, the present blessings have come to David because he has a relationship with the LORD, the source of blessing and provision. Without the LORD there is no blessing. David in turn offers blessing to God (v. 7), which is to acknowledge that God is the source of all the blessings in life.[28] Part of that blessing is the counsel of the LORD, who continues to guide David even in the difficult times. David lives his life in full recognition of the presence of God, which is the foundation of his unassailable confidence in verse 8: 'I will not be shaken.'

The reason David will not be shaken is because the LORD is at his right hand (v. 8), and the results of that confidence are laid out in verses 9-11. The confidence that David has in the LORD influences his whole being and every aspect of his life. He is full of joy because he is safe in the LORD even beyond this life. He is secure and protected in body because God will not abandon him to Sheol (v. 10). Some try to limit the statements of verses 9-11 to the immediate crisis the psalmist is facing. Deliverance, in this view, is from the immediate threat of death, and restoration takes place in this life.[29] However, the language of the psalm presses toward an unbroken relationship with the LORD beyond this life.[30] Even if the word 'corruption' in verse 10, in parallel with Sheol, just means 'pit,' the idea of not abandoning my soul to Sheol means that God will not leave the psalmist in Sheol, which generally refers to the place of the dead. Certainly this includes more than deliverance from death in this life. There is expressed here a confident hope beyond this life and beyond the grave.[31] Thus the path of life in verse 11 refers to eternal life,[32] which is reinforced by *fullness* of joy in God's presence and pleasures forevermore at his hand.

Psalm 16 is considered a Messianic psalm because verses 9-11 are used in Acts 2:24-32. The passage from 16:9-11 is quoted and then applied directly to the resurrection of Christ. The justification for this is that 16:10 could not have been about David because he was dead and buried in a tomb, thus he experienced corruption. David was not speaking of himself but of one of his descendants. His statement is based on the oath of the covenant promise that one of his descendants would sit on the throne. Peter says that David was a prophet and thus foresaw and spoke about the resurrection of Christ. Christ did not see the corruption of the grave because God raised him from the dead.

It is interesting to compare Peter's interpretation of 16:10 in the light of some explanations of the verse in the Old Testament context. S. R. Driver bluntly says that the declaration of faith and hope of the Old Testament saint in 16:10 cannot support the argument made by Peter in Acts 2.[33] Others are more subtle in describing the relationship between 16:10 and Acts 2:29-32. Kraus comments that the meaning of 16:10 is preservation from an evil death and that any premature spiritualization of the text blunts the psalm's essential assertions. Yet, mankind is destined for life, which is not fully revealed until Christ. The assurance found in the resurrection of Christ was hidden from the people of God in the Old Testament.[34] Craigie comments that the initial meaning of 16:10 is not messianic or eschatological, but the psalm took on a new, changed meaning in a different context. In the Old Testament the psalmist rose above imminent death to know the fullness of life in God's presence, an escape from an untimely death in this life. Jesus, on the other hand, rose in confidence from death itself. Thus there is a new meaning to this psalm in light of Jesus Christ.[35] These interpretations are hindered by their understanding that there is no clear concept of life beyond this earthly life, other than a shadowy existence in Sheol, until later in the Old Testament, when a resurrection is mentioned. Such a view makes the New Testament teaching seem radically new.

On the other hand, Kaiser uses this text to argue that meaning is rooted in the human author and that a prophet could foresee all the future fulfillments of his prophecy. The prophet not only saw the meaning of the prophecy for his own day (the literal historical sense called *historia*), but he also perceived the meaning of the prophecy for the future (*theoria*). Thus every Old Testament prophet foresaw the future fulfillment(s) of his prophecy. Peter specifically says that David was a prophet and he foresaw and spoke about the resurrection of the Christ (Acts 2:30-31).[36]

One has to take seriously the statements of Peter in Acts 2:29-32. David was a prophet and foresaw and spoke about the resurrection. Any attempt to downplay this angle should be avoided. However, this does not mean that Kaiser's view of *theoria* must be embraced. Not every prophet fully understood all the future fulfillments of his prophecy. Sometimes a prophecy is not understood until the fulfillment has taken place. Peter says two things in Acts 2:24-32 that would be evident to anyone familiar with the Old Testament. First, Peter points to the tomb of David, which means that 16:10 could not refer to him because he saw corruption. Second, David understood the oath of God that one of his descendants would sit on the throne. Putting these two together leads to the conclusion that a descendant of David who would sit on the throne would not see corruption. In this way David spoke of the resurrection of 'the Messiah' ('the Christ' in Acts 2:31). This would not be fully understood until after the resurrection of Christ. We are still dependent on the unity of Scripture, the progress of revelation, and the coming of the fullness of revelation, which are dependent on the divine author, to completely understand this Old Testament psalm.

The rest of Psalm 16 also relates to Christ. There are aspects of his work as priest in the psalm, with glimpses of his kingship in verse 11 ('your right hand'). Even though Christ struggled in the garden of Gethsemane with the 'cup' that he was about to drink, his confidence was never shaken (Luke 22:43: 'not my will, but yours be done'). Christ could pray for God to preserve him from death because he took refuge in his Father in heaven. He showed confidence in the timing of his own death in his statements to his disciples in John 11:7-10. He took great delight in the saints given to him by the Father (John 17). He pointed out the sorrows of the hypocrites who had made idols of the law in their hearts (Matt. 22:23-24). Jesus had a vital relationship with his Father and could do nothing of his own accord (John 5:19-24). The Father was his portion, the source of all his blessings (much like the priests of the Old Testament), and the one who gave him counsel. Because his whole life was focused on doing the will of the Father, he was not shaken. Even in facing the cross, a bitter cup, he knew that he had a beautiful inheritance and that eventually his cup would overflow. He could rejoice because he knew that the Father would not abandon him to Sheol and he would not see corruption. Jesus' confidence extended to life beyond the grave in the knowledge of his resurrection and the fullness of joy at the right hand of his Father. Such confidence can also be ours through this One who has conquered death, our priest and king, Jesus Christ.

Psalm 22: From the Crisis of Suffering to the Exuberance of Victory

The connection of Psalm 22 to Christ is obvious because Christ utters the cry of verse 1 from the cross: 'My God, my God, why have you forsaken me?' His use of this verse invites the reader to look at the whole psalm in light of his work and there are many connections between Psalm 22 and Christ.[37] But should Psalm 22 only be understood in relationship to Christ or is it appropriate to reflect on the meaning of the psalm in light of the experience of the author? Some argue that the psalm speaks only of Christ while others tend to limit the meaning of the psalm to the historical situation of the psalmist.[38] However, there is a growing recognition of the importance of understanding the words of Psalm 22 both in the context of the Old Testament and in reference to the death of Jesus Christ. There is a long history of the use of this psalm within the history of faith before Jesus used it, which should inform believers how to respond in situations of suffering when God seems absent.[39] However, many also recognize that the words of Psalm 22 go beyond any individual experience of suffering in the Old Testament.[40] As Mays notes,

> One senses in simply reading the text a difference, a development of the type that raises it to its very limits and begins to transcend them. There is an intensity and a comprehensiveness about the psalm that presses toward the ultimate possibilities that lie in the event sketched in the psalm ... the intensity and the comprehensiveness are a fact of the psalm's composition; it is there in the text itself.[41]

The intensity and the exuberance of poetic expression in Psalm 22 sets the stage for a new and expanded vision in relationship to the death of Jesus Christ.[42] This is not a new approach to Psalm 22 but is in line with viewing the suffering of the individual in Psalm 22 as a type of Christ's suffering.[43]

Psalm 22 is an individual lament (vv. 1-21)[44] with an expanded section of praise and thanksgiving for God's answer of the lament (vv. 22-31). The lament section moves back and forth between the psalmist's horrible experience of suffering (vv. 1-2, 6-8, 12-18) and statements of confidence (vv. 3-5, 9-11), with a plea for help ending the lament (vv. 19-21). The praise and thanksgiving section shows the implication of God's answer of the lament not only for Israel (vv. 22-26), but for all the earth (vv. 27-29), including future generations (vv. 30-31).

The lament begins with questions concerning God's absence and lack of response (vv. 1-2) and ends with an appeal for God to deliver the psalmist from his distress (vv. 19-21). The keynote of the lament is for God to respond to the psalmist's cries for help. The necessity for God to deliver is seen in the description of the psalmist's suffering (vv. 1-2, 6-8, 12-13). Such confidence in the ability of God to deliver is based on the character of God and how he has delivered his people in the past (vv. 3-5, 9-11). Part of the dilemma is that the psalmist's experience does not line up with what he knows to be true about God, and so he goes back and forth between his own experience of suffering and God's ability to deliver. Both of these ideas are expressed in the opening line, 'My God, My God, why have you forsaken me?' The cry 'my God' shows a close relationship with God that is explained in the statements of confidence in him (vv. 3-5, 9-11).[45] The psalmist is a part of a community that worships God for his holy character and trusts him in times of distress. When they cry to God he delivers them so that they are not ashamed (vv. 3-5). The concept 'trust' is repeated three times, showing the foundation of God's deliverance and matching the threefold use of 'my God' in verses 1-2. The faith of the ancestors and the faith of the psalmist is the same, but their situation is so different because the psalmist has not experienced the same deliverance.[46] The note of personal relationship ('my God') is emphasized in verses 9-11 where the psalmist expresses his own relationship with God even from the womb. There is an emphasis on God's involvement in the psalmist's life from birth, which is so different from his present experience. But this prior, life-long relationship is the basis for the appeal for God to draw near to the psalmist to help him (v. 11). This appeal for help is renewed in verses 19-21.

The statements of suffering are strongly contrasted with the statements of confidence in God's ability to deliver. The opening question in verse 1 sets the tone of alienation and abandonment by God. God has been silent and has left the psalmist to suffer without any help. The fact that God has delivered the fathers when they trusted in him makes the situation of the psalmist even worse. Because of God's deliverance they were not ashamed (v. 5), but the psalmist is experiencing the shame and powerlessness of suffering (vv. 6-8).[47] He has lost a sense of human dignity due to the ridicule of others because it appears that God has abandoned him.[48] Five phrases are used to describe how others view the psalmist: reproach, despised, ridicule, shoot out the lip, and shake the head. The last two phrases may be insulting or mocking gestures.[49] This contempt culminates in the taunts of the people for God to deliver the psalmist because he trusts in him. In other words, if he truly trusted in God he would not be suffering in this way. This taunt also contrasts with his own experience expressed in verses 9-11.[50]

The longest description of his suffering comes in verses 12-18 where the focus is on the enemies and the results of the suffering. The enemies are described as animals who are intent on destroying him. The enemy is strong as a bull, pursues the psalmist as a lion pursues prey,[51] and hounds the psalmist in the same way a pack of dogs moves in for the kill.[52] The psalmist is surrounded by the enemies and is considered as good as dead, for they are already casting lots for his garments (v. 18).[53] The physical effects of fear, terror, and anxiety are described in verses 14-15 and 17.[54] He is no longer able to function as a human being as his body is physically deteriorating. His heart, bones, tongue, hands, and feet are all affected. He is a broken man who is unable to cope with the situation as he approaches death.[55]

In one last plea the psalmist calls on God to deliver him from his enemies (vv. 19-21). The final plea is set off from the previous verses by an emphatic contrast, 'but you,' as the psalmist addresses the LORD directly as his only hope.[56] There is some debate about whether the last phrase of verse 21 stands alone ('you have answered me,' NKJV) or goes with the preceding words of the verse ('you have rescued me from the horns of the wild oxen,' as in ESV, NIV, NASB). Either way the transition in this verse is from appeal (the verb at the beginning of the verse is imperative) to a statement of deliverance (the verb at the end of the verse stresses completed action).[57] Here is the answer to the prayer of the psalmist, which is demonstrated in the drastic change of tone in the following section of thanksgiving.[58]

The praise section (vv. 22-32) is framed by the idea of proclamation or declaration and contains the verb 'praise' in every verse except verse 24, which gives the reason for the praise.[59] Such a reversal of fortunes invites widespread proclamation. The psalmist begins by declaring God's name to the congregation of Israel, also called 'brothers' (v. 22), 'you who fear the LORD,' and 'offspring' of Israel and Jacob (v. 23). Having been previously surrounded by enemies the psalmist is now surrounded by the congregation of faith.[60] The reason for praise is given in verse 24, which affirms that God did not abhor the affliction of the afflicted but responded to the plea for help. This answers the cry of verses 1-2 and demonstrates that ultimately the psalmist was not forsaken by God.[61] Such praise encourages further praise by the faithful.

There is a widening circle of praise as all the ends of the earth worship the LORD because the reign of God is not limited to Israel but includes the nations (vv. 27-29). The deliverance of the psalmist has universal significance that includes all different types and conditions of people, from the rich and prosperous to the lowly and dying. Not only will Israel and the nations hear of this deliverance and give praise, but future generations will hear what the LORD has accomplished and will serve the LORD (vv. 30-31). Thus Psalm 22 moves from the depths of despair to exuberant praise of God because he heard and answered the cry of his servant. Such deliverance has a transforming effect on all the world.

The psalmist serves as a model of persistence when God seems absent in the midst of suffering, which is in line with New Testament exhortations for the faithful to persevere in suffering when surrounded by lions and dogs (Romans 5:3-5; Phil. 3:2; 2 Tim. 4:17).[62] But the basis for our perseverance, and the comfort that comes to those who suffer, is seen ultimately in what Christ experienced on the cross. The suffering of the psalmist, expressed in metaphorical terms, is in many ways vividly fulfilled in Christ, which means that Christ's experience of suffering is greater than David's.[63] The words of verse 1 are uttered by Christ to express his feeling of being abandoned by God as he hung on the cross (Matt. 27:46; Mark 15:34). According to his human nature Christ struggled with being abandoned by God to death on the cross even though he knew of the deliverance of his ancestors when they trusted in God (22:3-5). Jesus struggled with being abandoned by God even though he himself had a close relationship with God from the day of his human birth (22:9-11).[64] Christ experienced the shame and humiliation expressed in 22:6-8 as scoffers mocked him, shook their heads at him, and called on God to save him if he really trusted in God (Matt. 27:38-44; Mark 15:27-32). Christ was hounded by his enemies, surrounded by those who would do him harm (Matt. 27:27-31; Mark 15:16-20), and experienced the fear and terror of being crucified. This experience included both physical and emotional dissolution (22:14-15, 17).[65] The words 'I thirst' (John 19:28) can be related to 22:15, 'my tongue sticks to my jaws.' His garments were divided among those who crucified him (Ps. 22:18; Matt. 27:35; Mark 15:24). Not only are the first words of the psalm uttered by Christ from the cross, but the last words of the psalm ('he has done it') are reflected in the cry 'it is finished' (John 19:28).[66] The deliverance of the son of Jesse is a foreshadowing of the ultimate deliverance of the son of David.[67]

The results of the deliverance of Christ from death are much greater than the results of the deliverance of the psalmist. Although Psalm 22 describes a world-wide consequence, this was made possible by the work of Christ and his deliverance/resurrection. If it is appropriate to understand 22:1-21 in reference to the crucifixion of Christ, it is appropriate to understand 22:22-32 in light of the resurrection of Christ. The statement 'you have answered me' (v. 22) indicates that Christ has been delivered from the power of death. The event that redeems his people from the power of death and begins the process of the restoration of creation deserves exuberant and world-wide praise. The declaration of redemption begins in Jerusalem, among the congregation of Israel, but extends to the whole world – 'Judea, Samaria, and to the end of the earth' (Acts 1:8). The statement 'May your hearts live forever' (v. 26), which in the context of the meal of a fellowship offering may be a blessing of the host upon the guests,[68] is now a statement that reflects the reality of Christ's eternal redemption (Heb. 9:12). The resurrected king now reigns and his kingdom extends over all the earth so that now all families of the nations worship him (22:27-28). All types of people are affected by Christ's work of redemption (1 Tim. 2:3-4), including those who have already experienced death (Ps. 22:29; Matt. 27:52-53 [where the tombs are opened after Christ's resurrection]). This great message of redemption will continue to be proclaimed to future generations (22:30-31) until the resurrected king comes again to bring in the full restoration of creation. All aspects of the work of Christ come into view in Psalm 22: his priestly work of suffering on our behalf, his prophetic work of proclaiming his deliverance, and his kingly work of reigning over all things.

Psalm 40: Deliverance through the Obedient Servant

Psalm 40 is considered a Messianic psalm because verses 6-8 are quoted in Hebrews 10:5-7. But there are major questions concerning the relationship of this psalm to Christ. Is the whole psalm Messianic or only the verses quoted in Hebrews? The quotation in Hebrews is different from the Hebrew text, which raises questions concerning the relationship between the meaning of the quotation and the Hebrew text. Does the author of Hebrews quote Psalm 40 correctly? Is his meaning in line with the meaning in the Hebrew text? These questions will be addressed after an examination of the meaning of Psalm 40.[69]

There are also questions surrounding the unity of Psalm 40 because the psalm falls into two distinct parts. The first part is a song of thanksgiving (vv. 1-10) and the second part is a lament (vv. 11-18). The fact that verses 12-18 reappear as Psalm 70, with minor variations, leads some to argue that two independent psalms were brought together in Psalm 40.[70] Also, the normal order is for the song of thanksgiving to follow the lament, but in

Psalm 40 the lament follows the song of thanksgiving. However, many argue for the unity of the psalm based on strong verbal connections between the two parts and the relationship between the opening of the psalm and the closing of the psalm.[71] The order of lament followed by thanksgiving is not a problem because other psalms reflect this order (Pss. 9–10; 44; 89).[72] It makes sense that a deliverance in the past would be used as a basis for a prayer for help in a new situation of crisis.[73]

The song of thanksgiving begins by describing God's deliverance (vv. 1-3). It opens with a strong sense of hopeful expectation, 'I hoped intensely for Yahweh.'[74] This is followed by a series of verbs that describe God's action: he inclined to me, heard my cry, drew me up, set my feet, and put a new song in my mouth. The deliverance is from beginning to end the work of the LORD. The poetic language does not allow the specific danger to be identified, but 'pit of destruction' and 'miry bog' remind one of Joseph being thrown into the pit and Jeremiah being thrown into the cistern.[75] It gives the picture of being confined in a small space without sure footing and sinking in the mud. Some connect the 'pit of destruction' to Sheol and the realm of the dead, which may indicate that his life was threatened.[76] God's deliverance radically changes the situation so that the psalmist sings a new song and leads others to put their trust in God.

The effect of deliverance is further expressed in verses 4-10. The one who trusts in the LORD does not turn to the proud. He is blessed (v. 4), partly because of the character of God and his many wonderful deeds for the sake of his people. The psalmist places himself within the history of God's great acts of deliverance for his people that are numerous and worthy of being proclaimed to others (v. 5). Such proclamation of God's salvation would normally take place by offering a sacrifice and sharing a meal where the goodness of God could be celebrated. But there is something more basic than the offering of a sacrifice, and that is the offering of the self in obedience to God. Verses 6-8 should not be seen as a repudiation of the sacrificial system but as stressing the importance of an inner willingness to do God's will.[77] Verse

6 does have in view the whole sacrificial system as four words for sacrifice are used, but the key phrase occurs in the middle of the verse: 'you have given me an open ear.' Although there are difficulties with this phrase in the Hebrew, many argue that the meaning is a willingness to obey.[78] The psalmist presents himself in verses 7-8 as willing to do the will of God from an internal compulsion ('your law is within my heart'). In this way obedience is better than mere sacrifice (1 Sam. 15:22-23; Ps. 51:16-17). There is debate concerning the meaning of the 'scroll of the book' in verse 7 and whether one can determine what is written in that scroll (v. 8). Suggestions include the law of the king in Deuteronomy 17:14-20, the law of Moses, revelation up to the time of David, and an account of the deliverance itself, which would include the song of thanksgiving in Psalm 40.[79] Although certainty is not possible, several of the suggestions may be viable. If one takes seriously that this is a psalm of David, then the scroll could refer to the law in Deuteronomy 17:14-20, which lays out instructions for a godly king.[80] But the inclusion of this psalm in the Psalter also invites one to view David's experience as a model experience for God's people.[81] They should be committed to keep the Mosaic law from a desire that arises from an inner compulsion (v. 8). In Deuteronomy 6:1-9 it is clear that God's people are to delight in God's law and that it is to be a heart matter. Thus the scroll could refer to the law of Moses in general.[82] If these words are appropriately spoken by David and by God's people in worship or meditation, one can easily see how they would be appropriately spoken by Christ (see below). What is clear is the emphasis in verses 6-8 on obedience coming from the heart that issues forth in the public praise of God (vv. 9-10). This proclamation includes the basics of the covenant relationship rooted in the character of God: righteousness, faithfulness, salvation, and steadfast love.[83]

The lament section of Psalm 40 begins in verse 11 and is closely tied into the previous section by the use of similar vocabulary, which highlights the crisis situation the psalmist faces. He did not restrain from proclaiming the good news of deliverance in the great congregation (v. 9), and now he calls on the LORD not to restrain from showing mercy and to preserve him in steadfast love and faithfulness. The law of God was in his heart in the song of thanksgiving (v. 8), but now his heart fails him (v. 12). Previously the psalmist declared that the wonders of God were more than could be told (v. 5), but now evils have encompassed the psalmist 'without number' (v. 12; both verses use *mispār*). Previously the psalmist delighted to do God's will (v. 8), but now there are those who desire to hurt the psalmist (v. 14; both verses use *ḥpṣ*).[84] Add to the list of troubles not only the enemies who want to see the psalmist fall (vv. 14-15) but also the sins of the psalmist (v. 12), and one can understand that this has led to a loss of perspective: 'I cannot see' (v. 12).

Although there is no resolution to the problem in the lament of Psalm 40, there is a movement toward confidence. The psalmist moves from those 'who seek to snatch away my life' (v. 14) to those 'who seek' the LORD (v. 16; both verses use the verb *bāqaš*).[85] There is almost a statement of confession in verse 16, 'Great is the LORD.' Although the psalmist is poor and needy, he knows the LORD takes account of him (v. 17). Verse 13 calls on God to deliver and to help him, and verse 17 affirms that God is his helper and deliverer, which is the basis of the final plea, 'do not delay.'

Although it is easy to see how 40:6-8 refers to Christ, not everyone is agreed that all of Psalm 40 should be understood as Messianic. One of the difficulties is that there is a confession of sin by the psalmist in verse 12. Kaiser comments that just because a portion of a psalm refers to Christ does not mean the whole psalm does. Otherwise, he believes, 'enormous verbal gymnastics' are needed to avoid saying that the Messiah confesses his own sins.[86] On the other hand, Hengstenberg, who argues that Psalm 40 *only* refers to Christ and not to David, understands the confession of sin in light of the substitutionary work of Christ as our priest, which makes good sense in relation to how the author of Hebrews uses this psalm to show how Christ has abolished the sacrificial system.[87]

Another difficulty in understanding the whole psalm as Messianic is the movement of the psalm from deliverance to lament, without any resolution to the particular difficulty the psalmist is facing in the lament.[88] But this is no more of a problem than understanding the lack of resolution in Psalm 88. Throughout his life Jesus offered to God prayers and supplications with loud cries and tears to the one who was able to save him from death (Heb. 5:7). How many times did Jesus have to wait expectantly for God to deliver him from some situation because many plotted to kill him (John 8:40; 11:8)! He was dependent upon his Father throughout his whole life, looking to him to deliver him. He stood in the long line of those who praised God for his wonderful deeds of redemption (Ps. 40:5). In John 17 Jesus prays that he has glorified the Father on earth and that he manifested his name to his disciples (vv. 4, 6). Jesus would have had confidence that his Father would hear his prayer and would deliver him according to God's righteousness, faithfulness, and steadfast love. Jesus, however, understood the purpose of his coming and so could pray the song of thanksgiving in anticipation of his own work of redemption, a work which itself should be included in the wonderful works of God for his people. He knew what his sacrifice would accomplish so that in his own life he did not refrain from proclaiming the faithfulness of the Father. He knew that the Father would not abandon him in his hour of need, surrounded by enemies, enduring the punishment for sin, and suffering the shame of the crucifixion. He was poor and needy, but he knew the Father would be his help and deliverer and that he would not delay in bringing full salvation.

In the song of thanksgiving are the words of 40:6-8, quoted in Hebrews 10:5-7. The point of these verses in Psalm 40 is the willing obedience of the psalmist that flows from the law in his heart, which is more important than sacrifices and offerings. He is ready and willing to do the will of God. The author of Hebrews placed these verses in the mouth of Christ so that he affirms, 'I have come to do your will, O God, as it is written in the scroll of the book.' In light of Jesus' own words in Luke 24:44 the scroll might refer to all the Old Testament,[89] but in light of how the author to the Hebrews uses these words they specifically refer to the sacrificial system, which is fulfilled by Christ.[90] Christ abolishes the sacrificial system in order to accomplish the will of God and our salvation (10:9-10). The sacrificial system of the Old Testament was not effective because it was 'a shadow of the good things to come' and 'could not make perfect those who draw near' (Heb. 10:1). Christ submitted himself fully to obey his Father's will and offered himself as the sacrifice on the cross so that he is able to affirm, 'Behold I have come to do your will, O God.' He presents himself to die on the cross. The difficulty with the quotation in Hebrews 10:5 is that one line is very different from the Hebrew. The following is a comparison of the Hebrew and Greek:

Psalm 40:6 [7] you have given me an open ear – אזנים כרית לי
Hebrews 10:5 a body you prepared for me – σῶμα δὲ κατηρτίσω μοι

There are LXX manuscripts that have 'ears' (ōtia) so there is some debate as to whether the word 'body' is in the manuscript the author of Hebrews is quoting or whether he made the change himself. Either way the basic meaning is not altered for both express the idea of willing obedience. The word 'body' makes it more explicit what this obedience entails in terms of the work of Christ, but it is not necessary to convey the meaning.[91] However, it is a small step from ears that are willing to obey to the whole body that is involved in the obedience. What is implicit in Psalm 40 is made explicit by the author of Hebrews. In any event, Christ fulfills Psalm 40 in his priestly work on our behalf by bearing the punishment of our sin on the cross and by abolishing the sacrificial system of the Old Testament. His deliverance is the guarantee of our deliverance and we pray that he does not delay to bring about our full salvation.

Psalm 68: Distributing the Spoils from the Victory of the Divine Warrior

Psalm 68 is classified as a traditional Messianic psalm because Paul in Ephesians 4:8 refers to verse 18. However, Paul's use of this verse seems problematic and raises some interesting hermeneutical questions, which will be dealt with in the course of examining the psalm. There are other difficulties related to Psalm 68, which are recognized by almost all commentators. Some call it the most difficult psalm to interpret because of the abrupt transitions and the nature of the words used in the psalm.[92] There are a high number of words that are not found anywhere else in the Old Testament, as well as a number of words that are not used very often in the Old Testament.[93] These difficulties affect discussions of structure and setting, which are more complex than most psalms because of the possibility of different stages or layers in the psalm. Psalm 68 reflects older material, such as the song of Moses (Exod. 15), the shout of Numbers 10:35, the song of Deborah (Judges 5), and Israel's historical experience.[94] However, many argue that the psalm is post-Davidic because of the reference to the Jerusalem temple, or even postexilic.[95] Those who see the psalm as arising in a liturgical setting emphasize different cultic traditions from different cultic centers, such as the sanctuary at Mount Tabor, which are later incorporated into the Jerusalem tradition.[96] Others believe Psalm 68 arose as a song of victory after one of David's battles, particularly the Syro-Ammonite conflict in 2 Samuel 10.[97]

The difficulties of Psalm 68 have also impacted discussions of structure. One view is that the psalm has no structure but is a collection of 30 song fragments that tries to accommodate the Israelite faith to the Canaanite poems of the thirteenth to the tenth centuries BC.[98] Those who take a liturgical approach usually see a unity to the psalm produced by the context of some festival.[99] Many are beginning to stress the unity of the psalm based on a literary analysis and the major theme of the victory of God over his enemies. This theme suggests the genre of the psalm. Because of the variety of elements found in the psalm (praise, petition, thanksgiving, and oracles) the psalm is hard to classify, but the most common classification is a hymn with a victory emphasis.[100]

Although there seem to be unconnected elements in Psalm 68, a basic structure is discernible.[101] Verses 1-3 serve as an introduction to the psalm. The body of the psalm (vv. 4-35) is bracketed by a summons to sing praises to the God who is on the move (vv. 4 and 32-33).[102] The body of the psalm can be divided into two parts (vv. 4-18 and 19-33). The first part moves geographically from the Exodus to Sinai to Jerusalem, with verse 18 being the climax of the victory of God. The second part is bracketed by the doxological cries 'Blessed be the Lord' (v. 19) and 'Blessed be God' (v. 35). It focuses on the victorious presence of God in Jerusalem and the implications of that victorious presence for God's people and the whole world.

The introduction to Psalm 68 (vv. 1-3) is an affirmation that envisions the reality of God rising in victory over his enemies and how that will affect the righteous and the wicked.[103] Verse 1 is taken from Numbers 10:35 where the ark of the covenant went ahead of God's people in the wilderness.[104] The ark was the symbol of God's presence and represents his power to defeat all his enemies. This emphasis prepares for the rest of the psalm which will portray God as the divine warrior who leads his people to victory.[105] Verses 2-3 give the response of the wicked and of the righteous. The wicked have no chance of standing before God for they are as insubstantial as smoke and are like wax before fire. The righteous respond with joy for they recognize that in the coming of God is their victory.

The body of the psalm can be divided into two parts. The first part (vv. 4-18) begins with an exhortation to praise the character of the God who will arise (vv. 4-6). He not only manifests his power as he 'rides through the desert' (v. 4) but he demonstrates his compassion for the lowly, becoming a father to the fatherless, a protector of widows, a provider of the lonely with families, and a releaser of prisoners. God's power is used for the sake of his people, which leaves the rebellious in their barrenness (v. 6). An historical review of what God has done for his people follows in verses 7-14. Although the language is general, there is an allusion to the Exodus event when God brought his people out of Egypt (v. 7a).[106] He then marches them through the wilderness (v. 7b), demonstrates his power at Sinai in the theophany (v. 8), and provides for them in the land of their inheritance (vv. 9-10). It is clear that God leads his people into battle and gives them the victory. The source of that victory is the Lord who gives the word of victory (v. 11a) that is announced by a great host of women. They lead in the victory celebrations, much like the song of victory in Exodus 15 (see also 1 Sam. 18:6). They announce the good news that the kings of the armies have fled (v. 12). Although there are problems with verses 12-14, the focus is on the results of the victory, specifically the division of the spoils.[107]

The choice of a mountain for the LORD's dwelling place is recounted in verses 15-16. The majestic Mount Bashan looks with envy on the mountain that the LORD chose, which no doubt is Zion, even though it is not specifically mentioned. Other mountains may have been taller and grander, but the LORD chose Mount Zion, which is its claim to fame.[108] The LORD is represented as ascending Mount Zion as the victorious Divine Warrior accompanied by his thousands of chariots, which is no doubt a reference to his heavenly armies or messengers (Deut. 33:2; 2 King 6:15).[109] The LORD ascends 'on high' with captives he has taken in battle as a visible representation of his conquest.[110] He also receives gifts as tribute among those he conquered, even among the rebellious.[111] Thus the first part of Psalm 68 celebrates the victory and the exaltation of the great God of Israel who fights for his people and reigns from Zion. However, the heavenly armies make it clear that the LORD's place of rule is not limited to earthly Zion, but includes heaven itself, a connection that will be made in the second half of the psalm.

The second part of the psalm (vv. 19-35) focuses on the victorious presence of God in Jerusalem and the implications of that victorious presence for his people and the whole world. It is bracketed by an acclamation of blessing to the Lord (vv. 19, 35) who now reigns from his throne. For God's people, the victorious reign of God means salvation from every foe, including the daily burdens of life (v. 19), the enemies in life (vv. 21-23), and even death itself (v. 20). The completeness of God's victory is seen in his pursuit and slaughter of the enemies so that the feet of the warriors 'strike' the blood of the foe.[112] This reign emanates from the sanctuary in Zion and it is there that the tribes of Israel praise God their king in festal procession and song (vv. 24-27). There follows a prayer that God's victorious reign would continue to manifest its power in the subduing of kings who would bring tribute to Jerusalem (vv. 28-29). Egypt and Cush are specifically mentioned (vv. 30-31). The psalm ends with an exhortation to the kingdoms of the earth to sing praise to the God who reigns in heaven as the sovereign God of the universe. His kingdom includes all the kingdoms of the world.[113] 'Blessed be God!'

Psalm 68 is a psalm that celebrates the victory of God the Divine Warrior and the results of that victory. These concepts relate to Christ who as our great king has defeated all our foes. The people of God benefit greatly from his victory. It is hard not to see a connection between the affirmation that God will arise to scatter his enemies and the resurrection of Christ, which was the one event where death and the principalities and powers were defeated (Eph. 1:20-22; 1 Cor. 15:20, 50-57). Jesus came proclaiming the kingdom of God for those willing to receive him, which included the lowly and the outcast. He came proclaiming release to the prisoners (Luke 4:18-21). He redefined family relationships so that the fatherless would have fathers and the lonely would have the community of a family (Mark 3:31-34, 10:28-31). As God was active in leading his people from Egypt to the promised land, so Christ came for a new Exodus/departure (Luke 9:31). Instead of leading his people in physical holy war he leads us in spiritual warfare against the principalities and powers (Eph. 6:10-20). He reigns from Mount Zion, the city of the living God, the heavenly Jerusalem (Heb. 12:22-24). Following his resurrection, Jesus ascended on high. He sits at the right hand of the Father as the ruler of the universe for the sake of his people (Eph. 1:22), who now share in the spoils of that great victory (justification by faith, peace with God, and hope are just a few listed in Romans 5:1-5).

With that background we come to the use of 68:18 in Ephesians 4:8. A comparison of the Hebrew text, the Septuagint, and Ephesians 4:8 shows some significant differences related to an important clause:

Hebrew (Ps. 68:18 [19]): you received gifts among men
לקחת מתנות באדם

LXX (Ps. 67:19): you received gifts among men
ἔλαβες δόματα ἐν ἀνθρώπῳ

Ephesians 4:8: he gave gifts to men
ἔδωκεν δόματα τοῖς ἀνθρώποις

The Hebrew and the LXX are virtually identical but Ephesians 4:8 is very different in two places. First, there is a change from second person ('you') in the Hebrew and LXX to third person ('he') in 4:8. Second, there is a change of the meaning of the verb from the Hebrew and the LXX ('received gifts') to 4:8 ('gave gifts'), which brings along with it a change in preposition from 'among' to 'to' ('you received gifts *among* men' versus 'he gave gifts *to* men'). The change from 'you' to 'he' facilitates the move from Yahweh in Psalm 68 to Christ in Ephesians 4. The change from 'received' to 'gave' facilitates the change from Yahweh *receiving* gifts from the conquered after his victory to Christ *giving* gifts to his people after his victory.

There are a number of ways these changes are explained. Some believe the author of Ephesians is using a Jewish or rabbinical method of interpretation called midrash. The term 'midrash' is slippery but it usually carries the connotation that an author is not concerned with the original meaning of a text in its historical context.[114] Andrew Lincoln identifies 4:9-10 as the author's midrash on Psalm 68:18, where he fills in gaps concerning 'descent' that are not there in the Old Testament text. He comments that 4:8-10 seems to complicate the argument unnecessarily. Even though the language of ascent is derived from the Old Testament citation, it is not the most appropriate language for ascertaining the writer's awareness of an ascension tradition.[115] Markus Barth raises the question of whether the changes the author makes go against the literal understanding of Psalm 68 (especially the change from Yahweh to Christ and the presupposition of the writer of an earlier descent). His answer is that the author is continuing a practice in the Old Testament of relating the enthronement psalms to a descendant of David, a method used with surprising results by rabbinic teachers. Although this use of midrash may seem strange to us, it fits his own historical setting.[116] Although it is important to understand the hermeneutical environment of the New Testament authors, Paul is not using a Jewish midrash to interpret Psalm 68, especially if that means his understanding of the text is not in line with the original meaning of the psalm.

Others argue that Paul's use of Psalm 68:18 in Ephesians 4:8 is unpacking the literal meaning of Psalm 68 in line with historical grammatical interpretation. Gary Smith argues for the use of analogy, where an author can express the new on the basis of the already known. The issue is not the change from 'you received' to 'he gave' as much as it is understanding from the historical context that God has always given leaders to his people. The way that idea is expressed in Psalm 68 is that the captives in verse 18 are among the rebellious and that the gifts received made it possible for God to stay in his sanctuary. The captives are identified by Smith with the Levites, who were rebellious, but were given to God on the basis of faithfulness in relationship to the golden calf incident. They were given to perform at the tabernacle so that God might dwell among the people. This is supported in Numbers 8 where the Levites are separated from the people to serve God. They are specifically called 'gifts' to Aaron in Numbers 8:19, and in Numbers 18:6 they are said to be taken and given as a gift from the Lord. The Levites are both the captives and the gifts.[117]

Kaiser takes a similar approach in relationship to the Levites but argues that the second person of Psalm 68:18 is a direct reference to the Messiah. 68:18 celebrates a time in the past on Mount Sinai when God came down to speak with Moses face-to-face. Because the conversation takes place with God the Father on the Mount it would appear that verse 18 has in view an appearance of the Messiah, which explains the abrupt shift to second person from verse 17 to verse 18.[118] In this context one is reminded of the golden calf incident and the faithfulness of the Levites. Thus the argument is made that just as the Messiah, in a pre-incarnate form, came down from heaven to meet with Moses on Mount Sinai, so he will return to the Father. In the meantime he has taken captives in the form of Levites, whom he now offers to the Father as gifts to carry out the work of the ministry in his absence. The apostle Paul then draws the same inference from this psalm, except it is not only Levites who are given to the Father as gifts, but also those mentioned in Ephesians 4:11 (apostles, prophets, evangelists, pastors and teachers). The captives are those called to equip the saints for ministry.[119]

There is much to commend this view based on the historical grammatical approach. However, the meaning is limited to the human author and so everything that Paul says about Psalm 68 must be found in the psalm, as though there was no divine author, progressive revelation, and the coming of the fulfillment of the Old Testament in Christ. Perhaps this is why Kaiser tries to find a direct reference to the pre-incarnate Christ in 68:18 – he has to be there or Paul could not use the psalm in the way he did. The change in person may be significant at times but such abrupt changes are common in the psalms, especially Psalm 68. It is certainly not enough in itself to argue for a pre-incarnate appearance of Christ. Also, the whole experience of Moses on Mount Sinai that is supposed to lie behind 68:18 is not clear because Sinai seems to merge with Zion in verse 17.

It is possible that 68:18 has in view the Levites who were received as gifts among men so that God could dwell in his dwelling place; but such a view is not necessary to deliver Paul's use of this psalm from midrash and to keep it in line with the original meaning of the psalm. One must recognize some movement toward a fuller meaning between 68:18 and Paul's use of it in Ephesians 4:8. Psalm 68 speaks of the LORD (Yahweh) while Paul speaks of Christ. There is the change of pronoun from second person to third person and there is the change of the verb from 'received' to 'gave.' Paul makes explicit in 4:8 what is implicit in 68:18. The apostles operated from a hermeneutical framework that believed that the Old Testament Scriptures, including the psalms, were fulfilled in Christ and in the community that he came to establish. Once Jesus is accepted as God incarnate, he is the Lord (Yahweh), the Divine Warrior, who has won the victory for his people. What the Old Testament authors could not fully comprehend is now clear once the fulfillment has come. Thus there is no problem in changing the second person to third person to make the connection to Christ explicit in the context of Paul's argument. Paul goes on to explain that for the ascension to take place there had to be a 'descent' (Eph. 4:9-10), a reference to the humiliation of Jesus.[120] The change from 'received gifts' to 'gave gifts' also makes explicit what is implicit in Psalm 68 once a connection to Christ is acknowledged. God's people enjoy the spoils of victory, which include leaders for the building and edification of the church. Although Calvin argues for a typical relationship between Psalm 68:18 and Ephesians 4:8, he explains the change from 'received gifts' to 'gave gifts' on the basis of the relationship between the head and its members. In Psalm 68 God was not enriched with the spoils but his people were enriched, and so Christ did not seek his own advancement but adorned the church with the spoils.[121]

The rest of the psalm (vv. 19-35) focuses on the implications of the victorious reign of Christ for the church and the world. The victory of Christ in his resurrection and ascension into heaven means for his people salvation from every foe, including the daily burdens of life (68:19; 1 Peter 5:7), the enemies in life (68:21-23; 1 Cor. 15:25), and even death itself (68:20; 1 Cor. 15:26, 50-56). The church continues to pray that Christ will strengthen her for the battle that still rages as the gospel goes forth to bring many from the nations to submit to Christ. His victory will be completed when he comes a second time to finish what he has already started. He will bring to fulfillment the judgment of God in 'the great winepress of the wrath of God', with blood flowing from the winepress (Rev. 14:20). He will lead his forces into the last great battle to victory (Rev. 19:11-21), the nations will bring their tribute to the great king (Rev. 21:24-26), and his kingdom will encompass all the kingdoms of the world. 'Blessed be God!'

Psalm 118: Thanksgiving for God's Great Deliverance

A first reading of Psalm 118 would not lead one to conclude that it has anything to do with Jesus, but verses 22-24 are used in the New Testament to explain the work of Christ. Although few contend that the whole psalm is about Christ,[122] we have tried to show that the psalms are the prayers of Christ and relate in a broader way to his person and/or work. The same is true of Psalm 118, but the question is always how does it relate to Christ. An analysis of the psalm will lay the foundation for making these connections.

Many recognize Psalm 118 as a song of thanksgiving offered by an individual as part of a processional up to the temple. The individual comes to give thanks to God for deliverance from a life-threatening crisis.[123] The psalm is classified as a song of thanksgiving because it is framed by the exhortation to 'give thanks' (vv. 1, 29) and it recounts the experience from which the individual was delivered (vv. 10-12, 17-18). The processional nature of the psalm is seen in the shifting from singulars to plurals (vv. 23-27 shift to the plural). The singular represents the individual who has come to give thanks and the plural represents those who have come with him. The request to enter the 'gates of righteousness' in order to give thanks (v. 19) and the antiphonal nature of the psalm (vv. 1-4) also support the idea of a processional.[124]

Although there are questions related to who is the main speaker of the psalm and what is the particular situation from which he gives thanks for deliverance, those questions will be postponed until after a brief analysis of the psalm. Psalm 118 is composed of two main sections (5-18 and 19-28) set within a framework of hymnic praise (vv. 1-4, 29).[125] The first section (5-18) reviews in general terms the situation of distress faced by the psalmist, with an emphasis that it is the LORD who has the power to deliver. The second section begins with a request to enter the sanctuary in order to give thanks (vv. 19-20) and is framed by the theme of the psalmist giving thanks (vv. 21, 28). Verses 22-27 are the response of the community to the thanksgiving for deliverance, with an exhortation that the LORD would continue to deliver his people.

The framework of hymnic praise (vv. 1-4, 29) sets the tone for the whole psalm as a psalm of thanksgiving with various groups within Israel exhorted to give thanks for God's steadfast love (Israel, house of Aaron, those who fear the LORD). In essence, all Israel is included.[126] The LORD's steadfast love refers to his covenant faithfulness, which is the basis for the deliverance recounted in verses 5-18. The LORD is faithful to his covenant promises and how he demonstrates that faithfulness will become clear in the psalm.[127]

The first section (vv. 5-18) of the main body of the psalm reviews the situation from which the Lord brought deliverance. As is usual in psalms of thanksgiving, the situation is described in general terms. It is a situation of distress (v. 5), a word that emphasizes being confined to a narrow place or being in a tight spot.[128] This idea fits the description of being surrounded by all nations (the word 'surrounded' is repeated numerous times in verses 10-12). The fierceness of the opposition is shown in describing them as 'those who hate me' (v. 7) and as bees (v. 12), which can be fierce and unrelenting in their attacks on humans. The desperate nature of this crisis is seen in the fact that the psalmist was pushed so hard that he was about to fall (v. 13).[129] He was also brought face-to-face with death (vv. 17-18).

This situation of distress was no match for the covenant LORD with whom the psalmist had a relationship. Instead of facing this situation alone, the LORD was 'for me' (repeated several times in vv. 6-7), which is translated 'on my side.' This relationship included the privilege of being heard in prayer (v. 5), having the LORD as a helper in distress (vv. 7, 13), and being given the courage to act ('I cut them off' in vv. 10-12). Such trust in the LORD leads to deliverance, described as being 'set free' from the place of confinement,[130] destruction of those who were causing the trouble (vv. 7, 12), and deliverance from death (vv. 17-18). All this is accomplished by the power of the LORD (the right hand of the LORD is repeated three times in v. 16), leading to songs of rejoicing (vv. 14-15).

The second section (vv. 19-28) of the main body of the psalm begins with a request to enter the 'gates of righteousness,' which is a request to enter the temple.[131] This section is framed by the intent of the psalmist to give thanks (vv. 21, 28). The intent to give thanks in verse 21 is specifically connected to God's deliverance of the psalmist from his distress. Thus verses 22-24 relate to that deliverance, with verses 22-23 being a proverbial saying that emphasizes a reversal of fortunes.[132] Just as a stone rejected by the builders later becomes the cornerstone of the building, so the psalmist was as good as defeated by his enemies and close to death, but his mighty deliverance by the LORD brought about a great reversal. It was marvelous, even unbelievable, making possible the festival day of rejoicing (v. 24). Such a magnificent demonstration of God's power is an encouragement for others to petition God for his continuing help (v. 25): 'Save us, we pray, O LORD.' There follows a priestly benediction (v. 26) that pronounces a blessing on the one who comes to the temple in the name of the LORD, a blessing that includes all those who have come with the one giving thanks: 'we (priests) bless you (plural) from the house of the LORD.'[133] It is unclear if verse 27 is spoken by the priests or the people. Many take verse 27a as a confession of the people that alludes to the priestly benediction in Numbers 6:25.[134] Although the meaning of verse 27b is not clear, it seems to refer to some aspect of their celebration of thanksgiving.[135]

One of the main questions in Psalm 118 concerns the identity of the individual that is the main speaker in the psalm. Related to this is the identification of the particular situation from which the speaker was delivered. The answers to these questions have implications for how this psalm relates to Christ. Several different possible scenarios are put forth by different scholars. Some argue that the thanksgiving for deliverance arises out of a military victory over national enemies (vv. 10-12), which makes it likely that the main speaker of verses 5-21 is the king. Thus Allen calls it a royal psalm of thanksgiving for military victory.[136] Others go a step further and connect the psalm to David even though the psalm is not specifically said to be a psalm of David. The main argument supporting Davidic authorship is the accumulation of allusions to events in David's life reflected in Psalm 118. For example, the phrase 'I cut them off' (which ends verses 10, 11, and 12) can literally be translated 'I circumcised them,' and could be a reference to when David killed 200 Philistines for their foreskins (1 Sam. 18:25-27). Also, being surrounded by all nations could refer to the distress of the enemies David faced in Moab, Ammon, Edom, Syria, and Philistia before he became king over all Israel and conquered them.[137]

If the main speaker is the king then it is easy to see how this psalm came to be connected to Christ. Allen comments that like other royal psalms this psalm came to have Messianic meaning.[138] Those who argue for the Davidic authorship of the psalm argue for a typological relationship between David and Christ. The rejected stone that became the cornerstone relates to David's rise to the kingship. His father did not think him suitable to be king, and his brothers scorned and misunderstood him. King Saul tried to kill him many times. What humans rejected God had chosen as the ruler of his people. One can see how this could relate to the rejection of Christ by the religious leaders and the people of his day.[139] Although such connections are appropriate, it is not certain that David is the author of this psalm. Although some of the historical allusions seem to fit, it is almost as if the identification of the author of the psalm is not significant and has been deliberately downplayed. In a book where there are many psalms attributed to David, it seems significant that Psalm 118 is not attributed to David. The same thing can be said about whether the main speaker is a king. Although verses 10-12 seem to be referring to a king, there may be other factors that make the identification of the speaker as a king less important (see below).

If the speaker is the king then Psalm 118 originates before the destruction of the monarchy and the exile.[140] Others argue for a postexilic date for the psalm. Delitzsch gives three possible occasions: the celebration of the Feast of Tabernacles in the seventh month of the first year of the people's return from exile when only an altar stood on the Holy Place (Ezra 3:1-4), the laying of the foundation stone of the temple in the second month of the second year (Ezra 3:8ff), or the dedication of the completed temple

(Ezra 6:15). He favors the third view because the difficulties which surrounded the building of the second temple are reflected in the psalm, especially the hostility of the neighboring peoples. Also, verse 22 makes more sense if the temple is already completed. He does not seek to identify the main speaker but sees verses 1-19 as spoken by the festive procession led by the priests and Levites.[141] The connection to Christ comes from the fact that 118:22 is combined with the Messianic prophecy of Isaiah 28:16, which gives 118:22 Messianic meaning. Such meaning is warranted by a typological relationship between Christ and Israel. The history of Israel is recapitulated and culminates in the history of Christ. The parallel is that just as Israel despised the small beginning of a new era that was dawning in the building of the temple after the exile, so the people of Jesus' day despised the dawning of a new era in Christ related to the building of a new temple (John 2:19).[142] Such a parallel between Israel and Christ is plausible given the historical setting proposed by Delitzsch, but it is not certain that the situation proposed by Delitzsch is the situation behind Psalm 118. It is very difficult to nail down the precise historical setting of the psalm.[143]

The elusive nature of the speaker and the setting of Psalm 118 may be due to the literary context of the psalm. First, it is the last psalm in a group of psalms called the Egyptian Hallel psalms. These psalms have the theme of deliverance and are connected to the Exodus event. Psalm 113 praises the LORD as the one who reverses difficult situations and lifts up the needy. Psalm 114 tells the story of the Exodus as a manifestation of God's rule in the world. Psalm 115 contrasts the LORD with the nations and their gods. Psalm 116 thanks the LORD for deliverance from death and Psalm 117 calls on the nations to praise the LORD. These psalms anticipate the themes of Psalm 118. It is possible that these psalms were sung at the Passover.[144] They seem to have been grouped together because of their deliverance and Exodus emphases. The psalms in this group focus mainly on the power of the LORD to deliver, as he delivered his people from Egypt. Any focus on a leader is subordinated to the emphasis on the LORD as deliverer and on the people of God as a whole. Thus the servant of the LORD is not identified in 116:16, just as the main speaker and the one who comes in the name of the LORD is not specifically identified in Psalm 118.

Second, this group of Hallel psalms occurs in Book V of the Psalter and, like Book V, it reflects the concerns of the exilic community. The first and last verse of Psalm 118 is the first verse of Psalm 107, the psalm that opens Book V and gives thanks for the return from exile.[145] Although Book V of the Psalter seeks a king like David (as is evident from the placement of the Davidic psalms in Book V: 108–110 and 138–145), the emphasis on deliverance by the LORD in the Exodus parallels the deliverance of God's people from exile. The Exodus event is a paradigm for the deliverance from exile, which becomes the basis for the future deliverance of God's people. Thus there is an open-endedness to Psalm 118 in terms of the one who comes in the name of the LORD and in terms of a future deliverance of God's people.[146]

With such a background one is not surprised that Psalm 118 is related to Jesus as the one who comes in the name of the LORD to bring deliverance for his people, a deliverance much greater than the Exodus or the exile. The festal procession in Psalm 118 fits the procession into Jerusalem on Palm Sunday. The crowds went before Jesus with shouts of 'Hosanna' to the one who comes in the name of the Lord, a joyful shout of acclamation (Ps. 118:25-26; Matt. 21:6-11; Mark 11:6-10).[147] Luke 19:37-38 mentions that the whole multitude of the disciples praised God with a loud voice for all the mighty works they had seen. There is no doubt that this one coming into Jerusalem could bring the long-awaited deliverance. At the end of this procession Jesus goes up to the temple, but instead of asking for entry he cleanses it (Matt. 21:12-13; Mark 11:15-17; Luke 19:45-46) because he has come to establish a new temple (John 2:19). The one who came in the name of the Lord to deliver his people is rejected, which is brought out in the parable of the tenants following the triumphal entry. At the end of the parable Jesus quotes 118:22-23 (Matt. 21:42; Mark 12:10-11; Luke 19:17) to show that just as the builders rejected the stone so the religious leaders of Israel had rejected Jesus, which leads to the loss of their kingdom privileges.[148] The rejection of Jesus is a moment of Messianic disclosure.[149] Peter picks up on this idea in Acts 4:11 to argue that although the leaders of Israel, the builders, rejected Jesus Christ, he has become the cornerstone. Thus there is salvation in no other name under heaven. The idea of Christ as a cornerstone is also used by Paul in Ephesians 2:8-10 to refer to the new temple Christ is building as a dwelling place for God's Spirit. Peter calls Christ a living stone, rejected by men, but chosen by God, in whom the church is being built up into a spiritual house with living stones (in 1 Peter 2:6-7 he combines Isaiah 28:16 and Psalm 118:22). Those who reject this stone and do not believe stumble (1 Peter 2:8) and will be crushed by that stone (Matt. 21:44; Luke 20:18).

The great act of deliverance that makes possible Christ becom-ing the cornerstone of a new spiritual temple becomes clear if Psalm 118 is seen as a prayer of Christ, with Christ as the main speaker of the psalm. In fact, it is enlightening to read Psalms 113–118 in the context of the Passover meal just before the crucifixion. Psalm 113 would have reminded Christ that God is the God of great reversals who lifts up the needy. Just as God delivered his people from the Exodus and the exile, so he has the power to deliver his true Son (Psalm 114). This is made explicit in Psalm 115, which states that the dead do not praise the LORD (115:17). Psalm 116 confirms this statement by thanking the LORD for deliverance from death. The situation of distress in Psalm 118 fits Christ's situation. He felt confined with no way of escape (118:6), surrounded by enemies (118:7, 10-12), and pushed hard to the brink of death. He was not given over to the power of death completely, but received full resurrection life (118:17-18). He was delivered because he trusted in the Lord as his helper (118:6-7). He did not fear what man could do to him (118:6). Even though he was rejected in his humiliation, God did a marvelous thing in raising him from the dead, setting off a great day of rejoicing for God's people (118:22-24). God opened for Christ the gate of righteousness and all who are righteous in

Christ will follow him through it (118:19-20). His work as our priest and our king is the basis for our cry for him to save us and all the blessings we receive as God's people (118:26-27). What God has done for us in Christ is a marvelous, unbelievable thing that demonstrates his enduring covenant faithfulness.

O give thanks to the LORD for he is good;
his steadfast love endures forever!

Chapter 9

Conclusion: The Majesty of Christ in the Psalms

The basic thesis of this book is that all the psalms, either directly or indirectly, relate to the person and/or work of Christ. Such an approach takes into consideration the context of the psalm in its historical or literary setting, the unfolding of revelation through redemptive history, the unity of the purposes of God for his people, and the fullness of revelation in Jesus Christ. Both the human author and the divine author are important for this approach. Without taking into account the implications of a divine author one is left with trying to bridge the gap between the historical meaning of a psalm and a later meaning related to Christ. Focusing only on a human author limits the meaning to the historical or literary context and does not allow the development of legitimate connections to Christ. Such connections arise when the major concepts of a psalm are understood in their Old Testament context and when the development of those concepts in redemptive history are also understood. This lays a foundation for seeing how Christ fulfills those concepts. Christ is truly the goal of the Old Testament, which cannot be fully understood apart from him.

Such an approach is in line with the way the New Testament handles the psalms. Jesus teaches his disciples that all the Old Testament, including the Psalms, speak of his work and his person (Luke 24:44-47). The New Testament authors use more than the traditional Messianic psalms to set forth the person and/or work of Christ. In fact, the New Testament authors approach the Old Testament with a Christological lens showing how the Old Testament speaks of Christ. They are willing to draw out Christological implications from the Psalms, many times making an explicit connection to Christ of what may only be implicit in the Psalm (see the discussion of Psalm 40:6-8 and Psalm 68:18). The New Testament is also full of allusions to the psalms which relate to Christ. Understanding the psalms as the prayers of Christ opens up possibilities concerning how the psalms relate to Christ as our covenant mediator, especially his work as prophet, priest, and king. The person of Christ as both human and divine also allows many connections to be made to him from the psalms. In fact, neither his humanity nor his deity can be separated from his role as prophet, priest, and king. Because Christ is fully God, any psalms that speak of God or Yahweh (the LORD) can legitimately apply to him. Because he is fully man he is able to fulfill the offices of prophet, priest, and king.

The complexity of the person of Christ (that he is both fully God and fully man in one person) and the complexity of the work of Christ (that prophet, priest, and king can refer both to his humiliation and exaltation) open up a variety of ways that a psalm can relate to Christ.[1] Once the major concepts in a psalm are understood in their own context, one can reflect on whether those concepts relate to the humanity or deity of Christ, and whether those concepts refer to his work as prophet, priest, and king in his humiliation and/or his exaltation. Many times the humanity and deity of Christ are both important for discussing his work as prophet, priest, or king. Also, it may be appropriate to discuss his work from both aspects of humiliation and exaltation. It is interesting that the New Testament uses Psalm 2:7 in reference to both the baptism (Matt. 3:17) and resurrection (Acts 13:30-33) of Jesus.

The psalms examined in this book have been categorized according to genre or type of psalm, partly because genre helps one to understand a psalm in terms of content, mood, and structure.[2] The genre of a psalm also has implications for how a psalm relates to Christ. Hymns are full of praise for who God is and what he has done and naturally leads to reflecting on the deity of Christ and how that relates to his work. Thus there are legitimate connections to Christ as God and the emphasis on his deity underscores his power to accomplish the things for which he is praised. In Psalm 103 the major concepts are Creator, a name worthy of being praised, and the power to abundantly bless God's people (for example, forgiveness of sins, healing from disease, administering justice, and providing the necessities of life). Christ's ability to do these things is assured because he is God, a point made in Mark 2:1-12 where the power to forgive sins and to heal are brought together as evidence of his deity. Thus his priestly role of forgiving sin and his kingly role of dispensing abundant life are related to his deity. In Psalm 93 the LORD is praised as king of the universe who enters into battle to defeat all his enemies. Christ is the LORD who defeats all his enemies and wins the battle for us. He is king in his humiliation as he defeated the power of sin and death on the cross and he is king in his exaltation as he sits at the right hand of the Father and will one day come back for the final victory.

Wisdom psalms set forth the goodness and order of life and deal with the major concepts of creation, the law, the family, and the community, including the different destinies of the righteous and the wicked. Some wisdom psalms struggle with the prosperity of the wicked. These psalms open up possibilities of connection to Christ in his humanity as a member of God's creation and the community of God's people. Christ no doubt enjoyed God's good creation, was taught the law, grew up in a family, and was a member of the covenant community. He was also considered a teacher of the law. Psalm 49 deals with the illusion of wealth and shows that wealth does not have the power to redeem because only God has the power to redeem. Christ would have affirmed the teaching of Psalm 49 and could have used it in the face of the temptation to envy the wealthy or to trust in riches. The fact that Christ is God has implications for the idea that only God can redeem from death because his priestly work of redemption is effective because he is God. Psalm 73 emphasizes the struggle of the psalmist concerning the prosperity of the wicked, even to the point that the psalmist almost slipped. The change of perspective came when the psalmist went into the temple and was reminded of the end of the wicked. Christ himself may have struggled with the apparent triumph of the wicked over him in his crucifixion. Hebrews 5:7 affirms that Jesus offered up prayers and supplications with loud cries and tears to him who was able to save from death. What an insight this passage gives to the struggles of Christ in his humanity which parallels many of the struggles reflected in the psalms! Christ did not just pray but he poured out his heart to his Father in heaven. Jesus did not stumble, however, because he was able to see beyond the cross to his ultimate triumph (Heb. 12:2).

Psalm 19 is a wisdom psalm that focuses on the revelation of creation and the law. The first part of the psalm examines the universal nature of God's revelation in creation, as displayed in the sun. Christ would have gloried in the beauty of God's creation and the way it reveals the power and eternity of God. He would also have affirmed the beauty and glory of the law laid out in the rest of Psalm 19, not only the law's characteristics but also the law's effect in the life of a believer. Here connections can be made to the prophetic ministry of Christ who taught the law to God's people. But Christ is more than a teacher of the law – he is the Word of God himself. The characteristics of the law apply to him (perfect, sure, right, pure, and clean) and he has the power to bring about the same effects of the law (reviving the soul, making wise the simple, rejoicing the heart, enlightening the eyes, and enduring forever). Thus the effectiveness of Christ's prophetic ministry is related to his deity.

In the psalms of confidence trust in God dominates and the difficulties of life are subordinated to strong statements of confidence in God. Christ in his humanity experienced the difficulties of life and would have learned to trust in God through those experiences. Psalm 91 encourages God's people to take refuge in him by asserting strong statements of confidence rooted in the blessings of the Mosaic covenant. Jesus would have affirmed that nothing can defeat the one who trusts in God, which he demonstrated all his earthly life. But Christ is also the covenant mediator who dispenses these covenant blessings to his people, which is an aspect of his kingship. Psalm 91 is ultimately about victory, which we will fully experience when Christ the king comes again. Similar ideas are expressed in Psalm 46, which focuses on community expressions of confidence based on the presence of God. The world is very unstable, but the place of God's dwelling is secure. The local temple and the city of Jerusalem were not that secure, but Christ came as the one who possessed the presence of God in order to build God's new house, the true temple. The security of Psalm 46 can be found now by those who trust in Christ, but the final manifestation of the power of God's presence will be in the new heavens and the new earth.

Psalms of lament arise out of situations of crisis and distress. They are full of questions to God and give evidence of the suffering and struggles of the psalmist in the face of the trials of life. These psalms are a window into the humanity of Christ and his struggles with such trials. Many of these psalms also relate to the priesthood of Christ. Psalm 79 is a community lament, probably in response to the destruction of Jerusalem and the temple in 587BC. As part of the covenant community Christ would have participated in such laments. In fact, he lamented over Jerusalem in light of her rejection of his ministry and the effects of that rejection. Christ showed tremendous compassion for those who rejected him. Psalm 88 is a psalm of darkness that fits Christ's experience in the Garden of Gethsemane as he struggled with the pain and suffering of crucifixion and the prospect of bearing the wrath of God as the sinbearer. We get insight into wrestling with God over a situation that does not seem to have any resolution. There is a desperate, continuous appeal to God, which is full of questions, with no answer to be found within the psalm itself.

Jesus experienced this wrestling with the will of God; however, he always submitted himself to the will of his Father. He secured our salvation through his priestly work of offering himself as our sacrifice, so darkness does not have the last word for us. Psalm 51 is a lament psalm where the confession of sin dominates. There is not a direct connection to the humanity of Christ, because he is sinless, but there is a connection to his work as priest in his making intercession for sinners. Psalm 51 shows that Christ understands the depth of sin, the burden of sin, and the consequences of sin. As priest he confesses our sin and offers himself as our sacrifice for sin, which is the basis for our forgiveness and renewal. Psalm 26 is a psalm of vindication where the psalmist affirms his integrity against false accusations. Many of Christ's claims were rejected and at his trial he was accused of false statements and blasphemy. Jesus affirmed his integrity. He was without sin and so could offer himself as our sacrifice 'without blemish'. Psalms 79, 88, and 51 relate to the priestly work of Christ, but refer to his ability as our high priest to sympathize with our weaknesses and struggles, even though he was without sin.

Psalms 109 and 137 are lament psalms, with a major part of each psalm given over to imprecation (cursing of the enemies). Psalm 109 is an individual lament that arises out of a situation of betrayal and Psalm 137 is a community lament over the destruction of Jerusalem and the exile of the community. Both psalms are concerned with the establishmet of the righteousness of God's cause and call on him to intervene in a way that will remove the threat against his people so that his ultimate purposes can be established. Psalm 109 fits the betrayal of Jesus. Psalm 137 can relate to the church under severe persecution but the final victory will not come until Jesus the judge appears. The cursing psalms are ultimately fulfilled in his role as our king where he defeats and judges all our enemies.

Psalms of thanksgiving give thanks to God for a specific act of deliverance from a situation of distress. Many times vows are made to God in the face of the trouble, which must be fulfilled when the psalmist is delivered. These psalms relate to the human nature of Christ, who at times prays for deliverance, but they cannot be separated from the divine nature of Christ, for Christ himself has the power to deliver. Psalm 32 is a psalm that gives thanks for the forgiveness of sin and the joy that results. Although Christ did not need forgiveness for his own sin, his priestly work is the basis for the forgiveness of our sin. Psalm 107 is a community psalm of thanksgiving praising God for his covenant faithfulness in bringing back his people from exile, which includes deliverance from several different types of situations (wandering without a permanent home, prison, illness, and perils at sea). Jesus himself experienced many of the situations that the exiles faced, such as hunger in the wilderness, no place to lay his head, and rude treatment by those who held him prisoner. Jesus could give thanks to his Father for deliverance from these situations. He also demonstrated the power to deliver because of his divine nature. He fed the hungry, healed the sick, and released prisoners from bondage.

Psalms of remembrance review the history of God's people for confessional and teaching purposes. The way God has acted in the past gives hope for what God can do in the future. The history recounted in these psalms is the history of Jesus' ancestors because he was 'born of woman, born under the law' (Gal. 4:4). Psalm 105 sets forth the message of the faithfulness of God to his covenant promises as that faithfulness is demonstrated in the history of God's people. As a part of the covenant community Jesus praised God for his covenant faithfulness with the encouragement that God would be faithful to deliver him as he delivered his people in the past. Psalm 106 also reviews the history of God's people, but the emphasis is on the faithfulness of God in light of the sinfulness of God's people. As a member of the covenant community, Jesus would identify with the community of God's people and their sinful history, but he would also recognize that his priestly work would be the basis for the removal of the problem of sin.

The royal psalms focus on the king and are related to the promises of the Davidic covenant. These psalms connect to the kingship of Christ. Although the human king is never considered divine, there is a close relationship between the human king and God as king. Christ is the human king, the son of David, who has come to fulfill the promises of the Davidic covenant; but he is also divine and what is said about God as king also relates to him. The royal psalms primarily focus on the human king, and within the structure of the Psalter there is a movement from the inauguration and righteousness of the reign of the king to humiliation and then victory. Psalm 2 sets forth the relationship between the human king and God and stresses that through the reign of this king, who is the son, the nations will be subdued. Psalm 72 lays out the righteous reign of the king and the abundant blessings that flow from such a reign. Psalm 89 emphasizes the humiliation and rejection of the king and laments that the promises to David are not being fulfilled. Other key royal psalms in the rest of the Psalter show a movement toward victory. Psalm 110 shows the king, who is now also identified as priest, victorious in battle. Psalm 132 demonstrates that the promises to David will be fulfilled. Psalm 144 stresses the final and complete victory of the king. When making connections to Christ several factors come into play. He is the son of David, the human king, but he is also the son of God, the divine king. The concept of 'son' in Psalm 2 now takes on fuller meaning in light of the person of Christ. His deity is important in his universal reign as king and in his power to deliver his people, to establish righteousness, and to confer abundant, covenant blessings, including the transformation of creation. However, his humanity is also important, not only in his humiliation, but also in his exaltation. A human king sits at the right hand of the Father in glory and a human king will return to defeat all his enemies. Christ thus fulfills the original design of God for mankind to rule and subdue the earth (Psalm 8).

When reflecting on how the royal psalms relate to Christ it is also important to consider his kingship in light of his humiliation and exaltation. The key royal psalms in the Psalter fit the movement from inauguration to humiliation to exaltation. Also, major concepts in the royal psalms might relate to either his humiliation or his exaltation.[3] Christ as king came to establish the kingdom, but it was a spiritual kingdom that manifested itself in spiritual blessings and spiritual warfare. He established this kingdom through his humiliation and death. The new creation has begun, we have a downpayment of the Spirit, and Christ now reigns at the right hand of the Father. The fullness of the kingdom, including full spiritual and physical blessings, will be established when Christ comes again to defeat all his enemies. Major concepts in the psalms might legitimately apply to both his first or second comings. Psalm 2 promises that the Son will rule the nations. He is now ruling the nations for the sake of the church, but that is evident only to those who have faith. One day his rule over the nations will be seen by all when he comes again to establish his rule on the earth. Psalm 72 describes the blessings of the righteous reign of a righteous king. Christ is that righteous king, who in his first coming demonstrated his power to bless his people, both physically and spiritually. The fullness of those blessings will not be experienced by God's people until he comes again. Psalm 89 is related to the humiliation and suffering of Christ as it laments the apparent rejection of the king and the tension between the promises of the Davidic covenant and the demise of the king. Psalm 110 speaks of the victory of the king, who is also priest, as he defeats all his enemies. The combination of king and priest in one person is fulfilled in Christ. Not just as king, but as priest, is Christ victorious over his enemies. These concepts relate to his humiliation and his exaltation. Our priest-king defeated death and Satan on the cross. Christ also now rules at the right hand of the Father, and continues to make intercession for his people. When he comes again to defeat all his enemies he will come as king, but he will also be wearing a robe dipped in blood. Even at the final victory his work as priest will be significant. Psalm 132 affirms the faithfulness of God to the promises of the Davidic covenant and the establishment of the reign of the king in Zion. Christ is the one who fulfills the promises to David and he reigns from Zion, not the earthly city of Jerusalem, but the heavenly city. His reign from Zion will one day be manifest in the new heavens and the new earth. Finally, Psalm 144 speaks of the final victory of the king, which will lead to an outpouring of blessings. Although this final victory cannot be separated from the victory of Christ on the cross, it is a victory for which we still wait as we look for the coming of our king. In this light Psalm 45, which describes a royal wedding, is important. The relationship of a bride and bridegroom is used to describe the relationship between Christ and his people. Jesus inaugurated this relationship in his first coming and his bride now waits and prepares herself for the great wedding feast that will occur when the king comes again.

Some of the traditional, or direct, Messianic psalms that were not covered in the chapter on the royal psalms were also examined. Although the focus was on what made these psalms directly Messianic, attention was also given to how the whole psalm relates to Christ. They were dealt with in the order in which they occur in the Psalter, but here they are organized in terms of their connection to the work of Christ. Psalm 8 is a hymn that contemplates the role of human beings in the world in light of God's majesty in creation. The original design for mankind of dominion over creation in Genesis 1:26-28 is fulfilled in Christ, who as a man exercises dominion over all creation (Gen. 1:26-28, Ps. 8:5-8, Heb. 2:5-9). He ensures that all who follow him will fulfill their God-given role of ruling over creation. As a hymn Psalm 8 praises the name of God and his glory in creation, which can be related to both the name of Christ that is above every name and to his role as Creator.

Psalm 118 is a song of thanksgiving which gives thanks to God for deliverance from a life-threatening situation. The deliverance is described as a reversal of fortunes where a rejected stone later becomes the cornerstone (vv. 22-24). Psalm 118 is used in the New Testament to refer to Jesus as the one who comes in the name of the LORD to bring deliverance. The procession of the psalm fits the triumphal entry into Jerusalem of the king with the crowds shouting 'Hosanna'. However, the one who came to deliver his people was rejected, but this rejected stone has become the cornerstone of a new temple that is being built into a spiritual house with living stones.

Psalm 22 is a lament psalm that expresses deep anguish over a situation in which the psalmist is near death. The psalmist feels abandoned by God because help is not coming from him, even although he has in the past been a help to the psalmist. The opening cry of Psalm 22 is uttered by Christ on the cross and some of the ways the psalmist metaphorically describes his situation of suffering is literally fulfilled in Christ's suffering on the cross. As a lament the psalm expresses the struggle and anxiety of someone who is in a hopeless situation. As with most laments, however, there is a movement toward confidence and praise, which dominates the second half of Psalm 22. Praise is given for deliverance, and the impact of such praise is demonstrated not only in the congregation of God's people but in all the world. Psalm 22 relates to the suffering of Christ in his death, his deliverance from death in the resurrection, and the power of the proclamation of his victory for all the world. All aspects of the work of Christ come into view in Psalm 22: his priestly work of suffering on our behalf, his prophetic work of proclaiming his deliverance, and his kingly work of reigning over all things.

Psalm 40 contains a song of thanksgiving and a lament. The deliverance of the past, celebrated in the song of thanksgiving, is used as a basis to pray for help in a new situation of distress. In the song of thanksgiving, verses 6-8 show the willing obedience of the psalmist, which flows from an internalization of the law on the heart, to do the will of God. Such obedience is better than sacrifices and offerings. These verses are used in Hebrews 10:5-7 as the words of Christ indicating his willing obedience to do the will of God. The results of Christ's obedience is the abolishing of the sacrificial system because of his sacrificial death. As our priest he offers himself as the sacrifice. The priestly emphasis continues in the lament part of Psalm 40 where there is a confession of sin (v. 12), which relates to the work of Christ as our priestly mediator.

Psalm 16 is a psalm of confidence which expresses strong statements of trust in God that extend beyond the grave. It is used in the New Testament to support the resurrection of Christ (Acts 2:22-32; 13:35-37). The strong statements of confidence in the psalm relate to the ministry of Christ in the timing of his death and in his deliverance from it. Although he struggled in the Garden of Gethsemane, his confidence was not shaken because he was intent on doing the will of his Father. Even though he died and his body was put into the grave, he came forth from the grave on the third day.

Psalm 68 focuses on the victorious presence of God in Jerusalem and the implications of that presence for God's people and the whole world. The LORD is presented as the divine warrior who leads his people into battle and wins the victory, which is followed by his ascent of Mt. Zion accompanied by his heavenly army and captives taken in battle. Gifts are received as tribute to this great victorious king. The victorious reign of God means God's people will also experience victory over every foe. Christ is our victorious king who scatters all our enemies. He was raised from the dead in victory over death, he ascended on high, and now sits at the right hand of the Father, reigning from Mt Zion, the city of the living God, the heavenly Jerusalem. As the victorious king he distributes gifts to his people as they now enjoy the spoils of his victory (Eph. 4:8).

The chart at the end of the chapter reviews the psalms that have been covered in this book and shows how those psalms relate to Christ. However, the connections to Christ listed in the chart are by no means exhaustive but are only suggestive. The richness of the psalms and the complexity of the person and work of Christ make many connections possible.[4] Although not all the psalms have been examined, the goal has been to show how all types of psalms relate to Christ in order that the reader can then understand how other psalms relate to Christ. In the process we hope the majesty of Christ in all his human and divine glory has been set forth.

The Relationship of the Psalms to Christ

Psalm	Genre	Relation to Christ
103	Hymn	deity
93	Hymn	deity and king

49	Wisdom	humanity: illusions of wealth
73	Wisdom	humanity: prosperity of wicked
19	Wisdom	prophet
91	Confidence	humanity: trust
46	Confidence	priesthood: temple and God's presence
79	Comm lament	humanity: lament over Jerusalem
88	Ind lament	humanity: struggle
51	Lament	priest: intercession, confession
26	Vindication	humanity: falsely accused
109	Lament /imprecation	humanity: betrayal / king as judge/cursing
137	Lament/ imprecation	humanity: persecution / king as judge/cursing
32	Thanksgiving	priest, forgiveness
107	Comm thanksgiving	humanity: thankfulness for deliverance; deity: power to deliver
105	Psalm of remembrance	humanity: praise for God's God's faithfulness
106	Psalm of remembrance	priest: getting rid of the sin of the community
2	Royal	king; status as son
72	Royal	king; righteous reign
89	Royal	king; rejection
110	Royal	king/priest; victory in battle
132	Royal	king; Davidic covenant
144	Royal	king; final victory
45	Royal	king and his bride
8	Hymn	humanity: fulfills dominion over creation; deity: name above every name
118	Thanksgiving	king: triumphal entry, rejection; cornerstone
22	Ind lament	crucifixion, resurrection
40	Thanksgiving/lament	willing obedience/priest
16	Confidence	resurrection
68	Hymn	king: resurrection/ascension/ victorious reign

Bibliography

Adams, James E. *War Psalms of the Prince of Peace*. Presbyterian and Reformed Publishing Co., 1991.

Alexander, T. D. 'The Old Testament View of Life after Death' (*Themelios* 11 [1986]: 41-46).

Alexander, T. D. 'The Psalms and the Afterlife' (*IBS* 9 [1987]: 2-17).

Alford, Henry. *Alford's Greek Testament*. Baker Book House, 1980.

Allen, Leslie C. *Psalms 101–150*. WBC. Word, 1983.

Anderson, A. A. *The Book of Psalms*. NCB. 2 vols. Eerdmans, 1972.

Anderson, Bernard W. *Out of the Depths: The Psalms Speak For Us Today*. Rev ed. Westminster Press, 1983.

Averbeck, Richard E. 'מהר (*ṭhr*)' (Pages 338-53 in *NIDOTTE*. Vol. 2. Ed. Willem VanGemeren. Zondervan, 1997).

Barth, Markus. *Ephesians 4-6*. AB. Doubleday, 1974.

Barton, John. 'The Messiah in Old Testament Theology,' in *King and Messiah in Israel and the Ancient Near East: Proceedings of the Oxford Old Testament Seminar*. Ed. John Day.Sheffield Academic Press, 1998.

Becker, Joachim. *Messianic Expectations in the Old Testament*. Trans. D. E. Green. Fortress Press, 1977.

Beisner, E. Calvin. *Psalms of Promise*. 2nd ed. P & R Publishing, 1994.

Bentzen, Aage. *King and Messiah*. Blackwell, 1970.

Berkhof, L. *Systematic Theology*. Eerdmans, 1941.

Best, Ernest. *Ephesians*. ICC. T & T Clark, 1998.

Birkeland, H. *The Evildoers in the Book of Psalms*. Oslo: Dybwad, 1955.

Bock, D. L. 'Evangelicals and the Use of the Old Testament in the New' (*BibSac* 142 [1985]: 209-23).

Bock, D. L. *Luke 9:51-24:53*. BECNT. Baker Books, 1996.

Bornkamm, Heinrich. *Luther and the Old* Testament. 2nd English ed. Trans. Eric and Ruth Gritsch. Sigler Press, 1997.

Brueggemann, Walter. *The Message of the Psalms*. Augsburg Publishing House, 1984.

Brueggemann, Walter. 'The Costly Loss of Lament' (*JSOT* 36 [1986]: 57-71).

Brown, Michael. בְּרַךְ (*brk* II)' (Pages 757-67 in *NIDOTTE*. Vol. 1. Ed. Willem VanGemeren. Zondervan, 1997).

Brown, Raymond. *The* Sensus Plenior *of Sacred Scripture*. St. Mary's University, 1955.

Bruce, F. F. *The Epistle to the Hebrews*. NICNT. Eerdmans, 1964.

Bullock, C. Hassell. *Encountering the Book of Psalms*. Baker, 2001.

Calvin, John. *Institutes of the Christian Religion*. 2 vols. The Westminster Press, 1977.

Calvin, John. *Joshua, Psalms 1-35*. Calvin's Commentaries 4. Trans. Henry Beveridge. Baker, 1996 reprint.

Calvin, John. *Psalms 36-92*. Calvin's Commentaries 5. Trans. Henry Beveridge. Baker, 1996 reprint.

Calvin, John. *Psalms 93-150*. Calvin's Commentaries 6. Trans. Henry Beveridge. Baker, 1996 reprint.

Cara, Robert J. 'Redemptive-Historical Themes in the *Westminster Larger Catechism*, *The Westminster Confession of Faith in the 21st Century*. Vol 3. Ed. Ligon Duncan, Christian Focus, 2006.

Carson, D. A. *The Sermon on the Mount*. Baker, 1978.

Carson, D. A. *The Gospel According to John*. PNTC. Eerdmans, 1991.

Carson, D. A. *New Testament Commentary Survey*. 4th ed. Baker, 1993.

Chapell, Bryan. *Christ-Centered Preaching*. Baker, 1994.

Charlesworth, J. H. 'From Messianology to Christology: Problems and Prospects,' in *The Messiah*. Ed. J. H. Charlesworth. Fortress Press, 1992.

Childs, Brevard S. *An Introduction to the Old Testament*. Fortress Press, 1979.

Clements, R. E. 'The Messianic Hope in the Old Testament' (*JSOT* 43 [1989]: 3-19).

Clines, D. A. 'The Tree of Knowledge and the Law of Yahweh (Psalm XIX)' (*VT* 24 [1974]: 8-14).

Clowney, E. P. 'The Final Temple' (*WTJ* 35 (1973): 156-89).

Clowney, E. P. 'The Singing Savior,' *Moody Monthly* 79 (1978): 40-43.

Coogan, Michael David. *Stories from Ancient Canaan.* Westminster Press, 1978.

Craigie, Peter C. *Psalms 1–50.* WBC. Word, 1983.

Crenshaw, James L. *The Psalms: An Introduction.* Eerdmans, 2001.

Dahl, N. A. 'Messianic Ideas and the Crucifixion of Jesus' in *The Messiah.* Ed. James Charlesworth. Fortress Press, 1992.

Davies W. D. and Dale C. Allison. *The Gospel According to Matthew.* 3 vols. T & T Clark, 1997.

Day, J. *Psalms.* OT Guides. Sheffield Academic Press, 1999.

Day, John N. 'The Imprecatory Psalms and Christian Ethics,' *BibSac* 159 (2002), 166-86.

Delitzsch, Franz. 'Psalms,' *Commentary on the Old Testament.* Vol 5. Eerdmans, 1978.

Dodd, C. H. *According to the Scriptures.* Scribner, 1953.

Domeris, W. R. 'ינק (*ynq*)' (Pages 472-74 in *NIDOTTE.* Vol 2. Ed. Willem VanGemeren. Zondervan, 1997).

Eaton, J. H. *Kingship and the Psalms.* SCM Press Ltd, n.d.

Ellingworth, Paul. *The Epistle to the Hebrews.* Grand Rapids: Eerdmans, 1993.

Ellis, E. Earle. 'Biblical Interpretation in the New Testament Church,' in *Mikra.* Ed. Jan Mulder. Fortress, 1990.

Enns, Peter. 'Apostolic Hermeneutics and an Evangelical Doctrine of Scripture: Moving Beyond a Modernist Impasse' (*WTJ* 65 [2003]: 263-87).

Fitzmyer, Joseph A. *The Gospel According to Luke (X-XXIV).* AB. Doubleday & Co., Inc., 1985.

Frame, John M. *The Doctrine of God.* P & R Publishing, 2002.

Gage, Warren Austin. *The Gospel of Genesis.* Eisenbrauns, 1984.

Geldenhuys, Norval. *Commentary on the Gospel of Luke.* NICNT. Eerdmans, 1977.

Gerstenberger, Erhard S. *Psalms Part 1.* FOTL. Eerdmans, 1988.

Gerstenberger, Erhard S. *Psalms, Part 2, and Lamentations.* FOTL. Eerdmans, 2001.

Gileadi, Avraham. 'The Davidic Covenant: A Theological Basis for Corporate Protection,' in *Israel's Apostasy and Restoration*. Ed. Avraham Gileadi. Baker, 1988.

Gillingham, S. E. 'The Messiah in the Psalms: A Question of Reception History and the Psalter,' in *King and Messiah in Israel and the Ancient Near East: Proceedings of the Oxford Old Testament Seminar*. Ed. John Day. Sheffield Academic Press, 1998.

Green, Joel. B. *The Gospel of Luke*. NICNT. Eerdmans, 1997.

Greidanus, Sydney. *Preaching Christ from the Old Testament*. Eerdmans, 1999.

Grogan, Geoffrey. *Prayer, Praise, and Prophecy: A Theology of the Psalms*, Christian Focus, 2001.

Gunkel, Herman. *Introduction to the Psalms: The Genres of the Religious Lyric of Israel*. Trans. James D. Nogalski. Mercer University Press, 1998.

Hamilton, James M. 'Old Covenant Believers and the Indwelling Spirit: A Survey of the Spectrum of Opinion' (*TrinJ* 24ns [2003]: 37-54).

Hamilton, James M. 'God With Men in the Torah' (*WTJ* 65 [2003]: 113-33).

Harman, Allan. 'The Syntax and Interpretation of Psalm 45:7,' in *The Law and the Prophets*. Ed. John H. Skilton. Presbyterian and Reformed, 1974.

Harman, Allan. 'The Continuity of the Covenant Curses in the Imprecations of the Psalms' (*RTR* 54.2 [1995]: 65-72).

Harman, Allan. *Commentary on the Psalms*. Christian Focus, 1998.

Harris, Murray J. 'The Translation of *Elohim* in Psalm 45:7-8' (*TynBul* 35 [1984]: 65-89).

Heim, Knut. 'The Perfect King of Psalm 72: An Intertextual Inquiry,' in *The Lord's Anointed*. Eds. Philip E. Satterthwaite, Richard S. Hess, and Gordon J. Wenham. Baker, 1995.

Hendriksen, William. *Exposition of Ephesians*. NTC. Baker, 1967.

Hendriksen, William. *Exposition of the Gospel According to Matthew*. NTC. Baker, 1973.

Hendriksen, William. *Exposition of the Gospel According to Luke*. NTC. Baker, 1978.

Hendriksen, William. *Exposition of Paul's Epistle to the Romans*. NTC. Baker, 1981.

Hengstenberg, E. W. *The Christology of the Old Testament*. Kregel Publications, 1970.

Hermission, H. J. 'Observations on Creation Theology in Wisdom,' in *Creation in the Old Testament*. Ed. B. W. Anderson. Fortress Press, 1984.

Hodge, Charles. *Systematic Theology*. 3 vols. Eerdmans, 1952.

Hodge, Charles. *The Epistle to the Romans*. The Banner of Truth Trust, 1972.

Howard, Jr., David M. 'Recent Trends in Psalms Study,' in *The Face of Old Testament Studies*. Eds. David W. Baker and Bill T. Arnold. Baker, 1999.

Howard, Jr., David M. *The Structure of Psalms 93–100*. Eisenbrauns, 1997.

Hubbard, David A. 'The Wisdom Movement and Israel's Covenant Faith' (*TynBul* 17 [1966] 3-33).

Hughes, Philip E. *A Commentary on the Epistle to the Hebrews*. Eerdmans, 1977.

Jeremias, Joachim. *The Eucharistic Words of Jesus*. Fortress Press, 1964.

Jobes, Karen. 'Rhetorical Achievement in the Hebrews 10 "Misquote" of Psalm 40' (*Biblica* 72 [1991]: 387-96).

Just, Jr., Arthur A. *Luke 9:51–24:53*. Concordia Commentary. Concordia Publishing House, 1997.

Kaltner, John. 'Psalm 22:17b: Second Guessing "The Old Guess".' (*JBL* 117:3 [1998]: 503-14).

Kaiser, Jr., Walter. C. 'The Present State of Old Testament Studies' (*JETS* 18 [1975]: 69-79).

Kaiser, Jr., Walter. C. 'The Promise to David in Psalm 16 and its Application in Acts 2:25-33 and 13:32-37' (*JETS* 23:3 [1980]: 219-29).

Kaiser, Jr., Walter. C. *Toward an Exegetical Theology*. Baker, 1981.

Kaiser, Jr., Walter. C. *The Uses of the Old Testament in the New*. Moody Press, 1985.

Kaiser, Jr., Walter. C. *The Messiah in the Old Testament*. Zondervan, 1995.

Kidner, Derek. *Psalms 73–150*. InterVarsity Press, 1975.

Kim, Jinkyu. *Psalm 110 in Its Literary and Generic Contexts: An Eschatological Interpretation*. PhD diss. Westminster Theological Seminary, 2003.

Kistemaker, Simon J. *Hebrews*. Baker Books, 1984.

Kistemaker, Simon J. *The Thessalonians, The Pastorals, and Hebrews*. NTC. Baker, 1984.

Kraus, Hans-Joachim. *A Theology of the Psalms.* Trans. Keith Crim. Fortress Press, 1992.

Kraus, Hans-Joachim. *Psalms 1–150.* 2 vols. Continental Commentary. Fortress Press, 1993.

Kugel, James. *The Idea of Biblical Poetry.* Yale University Press, 1981.

Kühlewein, J. 'אִישׁ *'îš* **man**' (Pages 98-104 in *Theological Lexicon of the Old Testament.* Vol 1. Eds. Ernst Jenni and Claus Westermann. Hendriksen Publishers, 1997).

Ladd, George. *The Gospel of the Kingdom.* Eerdmans, 1959.

Lane, William. *The Gospel According to Mark.* NICNT. Eerdmanns, 1974.

Lane, William. *Hebrews 1–8.* WBC. Word, 1991.

Lenski, R. C. H. *The Interpretation of St. Luke's Gospel.* Augsburg Publishing House, 1946.

Leupold, H. C. *Exposition of the Psalms.* Baker Book House, 1959.

Lewis, C. S. *Reflections on the Psalms.* Harcourt Brace Jovanovich, 1958.

Lincoln, Andrew T. *Ephesians.* WBC. Word Books, 1990.

Lloyd-Jones, D. Martyn. *Studies in the Sermon on the Mount.* 2 vols. Eerdmans, 1971.

Longenecker, Richard N. *Apostolic Exegesis in the Apostolic Period.* 2nd ed. Eerdmans, 1999.

Longman, III, Tremper. 'Form Criticism, Recent Developments in Genre Theory, and the Evangelical' (*WTJ* 47 [1985]: 46-67).

Longman, III, Tremper. *How To Read the Psalms.* InterVarsity Press, 1988.

Longman, III, Tremper and Daniel G. Reid. *God Is a Warrior.* Zondervan, 1995.

Longman, III, Tremper. *Old Testament Commentary Survey.* 3rd ed. Baker, 2003.

Luc, Alex. 'חטא (*ḥṭ'*)' (Pages 87-93 in *NIDOTTE.* Ed. Willem VanGemeren. Vol. 2. Zondervan, 1997).

Luc, Alex. 'עָוֹן (*'āwôn*)' (Page 351 in *NIDOTTE.* Ed. Willem VanGemeren. Vol. 3. Zondervan, 1997).

Luc, Alex. 'Interpreting the Curses in the Psalms' (*JETS* 42.3 [1999]: 395-410).

Luther, Martin. *First Lectures on the Psalms, Psalms 1–75.* Luther's Works. Vol 10. Ed. Hilton C. Oswald. Concordia Publishing House, 1974.

Marshall, I. Howard. *The Gospel of Luke: A Commentary on the Greek Text*. NIGTC. Eerdmans, 1978.

Mays, James L. *The Lord Reigns: A Theological Handbook to the Psalms*. Westminster John Knox, 1994.

Mays, James L. *Psalms*. Interpretation. John Knox Press, 1994.

McCann, J. Clinton, ed. *The Shape and Shaping of the* Psalter. JSOT Press, 1993.

McCann, J. Clinton. 'Books I–III and the Editorial Purpose of the Hebrew Psalter,' in *The Shape and Shaping of the Psalter*. Ed. J. Clinton McCann. JSOT Press, 1993.

McCann, J. Clinton, ed. 'Psalms,' *The New Interpreter's Bible*. Vol. 4. Abingdon Press, 1996).

McCartney, Dan. 'The New Testament's Use of the Old Testament,' in *Inerrancy and Hermeneutic: A Tradition, a Challenge, a Debate*. Ed. H. Conn. Baker, 1988.

McCartney, Dan and Charles Clayton. *Let the Reader Understand: A Guide to Interpreting and Applying the Bible*. Victor Books, 1994.

McCartney, Dan. '*Ecco Homo*: The Coming of the Kingdom at the Restoration of Human Vicegerency' (*WTJ* 56 [1994]: 1-21).

McFall, Leslie. 'The Evidence for a Logical Arrangement of the Psalter' (*WTJ* 62 [2000]: 223-56).

Miller, Patrick. *Interpreting the Psalms*. Fortress Press, 1986.

Miller, Patrick. 'The Beginning of the Psalter,' in *The Shape and Shaping of the Psalter*. Ed. J. Clinton McCann. JSOT Press, 1993.

Miller, Patrick. *They Cried to the Lord: The Form and Theology of Biblical Prayer*. Fortress Press, 1994.

Mitchell, David C. *The Message of the Psalter: An Eschatological Programme in the Book of Psalms*. Sheffield Academic Press, 1997.

Moberly, R. W. L. *The Bible, Theology, and Faith: A Study of Abraham and Jesus*. Cambridge University Press, 2000.

Moo, Douglas. 'The Problem of Sensus Plenior,' in *Hermeneutics, Authority, and Canon*. Eds. D. A. Carson and John D. Woodbridge. Zondervan, 1986.

Moo, Douglas. *The Epistle to the Romans*. NICNT. Eerdmans, 1996.

Mowinckel, Sigmund. *He That Cometh*. Blackwell, 1954.

Mowinckel, Sigmund. *The Psalms in Israel's Worship*. Abingdon, 1962. Republished by Eerdmans, 2004.

Murphy, Roland. 'A Consideration of the Classification "Wisdom Psalms",' in *Studies in Ancient Israelite Literature*. Ed. James Crenshaw. KTAV Publishing House, 1976.

Murphy, Roland. 'Wisdom-Theses and Hypotheses.' in *Israelite Wisdom: Theological and Literary Essays in Honor of Samuel Terrien*. Ed. J. G. Gammie. Scholars Press, 1978.

Murray, John. *The Epistle to the Romans*. Eerdmans, 1965.

Neusner, Jacob. *What is Midrash?* Guides to Biblical Scholarship. Fortress, 1987.

Neusner, Jacob. *Rabbinic Literature and the New Testament*. Trinity Press International, 1994.

Oswalt, John N. 'משׁח (*mšḥ*)' (Pages 1123-27 in *NIDOTTE*. Vol 2. Ed. Willem VanGemeren. Zondervan, 1997).

Parker, T. H. L. *Calvin's Old Testament Commentaries*. Westminster John Knox Press, 1986.

Patterson, Richard D. 'Psalm 22: From Trial to Triumph' (*JETS* 47.2 [2004]: 213-34).

Payne, J. Barton. *Encyclopedia of Biblical Prophecy*. Harper & Row, 1973.

Pink, A. W. *The Seven Sayings of the Saviour on the Cross*. Baker, 1958.

Pomykala, Kenneth E. *The Davidic Dynasty Tradition*. Scholars Press, 1995.

Poythress, Vern S. 'Divine Meaning of Scripture' (*WTJ* [1986]: 241-79).

Poythress, Vern S. *The Shadow of Christ in the Law of Moses*. P & R, 1991.

Poythress, Vern S. *God-Centered Biblical Interpretation*. P & R Publishing, 1999.

Puckett, David L. *John Calvin's Exegesis of the Old Testament*. Columbia Series in Reformed Theology. Westminster John Knox Press, 1995.

Perdue, Leo G. *Wisdom and Creation: The Theology of Wisdom Literature*. Abingdon Press, 1994.

Reimer, David J. 'Old Testament Christology,' in *King and Messiah in Israel and the Ancient Near East: Proceedings of the Oxford Old Testament Seminar*. Ed. John Day. Sheffield Academic Press, 1998.

Reymond, Robert L. *A New Systematic Theology of the Christian Faith*. Thomas Nelson, 1998.

Reymond, Robert L. *Jesus, Divine Messiah*. Christian Focus, 2003.

Ridderbos, Herman. *The Coming of the Kingdom*. The Presbyterian and Reformed Publishing Co., 1975.

Ridderbos, Herman. *Matthew*. Bible Student's Commentary. Zondervan, 1987.

Ridderbos, Herman. *The Gospel of John: A Theological Commentary*. Eerdmans, 1997.

Roberts, J. J. M. 'The Old Testament's Contribution to Messianic Expectation,' in *The Messiah: Developments in Earliest Judaism and Christianity*. Ed. J. H. Charlesworth. Fortress Press, 1992.

Robertson, O. Palmer. *Christ of the Covenants*. P & R, 1980.

Satterthwaite, Philip E. 'Zion in the Song of Ascents,' in *Zion, City of Our God*. Eds. Richard S. Hess and Gordon J. Wenham. Eerdmans, 1999.

Schaefer, Konrad. *Psalms*. Berit Olam. The Liturgical Press, 2001.

Schaper, J. *Eschatology in the Greek Psalter*. J. C. B. Mohr, 1995.

Schmid, H. H. 'Creation, Righteousness, and Salvation: "Creation Theology" as the Broad Horizon of Biblical Theology' in *Creation in the Old Testament*. Ed. B. W. Anderson. Fortress Press, 1984.

Silva, Moisés. 'The New Testament Use of the Old Testament: Text Form and Authority' in *Scripture and Truth*. Eds. D. A. Carson and John D. Woodbridge. Baker, 1992.

Smend, R. 'Julius Wellhausen and His Prolegomena to the History of Israel' (*Semeia* 25 [1982]: 1-20).

Smith, Gary V. 'Paul's Use of Psalm 68:18 in Ephesians 4:8' (*JETS* 18 [1975]: 181-89).

Strawn, Brent. 'Psalm 22:17b: More Guessing' (*JBL* 119:3 [2000]: 439-51).

Swenson, Kristin M. 'Psalm 22:17: Circling around the Problem Again' (*JBL* 123.4 [2004]: 637-48).

Tate, Marvin E. *Psalms 51–100*. WBC. Word, 1990.

Thomas, Derek. *The Essential Commentaries for a Preacher's Library*. Reformed Academic Press, 1996.

Thornwell, James Henry. 'The Priesthood of Christ,' in *Collected Writings*. Vol. 2. The Banner of Truth Trust, 1974.

Turretin, Francis. *Institutes of Elenctic Theology*. 3 vols. P & R, 1992.

Vall, Gregory. 'Psalm 22:17B: "The Old Guess".' (*JBL* 116:1 [1997]: 45-56).

VanGemeren, Willem. 'Psalms', *The Expositor's Bible Commentary*. Vol 5. Zondervan, 1991.

Van Groningen, Gerard. *Messianic Revelation in the Old Testament*. Baker Book House, 1990.

Van Leeuwen, Raymond. 'Wealth and Poverty: System and Contradiction in Proverbs' (*Hebrew Studies* 33 [1992]: 25-36).

Vos, Gerhardus. *The Teaching of Jesus concerning the Kingdom of God and the Church*. Presbyterian and Reformed Publishing Co., 1972.

Waltke, Bruce K. 'A Canonical Process Approach to the Psalms,' in *Tradition and Testament: Essays in Honor of Charles Lee Feinberg*. Eds. John S. Feinberg and Paul D. Feinberg. Moody Press, 1981.

Warfield, B. B. 'The Spirit of God in the Old Testament,' in *Biblical and Theological Studies*. The Presbyterian and Reformed Publishing Co., 1968).

Warfield, B. B. *The Person and Work of the Holy Spirit*. Calvary Press, 1997.

Weinfeld, Moshe. 'The Covenant Grant in the Old Testament and in the Ancient Near East' (*JAOS* 90 [1970]: 184-203).

Weiser, Artur. *The Psalms: A Commentary*. OTL. Westminster Press, 1962.

Westermann, Claus. 'The Role of the Lament in the Theology of the Old Testament' (*Int* 28 [1974]: 20-38).

Westermann, Claus. *The Psalms: Structure, Content, and Message*. Augsburg Publishing House, 1980.

Westermann, Claus. *Praise and Lament in the Psalms*. John Knox Press, 1981.

White, John B. 'The Sages' Strategy to Preserve Salôm,' in *The Listening Heart: Essays in Wisdom and the Psalms in Honour of Roland E. Murphy*. Ed. K. Hoglund. JSOT, 1987.

Wilson, Gerald H. *The Editing of the Hebrew Psalter*. Scholars Press, 1985.

Wilson, Gerald H. 'Shaping the Psalter: A Consideration of Editorial Linkage in the Book of the Psalms,' in *The Shape and Shaping of the Psalter*. Ed. J. Clinton McCann. JSOT Press, 1993.

Wilson, Gerald H. *Psalms Volume 1*. NIVAC. Zondervan, 2002.

Wood, Leon J. *The Holy Spirit in the Old Testament*. Zondervan, 1976.

Zenger, Eric. *A God of Vengeance?* Trans. Linda M. Maloney. Westminster John Knox Press, 1996.

References

Chapter 1: Key Issues in Interpreting the Psalms

[1]The Hebrew has *ʾîš* with the article: 'the man.' The word *ʾîš* basically means 'man' or 'husband' and is the opposite of '*iššāh*, 'woman' or 'wife'. Thus it primarily refers to the male gender. There are places, however, where *ʾîš* can mean 'person' (see J. Kühlewein, 'אִישׁ [*ʾîš*] man,' *Theological Lexicon of the Old Testament* [eds. Ernst Jenni and Claus Westermann; 3 vols.; Hendriksen Publishers], I:101, who points out that *ʾîš* is used as a person in legal texts [Exod. 21:12] and in texts of curses and blessings [Deut. 27:15]). It becomes clear in light of the whole psalm that the meaning 'person' is appropriate here, but as will be shown below, the translation 'man' keeps in view the reference to the king (see Patrick Miller, 'The Beginning of the Psalter,' *The Shape and Shaping of the Psalter* [ed. J. Clinton McCann; JSOT Press, 1993], 83-92).

[2]John Calvin, *Joshua, Psalms 1-35* (Calvin's Commentaries; trans. Henry Beveridge; 22 vols; Baker, 1996 reprint), 4:1-3.

[3]Martin Luther, 'First Lectures on the Psalms, Psalms 1-75,' *Luther's Works* (ed. Hilton C. Oswald; 56 vols.; Concordia Publishing House, 1974), 10:11.

[4]For modern evaluations of Calvin's exegesis, see David L. Puckett, *John Calvin's Exegesis of the Old Testament* (Columbia Series in Reformed Theology; Westminster John Knox Press, 1995), 7-12.

[5]See especially Calvin's comments in his Hosea commentary (chs. 6, 8, and 10) where he stresses sticking to the design and intention of the prophet (*Hosea*, 13:221 and 283 specifically, but all throughout his comments on Hosea he emphasizes what the prophet says; see also the discussion in Puckett, *Calvin's Exegesis*, 26-37 on the human writer's intention as an exegetical concern, and its relation to the Holy Spirit's intention).

[6]Calvin, *Psalms 36-92*, 5:100; Puckett, *Calvin's Exegesis*, 119.

[7]See the introductory comments to Psalm 22 in Calvin, *Psalms 1-35*, 4:333 and Puckett's comments on Calvin's handling of this Psalm, *Calvin's Exegesis*, 121-22.

[8]T. H. L. Parker, *Calvin's Old Testament Commentaries* (Westminster John Knox Press, 1986), 203-05.

[9]Calvin, *Psalms 93-150*, 6:295.

[10]Calvin, *Psalms 36-92*, 5:206; see Puckett, *Calvin's Exegesis*, 113-23 for a discussion of Calvin's view of typology.

[11]Puckett, *Calvin's Exegesis*, 113.

[12]Calvin, *Psalms 36-92*, 5:206.

[13]Thomas Aquinas, *Summa Theologica* (5 vols.; Christian Classics, 1981), vol 1, p 7.

[14]Luther, 'First Lectures on the Psalms, Psalms 1-75,' 6-7. For a brief analysis of Luther's approach to the Psalms, see the 'Introduction to Volume 10' in *Luther's Works*, ix-xii. Although Luther continued to use allegory, he greatly curtailed its use (see his warnings against allegory in 'Lectures on Isaiah 1–39,' *Luther's Works*, 16:326-37).

[15]For a discussion of Luther's exegetical method, see Heinrich Bornkamm, *Luther and the Old Testament* (2nd English ed.; trans. Eric and Ruth Gritsch; Sigler Press, 1997), 87-114.

[16]Luther distinguished between the literal, historical sense (the sense related to the kingdom of David and to the piety of David the king) and the literal, prophetic sense (the sense related to Christ). He justifies bypassing the literal, historical sense not because it is unimportant but because he believes the literal, prophetic sense was the most important to David, as he says in 2 Samuel 24:2, 'the Lord has spoken by me.' This statement is taken to mean that David spoke directly of Christ (see the 'Preface to the Scholia' in 'First Lectures on the Psalms, Psalms 1-75,' 9-10). Because Luther viewed the Old Testament as speaking directly of Christ, there is no concept of the Old Testament as foreshadowing the New Testament, and thus no use of typology in understanding the Old

Testament (Bornkamm, *Luther and the Old Testament*, 250-51). Thus much of Luther's exposition of the psalms seems arbitrary and forced in its relationship to Christ. Calvin, on the other hand, who emphasizes the historical context and comments specifically on the relationship of the Old Testament to New Testament in terms of shadow and substance, does use typology (see the *Institutes of the Christian Religion*, Book 2, Ch. 11).

[17]See David M. Howard, Jr., 'Recent Trends in Psalms Study,' *The Face of Old Testament Studies* (eds. David W. Baker and Bill T. Arnold; Baker, 1999), 329-50 for a good review of the various positions.

[18]A doxology brings each of the five books to a close. Book I includes Psalms 1–41, Book II includes Psalms 42–72, Book III includes Psalms 73–89, Book IV includes Psalms 90–106, and Book V includes Psalms 107–150.

[19]For a succinct review of the developments in Psalm study related to the editing of the Psalter, see the articles in *The Shape and Shaping of the Psalter* (ed. J. Clinton McCann; JSOT Press, 1993).

[20]For a discussion of the differences between Books I–III and Books IV–V and the significance of those differences for the editing of the Psalter, see Gerald H. Wilson, *The Editing of the Hebrew Psalter* (Scholars Press, 1985), chapter 7. He stresses the importance of the placement of the royal psalms for understanding the structure of the Psalter.

[21]See David M. Howard, Jr., *The Structure of Psalms 93-100* (Eisenbrauns, 1997). He does not believe that human kingship and the Davidic covenant have been completely rejected and replaced by divine kingship. These can coexist together. The yearning for a king persisted in the exilic period.

[22]Jinkyu Kim (*Psalm 110 in Its Literary and Generic Contexts: An Eschatological Interpretation* [PhD diss., Westminster Theological Seminary, 2003]) tries to apply the concept of the positioning of the royal psalms that Wilson developed in relationship to Books I–III to Books IV–V. He argues for the important positioning of the royal psalms at or near the end of a group of psalms which are then followed by doxological psalms. Thus he groups together the doxological Psalms 111–118 which follow the royal Psalms 108–110. He also stresses the eschatological nature of the Psalter. Although an extremely valuable study, some of his groupings appear forced; for example, he takes psalms 90–110 as a group, which seems to overlook the major division between Books IV and V at Psalm 106–107.

[23]Willem VanGemeren, 'Psalms,' in *The Expositor's Bible Commentary* (12 vols.; Zondervan, 1991), 5:713.

[24]Wilson, *The Editing of the Hebrew Psalter*, Chapter 7. In addition to a 'royal covenantal frame' in the Psalms, Wilson also sees a 'final wisdom frame' that takes precedence over the royal covenantal frame (Wilson, 'Shaping the Psalter: A Consideration of Editorial Linkage in the Book of the Psalms,' *The Shape and Shaping of the Psalter* [ed. J. Clinton McCann; JSOT Press, 1993], 72-82; see also James L. Mays, *The Lord Reigns: A Theological Handbook to the Psalms* [Westminster John Knox, 1994]). For the editorial significance of the psalms that deal with the law (torah psalms) see James L. Mays, "The Place of the Torah-Psalms in the Psalter," *JBL* 106 (1987): 3-12. For the view that links the torah psalms with the kingship psalms and argues that the editors of the Psalter were trying to set forth the law of the king in Deuteronomy 17:14-20, see Jamie A. Grant, *The King as Exemplar: The Function of Deuteronomy's Kingship Law in the Shaping of the Book of Psalms* (Atlanta: SBL, 2004).

[25]David M. Howard, Jr., 'Recent Trends in Psalm Studies,' in *The Face of Old Testament Studies* (Baker Books, 1999), 334.

[26]Patrick D. Miller, 'The Beginning of the Psalter,' *The Shape and Shaping of the Psalter*, 88-92. See also Bruce K. Waltke, 'A Canonical Process Approach to the Psalms,' *Tradition and Testament: Essays in Honor of Charles Lee Feinberg* (ed. John S. Feinberg and Paul D. Feinberg; Moody Press, 1981), 3-18, who sees Jesus as the subject of the Psalms based on the argument that in the original composition of the Psalms the subject was the king.

[27]The following discussion of the role of the divine author in meaning is heavily indebted to the article by Vern S. Poythress, 'Divine Meaning of Scripture,' *WTJ* (1986): 241-79.

[28]This view has been called *sensus plenior*, or 'fuller meaning', which in Roman Catholic discussions has included church tradition in the development of meaning to account for dogmas like the immaculate conception of Mary (see Raymond Brown, *The* Sensus Plenior *of Sacred Scripture* [St. Mary's University, 1955]). We will limit our discussions to the biblical canon of the Old and New Testaments.

[29]See the concerns expressed by Walter Kaiser who wants to limit the discussions of meaning to the human author ('The Promise to David in Psalm 16 and its Application in Acts 2:25-33 and 13:32-37,' *JETS* 23:3 [1980]: 219-29). Other implications follow from this limitation.

He does not allow later revelation to be brought into a discussion of the meaning of an Old Testament text for fear that someone's theology might hinder the discovery of meaning. He also makes a distinction between meaning and application (Poythress, 'Divine Meaning,' deals with some of these concerns). Many of Kaiser's articles have been published in *The Uses of the Old Testament in the New* (Moody Press, 1985) and reprinted by Wipf and Stock.

[30]See Dan McCartney and Charles Clayton, *Let the Reader Understand: A Guide to Interpreting and Applying the Bible* (Victor Books, 1994), 164.

[31]Dan McCartney, 'The New Testament's Use of the Old Testament,' in *Inerrancy and Hermeneutic: A Tradition, a Challenge, a Debate* (ed. H. Conn; Baker, 1988), 101-16 and the discussion of the term 'Christotelic' (Christ as the goal of the Old Testament) in Peter Enns, 'Apostolic Hermeneutics and an Evangelical Doctrine of Scripture: Moving Beyond a Modernist Impasse,' *WTJ* 65 (2003): 263-87.

Chapter 2: Different Approaches to the Messianic Psalms

[1]Sigmund Mowinckel, *He That Cometh* (Blackwell, 1954), republished by Eerdmans, 2005. Mowinckel has had tremendous influence in psalm studies even among those who disagree with his conclusions. It is almost impossible to read a modern commentary on the Psalms without some interaction with his views. His foundational work on the Psalms (*The Psalms in Israel's Worship* [Abingdon, 1962], republished by Eerdmans, 2004) argues that the psalms should be understood in the context of a New Year's festival in Israel where the king, who represents Yahweh in a cultic drama, is depicted as victorious over all his enemies and is proclaimed ruler once again.

[2]J. H. Charlesworth, 'From Messianology to Christology: Problems and Prospects,' *The Messiah* (ed. J. H. Charlesworth; Fortress Press, 1992), 3-35.

[3]The historical-critical method developed during the Enlightenment. It emphasizes the importance of the historical context for interpreting Scripture but treats the Bible as only a human document. This method denies the divine origin of Scripture.

[4]Mowinckel, *He That Cometh*, 71-72, 96-98, 122-23, 125-26, and 150-57.

[5]John Day, *Psalms* (OT Guides; Sheffield Academic Press, 1999), 98.

[6]J. J. M. Roberts, 'The Old Testament's Contribution to Messianic Expectation,' *The Messiah: Developments in Earliest Judaism and Christianity* (ed. J. H. Charlesworth; Fortress Press, 1992), 39.

[7]Although proponents of this view do not believe that Messianic ideas fully develop until Judaism or early Christianity, some believe that early Messianic ideas can be found in Isaiah 7, 9, 11, Zechariah 9, and Daniel 9, which are further developed in the Septuagint and the Qumran texts (see Charlesworth, 'From Messianology to Christology,' 12; Kenneth E. Pomykala, *The Davidic Dynasty Tradition* [Scholars Press, 1995], 270-71; and J. Schaper, *Eschatology in the Greek Psalter* [J. C. B. Mohr, 1995]).

[8]John Barton, 'The Messiah in Old Testament Theology,' *King and Messiah in Israel and the Ancient Near East: Proceedings of the Oxford Old Testament Seminar* (ed. John Day; Sheffield Academic Press, 1998), 371.

[9]Joachim Becker, *Messianic Expectations in the Old Testament* (trans. D. E. Green; Fortress Press, 1977), 38.

[10]S. E. Gillingham, 'The Messiah in the Psalms: A Question of Reception History and the Psalter,' *King and Messiah in Israel and the Ancient Near East: Proceedings of the Oxford Old Testament Seminar* (ed. John Day; Sheffield Academic Press, 1998), 220, n. 29. Gillingham believes that the concept of the Messiah in the Psalms is not a theological concept that arises from the psalms themselves, but is an agenda which has been imposed upon the psalms (p. 237).

[11]Aage Bentzen, *King and Messiah* (Blackwell, 1970), 35.

[12]See the discussion at the beginning of R. E. Clements, 'The Messianic Hope in the Old Testament,' *JSOT* 43 (1989): 3-19.

[13]Barton, 'The Messiah,' 375-78.

[14]Becker, *Messianic Expectations*, 91-96.

[15]David J. Reimer, 'Old Testament Christology,' *King and Messiah in Israel and the Ancient Near East: Proceedings of the Oxford Old Testament Seminar* (ed. John Day; Sheffield Academic Press, 1998), 383, 390-400.

[16]Bruce K. Waltke, 'A Canonical Process Approach to the Psalms,' *Tradition and Testament: Essays in Honor of Charles Lee Feinberg* (ed. John S. Feinberg and Paul D. Feinberg; Moody Press, 1981), 5.

[17]The Historical Critical Method has historically led to a separation of the academy from the church. This can be seen in Wellhausen's strugggle as a professor of theology. He helped develop and popularize source criticism (JEDP). As a professor of theology he had the task of

preparing students for service in the church, but he eventually resigned from the position because he felt inadequate for the task. Instead of preparing students for ministry in the church, he felt he made them unfit for such an office (R. Smend, 'Julius Wellhausen and His Prolegomena to the History of Israel,' *Semeia* 25 [1982]: 6).

[18]David C. Mitchell (*The Message of the Psalter: An Eschatological Programme in the Book of Psalms* [Sheffield Academic Press, 1997], 65) notes that only from 1820 to 1970 were eschatological views denied to the Psalter.

[19]James L. Mays, *The Lord Reigns: A Theological Handbook to the Psalms* (Westminster John Knox, 1994), 87-89.

[20]The royal psalms are the psalms that deal specifically with the king, who is the central figure in the psalm. Generally, the royal psalms have included 2, 18, 20, 21, 45, 72, 89, 101, 110, 132, and 144.

[21]Clements, 'The Messianic Hope,' 14.

[22]Brevard S. Childs, *An Introduction to the Old Testament* (Fortress Press, 1979), 517.

[23]Mays, *The Lord Reigns*, 97-98.

[24]Clements, 'The Messianic Hope,' 17.

[25]Ibid., 16.

[26]Mays, *The Lord Reigns*, 100.

[27]Franz Delitzsch, 'Psalms,' *Commentary on the Old Testament* (10 vols.; Eerdmans, 1978), 5:66. Note also Walter Kaiser, *The Messiah in the Old Testament* (Zondervan, 1995), 33, who discusses direct prophecy as one of the types of prophecy.

[28]E. W. Hengstenberg, *The Christology of the Old Testament* (Kregel Publications, 1970), 10. J. Barton Payne, *Encyclopedia of Biblical Prophecy* (Harper & Row, 1973), 256 makes the same point in reference to Luke 24:44.

[29]Hengstenberg, *Christology of the Old Testament*, 42.

[30]Kaiser, *The Messiah*, 23.

[31]Payne, *Encyclopedia of Biblical Prophecy*, 76.

[32]Delitzsch, 'Psalms,' 5:68-70. Delitzsch' approach has also been called a literary historical approach (Waltke, 'Canonical Process Approach').

[33]Kaiser, *The Messiah*, 26-27.

[34]The authors discussed in this section would affirm the divine origin of Scripture, but do not adequately take into account the implications that Scripture has a divine author.

[35]Hengstenberg, *Christology of the Old Testament*, 42, 69.

[36]H. C. Leupold, *Exposition of the Psalms* (Baker Book House, 1959), 21.

[37]Kaiser, *The Messiah*, 93-94.

[38]Payne, *Encyclopedia of Biblical Prophecy*, 257-58.

[39]Gerard Van Groningen, *Messianic Revelation in the Old Testament* (Baker Book House, 1990). He identifies his approach as making use of grammatical, historical, and theological aspects, as well as a revelation-response method where not only is God's revelation to humanity ascertained, but there is also a study of the human response (12).

[40]Ibid., 13, 20.

[41]Ibid., 332.

[42]Ibid., these psalms are discussed by Van Groningen on pp. 327-407.

Chapter 3: The Christological Approach to the Messiah in the Psalms

[1]Even among scholars who agree on divine inspiration, there is disagreement on the relationship between the human and divine authors of Scripture (see D. Bock, 'Evangelicals and the Use of the Old Testament in the New,' *BibSac* 142 [1985]: 209-23). For an excellent analysis of the relationship of the divine author to the human author and its importance for interpretation, see Vern S. Poythress, 'Divine Meaning of Scripture,' *WTJ* 48 (1986): 241-79. For an approach to the psalms that has much in common with what is being developed here see Bruce K. Waltke, 'A Canonical Process Approach to the Psalms,' in *Tradition and Testament: Essays in Honor of Charles Lee Feinberg* (eds. John S. Feinberg and Paul D. Feinberg; Moody Press, 1981), 3-18.

[2]It is rather amazing that very few discussions related to the Messiah in the Old Testament, even among evangelicals, give Luke 24 any more than a passing reference. Critical scholars tend to dismiss it as Luke's own theology (N. A. Dahl, 'Messianic Ideas and the Crucifixion of Jesus,' *The Messiah* [ed. James Charlesworth; Fortress Press, 1992], 390-91), or they misrepresent the evangelical view as a product of 'timeless revelation' (David J. Reimer, 'Old Testament Christology,' *King and Messiah in Israel and the Ancient Near East* [ed. John Day; Sheffield Academic Press, 1998], 381). For a recent analysis of the implications of Luke 24 in understanding the Old Testament, see R. W. L. Moberly, *The Bible, Theology, and Faith: A Study of Abraham and Jesus* (Cambridge University Press, 2000), 45-70.

[3]The Hebrew Bible arranges the books of the Old Testament a little bit differently than the English Bible. Both agree on the Law (the first five books), but there is divergence in the Prophets. The former Prophets in the Hebrew Bible include Joshua, Judges, 1–2 Samuel, and 1–2 Kings. Then come the latter Prophets, which include Isaiah, Jeremiah, Ezekiel, and the 12 Minor Prophets. The third section of the Hebrew Bible is called the Writings. The first book in the Writings is the Psalms. It also contains Job, Proverbs, Ruth, Song of Songs, Ecclesiastes, Lamentations, Esther, Daniel, Ezra, Nehemiah, and Chronicles. Although it is possible that Jesus' reference to the Psalms in Luke 24:44 could only refer to the Psalms, in light of the comprehensive nature of the statements by Jesus, it is more likely that the reference to the Psalms stands for all of the third section of the Old Testament Scriptures.

[4]I. Howard Marshall, *The Gospel of Luke: A Commentary on the Greek Text* (NIGTC; Eerdmans, 1978), 903, 905.

[5]Arthur A. Just, Jr. (*Luke 9:51-24:53* [Concordia Commentary; Concordia Publishing House, 1997], 1021-36) has an Excursus on the Old Testament witness to Christ where he gives a full account of the Old Testament passages that are significant for Luke's Gospel in relationship to Jesus. Darrell L. Bock (*Luke 9:51–24:53* [BECNT; Baker Books, 1996]) notes that prophetic texts from the Psalter appear in Luke 13:35; 20:17, 41-44; 22:69 (p. 1937), and includes texts such as Psalm 118:22, 26; and Psalm 110:1. He also refers to various speeches in Acts that use key passages from the Old Testament, such as Deuteronomy 18:15, Psalms 2:7, 16:8-11; 110:1; 118; and Isaiah 53:8 (p. 1916).

[6]Commentators who stress that Jesus has in view all the Old Testament include Henry Alford, *Alford's Greek Testament* (4 vols.; Baker Book House, 1980), 1:670; Bock, *Luke 9:51–24:53*, 1918; Joel B. Green, *The Gospel of Luke* (NICNT; Eerdmans, 1997), 848; and William Hendriksen, *Exposition of the Gospel According to Luke* (Baker Book House, 1978), 1065.

[7]R. C. H. Lenski (*The Interpretation of St. Luke's Gospel* [Augsburg Publishing House, 1946], 1190) comments that Jesus did what many modern scholars do not seem to be able to do – find him in the Old Testament.

[8]See the discussion in Chapter 2 under the heading 'The Historical Critical Approach.'

[9]See Joseph A. Fitzmyer, *The Gospel According to Luke (X-XXIV)* (Doubleday & Co., Inc., 1985), 1565. He also notes that there is no concept of a suffering messiah in pre-Christian Judaism.

[10]Although it is very important to study the various Messianic views of pre-Christian Judaism as a part of the environment of early Christianity, Jesus looks to the Old Testament as the source of Messianic ideas about himself.

[11]Kaiser so emphasizes interpreting a passage in its historical context that he believes it is inappropriate for the interpreter to bring in later Scripture (either later Old Testament texts or the New Testament) as part of the process of interpreting the *meaning* of an Old Testament passage, although later passages can be brought in as conclusions or in summaries (Walter C. Kaiser, 'The Present State of Old Testament Studies,' *JETS* 18 [1975]: 73 and *Toward an Exegetical Theology* [Baker, 1981], 134-40).

[12]Bock, *Luke 9:51–24:53*, 1939.

[13]It is beyond the scope of this chapter to argue for the deity of Jesus Christ. For discussion of this issue, see Francis Turretin, *Institutes of Elenctic Theology* (3 vols.; P & R Publishing, 1992), 2:282-93, John M. Frame, *The Doctrine of God* (P & R Publishing, 2002), 663-80, and Robert L. Reymond, *Jesus, Divine Messiah* (Christian Focus, 2003).

[14] See John N. Oswalt, מָשַׁח, in *NIDOTTE* (ed. Willem VanGemeren; 5 vols.; Zondervan, 1997), 1123-27. For a systematic presentation of the offices of prophet, priest, and king in relation to Christ, see Charles Hodge, *Systematic Theology* (3 vols.; Eerdmans, 1952), 2:459-67, 596-609 and L. Berkhof, *Systematic Theology* (Eerdmans, 1941), 356-66, 406-12. See also Larger Catechism questions 43-45 in the Westminster Standards.

[15]See the 'Index of Quotations' and the 'Index of Allusions and Verbal Parallels' at the back of *The Greek New Testament* (eds. Aland, Black, Martini; 3rd ed.; United Bible Societies, 1983).

[16]Moisés Silva ('The New Testament Use of the Old Testament: Text Form and Authority,' in *Scripture and Truth* [eds. D. A. Carson and John D. Woodbridge; Baker, 1992], 164) comments, 'If we refuse to pattern our exegesis after that of the apostles, we are in practice denying the authoritative character of their scriptural interpretation – and to do so is to strike at the very heart of the Christian faith.' For an alternative view, see Richard N. Longenecker, *Apostolic Exegesis in the Apostolic Period* (2nd ed.; Eerdmans, 1999), xxxiv-xxxix.

[17]Sigmund Mowinckel laid the groundwork for the origin and use of all the psalms in an annual festival (*The Psalms in Israel's Worship* [Abingdon, 1962]). Although many have rejected his basic analysis of the

festival, they still argue for the importance of a festival for the setting of the psalms (see especially Artur Weiser, *The Psalms: A Commentary* [OTL; Westminster Press, 1962], who argues for an annual covenant festival, and Hans-Joachim Kraus, *Psalms 1–150* [2 vols; Continental Commentary; Fortress Press, 1993], who argues for an annual royal Zion festival). It is faulty to assume that all the psalms were composed for a festival, or even that all the psalms were composed for worship at the temple. Some of the psalms were composed specifically for worship, but many of the psalms reflect a variety of situations of life from which they arose. 2 Samuel 22 represents the origin of Psalm 18 in relation to an event in David's life (see C. Hassell Bullock, *Encountering the Book of Psalms* [Baker, 2001], 125, who argues that not all psalms move from public to private use but that some move from private to public use). Thus, even psalms that were not specifically composed for worship came to be used in worship.

[18]See especially Patrick D. Miller, *They Cried to the Lord: The Form and Theology of Biblical Prayer* (Fortress Press, 1994), who bases a lot of his discussion of prayer on the Psalms.

[19]Derek Kidner, *Psalms 73-150* (InterVarsity Press, 1975), 401 and Willem VanGemeren, 'Psalms,' *The Expositor's Bible Commentary* (12 vols.; Zondervan, 1991), 5:713. For a discussion of the Passover liturgy and the place of the Hallel psalms in that liturgy, see Joachim Jeremias, *The Eucharistic Words of Jesus* (Fortress Press, 1964), 84-88. Since much of the information that relates to Jewish practices in the first century comes from the Mishnah, which was compiled later than the New Testament period, caution is needed in using this material (see Jacob Neusner, *Rabbinic Literature and the New Testament* [Trinity Press International, 1994]).

[20]William Lane, *The Gospel According to Mark* (NICNT; Eerdmanns, 1974), 509.

[21]It is clear that the author of Hebrews considers God to be the ultimate author of the Old Testament. His favorite way of introducing an Old Testament passage is to use the verb 'to say' (*legō*). William Lane (*Hebrews 1-8* [WBC; Word, 1991], cxvii) notes that twenty times God is the grammatical subject of these quotations, four times it is the Son (2:12, 13a, 13b; 10:5-7), and five times it is the Holy Spirit (3:7b-11; 4:3, 5, 7; and 10:16-17). God continues to speak to God's people today through the Old Testament.

[22]F. F. Bruce (*The Epistle to the Hebrews* [NICNT; Eerdmans, 1964], 46) notes that the quotation of Isaiah 8:17b in Hebrews 2:13 supports

C. H. Dodd's contention that the principal Old Testament quotations in the New Testament are not isolated proof-texts but carry their Old Testament contexts by implication (see Dodd, *According to the Scriptures* [Scribner, 1953]).

[23]Simon J. Kistemaker, *Hebrews* (Baker Books, 1984), 73. Bruce (*Hebrews*, 46-48) connects the concept of the righteous remnant that emerges in Isaiah with the people whom Christ came to save.

[24]Bruce, *Hebrews*, 232-33. The key phrase is in 10:5, 'when he came into the world' (Kistemaker, *Hebrews*, 275). It is a bit unusual that Paul Ellingworth (*The Epistle to the Hebrews* [Eerdmans, 1993], 499-501) argues that this psalm was spoken by Christ before the incarnation.

[25]Hebrews 10:5-7 quotes from the Greek Old Testament (39:7-9 LXX), which may be different from the Hebrew text (MT), although this is debated (see Karen Jobes, 'Rhetorical Achievement in the Hebrews 10 "Misquote" of Psalm 40,' *Biblica* 72 (1991): 387-96). The MT states 'my ears you have pierced' while the LXX has 'a body you prepared for me'. The use of 'body' in the LXX fits the emphasis on the incarnation in Hebrews 10:8-10. Many commentators note that the differences between the two are not great and that in reality the MT and the LXX are both emphasizing submission (Bruce, *Hebrews*, 232; Phillip E. Hughes, *A Commentary on the Epistle to the Hebrews* [Eerdmans, 1977], 396-97; and Kistemaker, *Hebrews*, 274). See the discussion of Psalm 40 in Chapter 8.

[26]Hughes (*Hebrews*, 397-98) understands the phrase 'in the volume of the book it is written of me' in Psalm 40:7, quoted in Hebrews 10:7, to be a reference to the law and what it set forth about the king, as in Deuteronomy 17:14-20 (see also Peter C. Craigie, *Psalms 1–50* [WBC; Word, 1983], 315). Placing this phrase in the mouth of Jesus underscores the idea that the Old Testament speaks of him.

[27]Lane, *Hebrews 1-8*, 265.

[28]For further development of this idea, see E. P. Clowney, 'The Singing Savior,' *Moody Monthly* 79 (1978): 40-43 and James E. Adams, *War Psalms of the Prince of Peace* (Presbyterian and Reformed Publishing Co., 1991), 21-38. Adams contemplates the imprecatory psalms as the prayers of Jesus. It would also be an interesting study to look at the conversations that Jesus has with the Father in the Gospels in light of the major theological concepts in the Psalms.

[29]Hebrew should be consulted as much as possible as a foundation for understanding a psalm. Hebrew is also very beneficial when comparing how English translations differ from each other.

³⁰For understanding how Hebrew poetry operates, see James Kugel, *The Idea of Biblical Poetry* (Yale University Press, 1981) and Tremper Longman, III, *How To Read the Psalms* (InterVarsity Press, 1988), 89-122.

³¹For evaluation of commentaries, see Tremper Longman III, *Old Testament Commentary Survey* (3rd ed.; Baker, 2003), Derek Thomas, *The Essential Commentaries for a Preacher's Library* (Reformed Academic Press, 1996), and D. A. Carson, *New Testament Commentary Survey* (4th ed.; Baker, 1993).

³²The challenge for any teacher, and especially for a preacher, is to take the above information and put it into a format that will impact the hearers. In one sense the hard work now begins as one must refine what is the message of the psalm and how that message should be developed and presented, which is the area of homiletics (see especially Bryan Chapell, *Christ-Centered Preaching* [Baker, 1994]), as well as Sydney Greidanus, *Preaching Christ from the Old Testament* [Eerdmans, 1999]).

³³How a psalm that confesses sin can relate to Christ or be a prayer of Christ is taken up in Chapter 5 where Psalm 51 is discussed.

³⁴Reymond, *Divine Messiah*, 193-98.

³⁵Hughes, *A Commentary on the Epistle to the Hebrews*, 180.

³⁶A related issue is how the unity of God as one, as well as the complexity of God as triune, affects meaning. The meaning of any passage is one, but it is a complex unity that reflects the complexity of the triune God. Any passage of Scripture has a center, the main idea that the author is trying to get across, but there will also be minor themes in a passage. Although it is good to seek the center of a passage when preaching from a passage, there is nothing wrong with preaching a minor theme of a passage. For example, the main teaching of the Great Commission (Matt. 28:19-20) is that the church should be making disciples (the center of the passage), but it is also appropriate to teach on the triune nature of God from this text (a minor theme). If one believes that only the center of a passage can be taught, one is limiting the concept of meaning (meaning is a dot), but if one believes it is appropriate to teach a minor theme of a passage, then the full-orbed reality of meaning is taken into consideration (meaning is a circle). It follows that there is not just one way to preach Christ from the psalms. For an approach that develops the concept of meaning in light of the nature of the triune God, see Vern S. Poythress, *God-Centered Biblical Interpretation* (P & R Publishing, 1999).

[37]Longman, *How To Read the Psalms*, 67-68.

[38]Directly Messianic psalms do not have to be divorced from their Old Testament context.

Chapter 4. Indirect Messianic Psalms: Psalms of Orientation

[1]Herman Gunkel laid the foundation for modern genre analysis (*Introduction to the Psalms: The Genres of the Religious Lyric of Israel* [trans. James D. Nogalski; Mercer University Press, 1998], originally published in 1933). Although his work is foundational, he operated with faulty presuppositions concerning genre. For a summary review and critique of Gunkel's view of genre with the goal of a more positive use of genre analysis for interpreting Scripture, see Tremper Longman III, 'Form Criticism, Recent Developments in Genre Theory, and the Evangelical,' *WTJ* 47 (1985): 46-67.

[2]Thus to translate Genesis 11:1 as 'Once upon a time the whole world spoke a single language' (*New English Bible with the Apocrypha* [Cambridge University Press, 1971) gives the reader the wrong impression that Genesis 11 is a fairy tale.

[3]See Longman's discussion of how genre determines the reading strategy of a particular text and his excellent example of a paragraph from a novel that is understood differently if the reader assumes a murder mystery or an autobiography is being read (*How To Read the Psalms* [InterVarsity Press, 1988], 20-23).

[4]It is important, however, not to operate with a rigid or fixed view of genre that tries to force psalms into a particular mold. There may be significant differences between psalms in a particular genre and some psalms may seem to defy genre analysis (see the discussions in the commentaries on Psalm 73). Longman develops a fluid concept of genre that operates at several levels. All the psalms are poetry, a broad genre category, but some psalms are hymns, and some hymns can be further delineated based on specific content (see his discussion of Psalm 98 in 'Form Criticism,' 57-58 and *How To Read the Psalms*, 125-31, where he classifies Psalm 98 as a poem, a hymn, a hymn concerning God's kingship, or even a divine warrior victory psalm).

[5]Gunkel (*Psalms*, 19) operated with the following major genres: the hymn, the communal complaint song, the complaint of the individual, and the thanksgiving song of the individual. Claus Westermann (*The Psalms: Structure, Content, and Message* [Augsburg Publishing House, 1980], 24-25) divided the psalms into two major dominant poles, lament

and praise. He used the main genre categories of community psalm of lament (CL), individual psalm of lament (IL), community psalm of narrative praise (CP), individual psalm of narrative praise (IP), and psalm of descriptive praise (H). The community psalms of narrative praise are usually called songs of thanksgiving and the psalms of descriptive praise are usually called hymns. Artur Weiser (*The Psalms: A Commentary* [OTL; Westminster Press, 1962], 52) lays out the main types of psalms as hymns, laments, and thanksgivings, with the thanksgivings occurring in association with the lament. Hans-Joachim Kraus (*Psalms 1–150* [2 vols; Continental Commentary; Fortress Press, 1993], 1:41) develops genre categories that are derived from the terminology in the psalms themselves in order to avoid foreign categories and designations. He lays out six groups of psalms: songs of praise (*tehillah*, תהלה), songs of prayer (*tephillah*, תפלה), royal psalms (*verses for the king*, מעשי למלך, Ps. 45:1), songs of Zion (שיר ציון), didactic (wisdom) poems, and liturgies or festival psalms. For a criticism of his approach, see J. Day, *Psalms* (OT Guides; Sheffield Academic Press, 1999), 14, who notes that his category 'Songs of Prayer' covers too broad a range of psalms to be useful. Although there may be some benefit to genre designations that are intrinsic to the psalms, Longman ('Form Criticism,' 53-56) shows the benefit of using genre terms that are not native to the time of the literature. I basically follow Longman's genre terms (*How To Read the Psalms*, 23-35).

[6]Longman (*How To Read the Psalms*, 23-35) uses structure, mood, and content to identify the genres of the psalms.

[7]Walter Brueggemann (*The Message of the Psalms* [Augsburg Publishing House, 1984], 9-13) develops these categories in showing how the psalms are related to life. Brueggemann is dependent on the psychological insights of Paul Ricoeur but he also recognizes the pastoral value of these categories. They are a convenient way to characterize the psalms in terms of their general tone and outlook. The royal psalms, depending on their content, could fit any of the broad categories (for example, Psalm 89 laments the seeming failure of the Davidic covenant). We will take up the royal psalms in a later chapter.

[8]Although Brueggemann (*The Message of the Psalms*, 158) deals with hymns of praise under the category of New Orientation, he acknowledges that they could be discussed under Psalms of Orientation. He places them under New Orientation because their extravagant form of celebration does not seem fatigued with old orientation. However, it seems that the phrase 'old orientation' is rather slanted against the order, stability, and blessings that are expressed in the hymns.

[9]Bernhard W. Anderson, *Out of the Depths: The Psalms Speak For Us Today* (rev.; Westminster Press, 1983), 135. This book has a useful appendix where all the psalms are listed according to their genre.

[10]Longman, *How To Read the Psalms*, 24.

[11]Anderson (*Out of the Depths*, 138-39) groups hymns around the categories God's creation (redemption) of Israel (66:1-12, 100, 111, 114, 149), God's creation of the world (8, 19:1-6, 95:1-7a, 104, and 148), and God's sovereignty over history (33, 103, 113, 117, 145, 146, and 147). Kraus (*Psalms*, 45-46) uses the following thematic groupings: the praise of the Creator (8:19A, 33, 104), the hymns of Yahweh as king (47, 93, 96, 97, 98, 99), hymns of praise to the Lord of the harvest (65 and maybe 145), praise to the great acts of Yahweh in history, also called historical hymns (105, 114, 135), and entrance hymns (24, 95, 100) that are used in connection with festival processions. Mays (*The Lord Reigns: A Theological Handbook to the Psalms* [Westminster John Knox Press, 1994], 27) mentions special topics like Zion and kingship.

[12]Kraus, *Psalms 1–150*, 2:290. For a review of the discussion of whether Psalm 103 is a song of thanksgiving or a hymn, see Leslie C. Allen, *Psalms 101–150* (WBC; Word, 1983), 19-22.

[13]Anderson, *Out of the Depths*, 128.

[14]John Calvin, *Psalms 93-150* (Calvin's Commentaries; trans. Henry Beveridge; 22 vols; Baker, 1996 reprint), 6:125.

[15]Allen (*Psalms 101–150*, 22) notes that the psalm opens out to ever widening circles, which is an attempt at total praise.

[16]The Hebrew word *bārak* (ברך), which the NIV translates as 'praise' is a word that means 'bless' (NKJV, ESV, NASB). This word is used in other places of the Old Testament to refer to God blessing people and people blessing God (Ps. 134:2-3; 2 Chron. 31:8). But how do we as humans bless God? As Michael Brown ('ברך,' in *NIDOTTE* [ed. VanGemeren; 5 vols.; Zondervan, 1997], 1:764) notes, 'God blesses human beings by speaking well of them, thereby imparting "blessing" (good things) to them, and so they are blessed; human beings bless God by speaking well of him, attributing "blessing" (good qualities) to him, and so he is blessed, ie, praised and praiseworthy.' God blesses people by conferring good on them; we bless God by praising the good in him.

[17]There are a series of participles in verses 3-6 describing the covenant blessings given by God. Brueggemann (*The Message of the Psalms*, 160) notes that these participles describe the way God characteristically acts toward his people.

[18]The meaning of the word *'edyēk* is disputed. It is translated a variety of ways: 'desires' (NIV and the LXX), 'mouth' (NKJV), 'years' (NASB), and 'you' (ESV). The Hebrew word *'ªdî* means 'ornament,' which is not followed by any of the major translations. Allen (*Psalms 101–150*, 18) follows the 'standard emendation' (*'ōdēkî*) and translates it 'your existence.' The ultimate meaning is not affected, although 'mouth' brings out a little stronger the connections to covenant blessings.

[19]Although Sigmund Mowinckel (*The Psalms in Israel's Worship* [Abingdon, 1962], 107-09) argues that the phrase *yhwh mālāk* should be translated 'Yahweh has become king,' which refers to a particular act in a yearly enthronement festival, the phrase is better translated 'Yahweh reigns' or 'Yahweh is king,' which emphasizes the eternal nature of Yahweh's reign (Kraus, *Psalms 60-150*, 2:233-34). The translation 'x has become king' would be expressed by the phrase *mālāk yhwh*, which occurs in 2 Samuel 15:10 and 2 Kings 9:13 (Marvin E. Tate, *Psalms 51–100* [WBC; Word, 1990], 472).

[20]Tate (*Psalms 51–100*, 474) states that hymns that declare the kingship of Yahweh display five characteristics: concern with all the earth and all the nations, references to other gods, signs of exaltation and kingship, characteristic acts of Yahweh (making, establishing, sitting, judging), and expressions of the attitude of praise before the heavenly king. These characteristics, however, are not found in every Yahweh kingship psalm.

[21]David M. Howard, Jr. (*The Structure of Psalms 93-100* [Eisenbrauns, 1997]) takes an in-depth look at Psalms 93–100 not only by analyzing each psalm but also by showing the relationship between each of these psalms by looking at their internal connections. For the significance of the placement of Psalms 93–99 in Book IV of the Psalter, see Chapter 1.

[22]Willem VanGemeren, 'Psalms,' in *The Expositor's Bible Commentary* (12 vols.; Zondervan, 1991), 5:608.

[23]Konrad Schaefer, *Psalms* (Berit Olam; Collegeville, MN: The Liturgical Press, 2001), 233.

[24]It is also interesting that the term for 'flood' (*nāhār*) is a title of Yam. For some of the ancient Baal myths, see Michael David Coogan, *Stories from Ancient Canaan* (Westminster Press, 1978). Some think it is possible that this as an historical reference to the roaring of hostile nations against Yahweh (Tate, *Psalms 51–100*, 480; A. A. Anderson, *The Book of Psalms* [NCB; 2 vols.; Eerdmans, 1972], 2:668).

[25]Franz Delitzsch, 'Psalms,' in *Commentary on the Old Testament* (10 vols.; Eerdmans, 1978), 5:72-73.

[26]Although James L. Crenshaw (*The Psalms: An Introduction* [Eerdmans, 2001], 87-95) denies that there are wisdom psalms, most acknowledge a wisdom category. C. Hassell Bullock (*Encountering the Book of Psalms* [Baker, 2001], 203) notes the following commentators and how they differ in their list of wisdom psalms: Sabourin (1, 37, 49, 112, 119, 127), Murphy (1, 32, 34, 37, 49, 112), Kuntz (1, 32, 34, 37, 49, 112, 127), and Scott (1, 19B, 32, 34, 37, 49, 78, 112, 119, 127). Bullock himself identifies 32, 34, 37, 49, 73, 112, 127, 128, and 133 as wisdom psalms. He deals with the Torah psalms (1, 19, 119) in a separate chapter, even though they exhibit wisdom characteristics. For an emphasis on the Torah psalms as providing the central clue to the way the Psalms, individually and as a book, should be understood and read, see Mays, *The Lord Reigns*, 128-35.

[27]Roland Murphy, 'A Consideration of the Classification "Wisdom Psalms,"' in *Congress Volume: Bonn, 1962* (Supplements to *VT* 9; Brill, 1963), 159-60. This article by Murphy is also found in *Studies in Ancient Israelite Literature* (ed. James Crenshaw; KTAV Publishing House, 1976). 456-567. Kraus (*Psalms 1–150*, 1:60) adds autobiographical stylization, which he sees in Psalm 73.

[28]Murphy, 'Wisdom Psalms,' 159-60. Others who stress a thematic approach to the wisdom psalms are Longman (*How To Read the Psalms* 33); Bullock (*Encountering the Psalms*, 203); Brueggemann (*The Message of the Psalms*, 42); and Kraus (*Psalms 1–150*, 1:60), among others.

[29]H. J. Hermission, 'Observations on Creation Theology in Wisdom,' *Creation in the Old Testament* (ed. B. W. Anderson; Fortress Press, 1984), 118-34; H. H. Schmid, 'Creation, Righteousness, and Salvation: 'Creation Theology' as the Broad Horizon of Biblical Theology,' in *Creation in the Old Testament*, 102-07; Roland E. Murphy, 'Wisdom-Theses and Hypotheses,' in *Israelite Wisdom: Theological and Literary Essays in Honor of Samuel Terrien* (ed. J. G. Gammie; Scholars Press, 1978), 35-42; Leo G. Perdue, *Wisdom and Creation: The Theology of Wisdom Literature* (Abingdon Press, 1994); and John B. White, 'The Sages' Strategy to Preserve Salôm,' *The Listening Heart: Essays in Wisdom and the Psalms in Honour of Roland E. Murphy* (ed. K. Hoglund; JSOT, 1987), 299-311.

[30]Anderson, *Out of the Depths*, 219 and Bullock, *Encountering the Psalms*, 207. It is significant that Psalm 1 and Psalm 19 bring together

the law with wisdom themes (the contrast between the righteous and the wicked in Psalm 1 and creation in Psalm 19). For a positive analysis of the relationship between wisdom and the covenant, see David A. Hubbard, 'The Wisdom Movement and Israel's Covenant Faith,' *TynBul* 17 (1966): 3-33.

[31]The wisdom psalms that struggle with the prosperity of the wicked will be examined in the section concerning Psalms of Disorientation (37 and 73).

[32]Craigie (*Psalms 1–50*, 180) discusses the differences between the two parts of the psalm and mentions the attempt to fix the background of 19:2-7 in Ugaritic poetry, which he does not believe is convincing. He traces the literary background to Genesis 1–3 (see D. A. Clines, 'The Tree of Knowledge and the Law of Yahweh [Psalm XIX],' *VT* 24 [1974], 8-14). Even in the context of the ANE the sun and justice are closely related concepts (Anderson, *Psalms*, 1:167).

[33]The characterization of Psalm 19:1-6 as a hymn is not conclusive because it does not address God directly and is more objective and meditative (Erhard S. Gerstenberger, *Psalms Part 1* [FOTL; Eerdmans, 1988], 101). However, Craigie (*Psalms 1–50*, 180) and VanGemeren ('Psalms,' 5:178) classify it as a wisdom hymn.

[34]Gerald H. Wilson, *Psalms Volume 1* (Zondervan, 2002), 360.

[35]This is evident in the participles in verse 1 and the alternation of day and night in verse 2: day after day and night after night (VanGemeren, 'Psalms,' 5:180).

[36]It is possible to understand verse 3 to be stating that the voice of creation is not audible: 'there is no speech, there are no words; their voice is not heard' (Wilson, *Psalms Volume 1*, 363 calls this the usual tack; see also Craigie, *Psalms 1–50*, 181; VanGemeren, 'Psalms,' 180; and Kraus, *Psalms 1–150*, 1:271).

[37]There is debate concerning the meaning of the Hebrew word translated 'line' (*kāv*) in verse 4. VanGemeren ('Psalms,' 5:181) wants to emend it to the Hebrew word for 'voice' used in verse 3 (*qōl*). Others try to make sense of the word 'line'. John Calvin (*Psalms 1-35* [Calvin's Commentaries; trans. Henry Beveridge; 22 vols; Baker, 1996 reprint], 4:313) connects *kāv* to Isa. 28:10 and understands it to signify a line in writing with the idea that a loud and distinct voice reaches the ears of all. Delitzsch ('Psalms,' 5:283) takes a little bit different angle in connecting *kāv* with the verb 'to go out' (as in Jer. 31:39), with the meaning that the measuring line of the heavens has gone out into all the earth – it

has taken entire possession of the earth. Either way the meaning is the universal nature of this revelation.

[38]VanGemeren, 'Psalms,' 5:180.

[39]Ibid.; Wilson, *Psalms Volume 1*, 364.

[40]God's wrath and glory should not be separated from each other, for God's glory is demonstrated through his wrath (Romans 9:22-23).

[41]Craigie, *Psalms 1–50*, 184.

[42]This pattern is adapted from Wilson (*Psalms Volume 1*, 368) who comments on the Hebrew of the text.

[43]Wilson (*Psalms Volume 1*, 370) notes that this last phrase breaks the pattern of participles with a Qal pft, which suggests that the righteous standard of Yahweh's judgment is an established certainty upon which one can rely.

[44]VanGemeren, 'Psalms,' 5:185.

[45]Wilson, *Psalms Volume 1*, 367.

[46]VanGemeren, 'Psalms,' 5:185.

[47]Wilson, *Psalms Volume 1*, 369.

[48]Delitzsch, 'Psalms,' 5:287. Wilson (*Psalms Volume 1*, 369) argues that the change in pattern in relationship to the participles (from piel or hiphil participles to a qal participle) in connection with the term 'Fear' suggests that 'Fear' is not a synonym for the law but is a characteristic of the believer. However, the parallel pattern, the adjective 'clean,' and the phrase 'enduring forever' supports the view that 'Fear' is a synonym of the law.

[49]Wilson, *Psalms Volume 1*, 366.

[50]Kraus, *Psalms 1–150*, 1:274.

[51]VanGemeren, 'Psalms,' 5:182 and Wilson, *Psalms Volume 1*, 367.

[52]VanGemeren, 'Psalms,' 5:182.

[53]Wilson, *Psalms Volume 1*, 367-68.

[54]For a discussion of the concept 'clean' in its figurative meaning of 'purity', see Richard E. Averbeck, 'rḥḥ ṭhr' *NIDOTTE*, 2:345-46.

[55]VanGemeren ('Psalms,' 5:182) takes honey here in the sense of 'fine food.'

[56]For an analysis of the law in light of Christ, see Vern Poythress, *The Shadow of Christ in the Law of Moses* (P & R, 1991).

[57]The Hebrew is a participle of the verb 'āman which is translated in the LXX with the noun *pistos*.

[58]The Hebrew yāšār means 'straight' and is translated in the LXX with *eutheia*, which can be used in the idea of a straight way (LXX Pss. 26:11; 142:10) or in the sense of what is right (LXX Pss. 57:2; 77:37).

[59]Calvin (*Acts 14-28, Romans 1-16*, 19:403) argues that Paul has not mishandled Psalm 19:4 by transferring what is said of creation to the apostles, but that the meaning is that God has already from the beginning manifested his glory to the Gentiles, though not by the preaching of men. Thus God did not withdraw from the Gentiles in the Old Testament the knowledge of himself; he spoke to the Gentiles at a distance by the voice of the heavens. See also Charles Hodge, *The Epistle to the Romans* (The Banner of Truth Trust, 1972).

[60]William Hendriksen, *Exposition of Paul's Epistle to the Romans* (NTC; Baker, 1981), 349.

[61]Many see Paul's use of Psalm 19:4 as referring to the preaching of the gospel through the apostles (Hendriksen, *Romans*, 352; Douglas Moo, *The Epistle to the Romans* [NICNT; Eerdmans, 1996], 667).

[62]A similar approach has been taken here in terms of the relationship of Psalm 19 and Christ. The way Paul handles Deuteronomy 30:11-15 in Romans 10 supports the statement in Romans 10:4 that Christ is the *telos* of the law. Although the meaning of *telos* is debated (end, termination, goal), the idea of goal cannot be completely ruled out, even if other meanings are present (see the discussion in Moo, *Romans*, 638-42). Thus Christ is what the law anticipated and pointed toward, he is the goal of the law. Calvin (*Romans*, 19:384) aptly comments: '... whatever the law teaches, whatever it commands, whatever it promises, has always a reference to Christ as its main object; and hence all of its parts should be applied to him.'

[63]Many commentators recognize the wisdom elements of Psalm 49 (for example, Craigie, Kraus, VanGemeren). Brueggemann (*The Message of the Psalms*, 106-107) places it in the category of disorientation because it is reflective, which shows distance from the first shock of disorientation. The problem has been worked through to a solution. Brueggemann, however, recognizes that these categories should not be pressed too tightly and that usage determines function (see his comment on p 201, n 57).

[64]Wilson, *Psalms Volume 1*, 664-65. J. Clinton McCann ('Books I-III and the Editorial Purpose of the Hebrew Psalter,' in *The Shape and Shaping of the Psalter* [ed. J. Clinton McCann; JSOT Press, 1993], 102) argues that the Korah psalms should be read as a group.

[65]Verse 12 uses the Hebrew *yālîn* (to remain) and verse 20 uses *yābîn* (to understand); otherwise the two verses are identical.

[66]The riddle in this psalm is not like one of the riddles of Samson (Judges 14:14), but is larger in scope than that, and may have the

connotation of a difficult or enigmatic question (VanGemeren, 'Psalms,' 5:368).

[67]The problem does not lie in the proverbs themselves but in the misuse of proverbs where there develops a rigid connection between the deed-consequence relationship, as expressed by Job's friends. The book of Proverbs is very nuanced in its teaching (see Raymond Van Leeuwen, 'Wealth and Poverty: System and Contradiction in Proverbs,' *Hebrew Studies* 33 [1992]: 29-31), and affirms the teaching of Psalm 49: 'Riches do not profit in the day of wrath' (Prov. 11:4).

[68]James L. Mays, *Psalms* (John Knox Press, 1994), 192.

[69]Wilson (*Psalms Volume 1*, 750) comments that the practice of naming lands after oneself was normally the perogative of kings, but here the rich do it to try to ensure immortality for themselves.

[70]Craigie (*Psalms 1–50*, 360) explains that humans are like beasts in that death ends the continuity of life and Brueggemann (*The Message of the Psalter*, 109) understands the comparison to be that both die helpless and abandoned, not worthy of respect.

[71]Schaefer, *Psalms*, 126. The rest of verse 14 is difficult. Some accept the text as it stands with the translation 'the upright will rule over them in the morning' (VanGemeren, 'Psalms, 5:371; Delitzsch, 'Psalms,' 5:118), while others emend the text to read that the wicked go down to Sheol (a change of the verb *rādad* to *yārad*; Wilson, *Psalms Volume 1*, 750-51).

[72]Brueggemann, *The Message of the Psalter*, 109. The psalmist puts this in very personal terms: 'God will ransom my soul from the power of Sheol.' Although Craigie (*Psalms 1–50*, 360) argues that verse 15 expresses the false confidence of the wicked, there is no indication that this is a false statement. Such a view would take away the distinction between the fate of the good and the wicked (T. D. Alexander, 'The Psalms and the Afterlife,' *IBS* 9 [1987]: 9).

[73]The allusion is found in the verb *lāqaḥ* ('to take') used in Psalm 49 and in reference to Enoch and Elijah.

[74]Schaefer, *Psalms*, 124.

[75]Alexander ('Psalms and the Afterlife,' 6-11) argues that Psalm 49 clearly has in view the afterlife.

[76]Robert L. Hubbard, Jr., 'פדה (*pdh*),' *NIDOTTE*, 3:578-79.

[77]These psalms are also called Songs of Trust. Gunkel (*Psalms*, 152), followed by Westermann (*Psalms*, 69), derives these psalms from the lament psalms. The movement in the lament psalms toward confidence in God dominates the whole psalm and pushes back the other motifs of the

lament genre. Brueggemann (*The Message of the Psalter*, 152) and Bullock (*Encountering the Psalms*, 166) relate the psalms of confidence to the Songs of Thanksgiving. Bullock notes that the specific crisis that the song of thanksgiving mentions has receded so that there are only hints of the occasion of trouble. Brueggemann comments that the psalms of confidence are not as immediate as the songs of thanksgiving, are more distant from the crisis, and are thus more reflective. He places these psalms under the category of New Orientation. Although such a development is possible, the psalms of confidence seem to look ahead and express trust in whatever situation the psalmist may face in the future, instead of looking back to the past. Thus we have covered them under Psalms of Orientation.

[78]Bullock (*Encountering the Psalms*, 166) lists six elements that he thinks are essential to the psalms of confidence (declaration of trust, invitation to trust, the basis for trust, petition, an interior lament, and the vow to praise the Lord), but he recognizes that there is no fixed order to the elements. Although looking for these elements can be helpful, they do not occur frequently enough in every psalm to make them essential elements. Thus tone and content, not structure, characterizes these psalms (Longman, *How To Read the Psalms*, 31).

[79]Longman (*How To Read the Psalms*, 31) and Bullock (*Encountering the Psalms*, 170). Longman lists the metaphors of refuge, shepherd, light, rock, and help.

[80]Longman, *How To Read the Psalms*, 31. The lists of the psalms of confidence vary greatly from one person to the next depending on how one develops this genre. Anderson (*Out of the Depths*, 205) includes 11, 16, 23, 27:1-6, 62, 63, 91, 121, 125, 131. Brueggemann (*The Message of the Psalms*, 200, n. 50) includes 11, 62, 63, 115, 121, 125, 129, and he discusses 23, 27, and 91. Bullock (*Encountering the Psalms*, 170) includes 4, 16, 23, 27, 62, 73, 90, 115, 123, 124, 125, 126. Gunkel (*Psalms*, 121) includes 4, 11, 16, 23, 27:1-6, 62, 131 and Westermann (*Psalms*, 69) includes 23, 27:1-6, 62, 63, 71, and 131.

[81]Although some classify Psalm 91 as a wisdom psalm (Gunkel, *Psalms*, 296 and VanGemeren, 'Psalms,' 5:598), the strong tone of confidence and trust is reason to see it as a song of confidence (Anderson, *Psalms*, 2:212; Mays, Psalms, 296-97; and J. Clinton McCann, Jr., 'Psalms,' in *New Interpreter's Bible* [Abingdon Press, 1996], 4:1047).

[82]Tate (*Psalms 51–100*, 458) points out the comprehensive nature of the promises in the alternating periods of light and darkness in vv. 5-6. There is a tendency to qualify the promises in this psalm. For example,

VanGemeren ('Psalms,' 5:601) comments concerning verse 10 that God does not guarantee that no evil will befall those who trust in him, but a person of trust will rest with the confidence that whatever happens on earth is with his knowledge. Anderson (*Out of the Depths*, 215) wonders whether the psalmist puts forth an elementary view of God's protection, not qualified by exceptions, possibly leading to an immature view of divine protection or a view of prayer as magic. Understanding the promises of Psalm 91 in context of the Mosaic covenant (see below) will give greater clarity to the promises.

[83]Experience can affect a person's perception of God and life. The experience of losing a son to leukemia led Rabbi Harold Kushner to argue that God cannot be both good and all-powerful at the same time or else these tragedies would not happen. He opted for a God who is good, but not all-powerful (see *When Good Things Happen to Bad People* [Avon Books, 1981]).

[84]McCann, 'Psalms,' 4:1047.

[85]Allan Harman, *Psalms* (Christian Focus, 1998), 311. Harman also points out that the mention of angels in 91:11 may be a reference to Exodus 23:20 (p. 312).

[86]McCann, 'Psalms,' 4:1047, and VanGemeren, 'Psalms,' 5:598.

[87]It is disappointing that few commentators recognize the relationship between Psalm 91 and the blessings and curses of the Mosaic covenant, which include both physical and spiritual promises. Apart from the covenant connection other explanations are given for these promises, such as 'idiomatic hyperbole' (Mays, *Psalms*, 297), the security of a safe place and safe travel (Brueggemann, *The Message of the Psalter*, 156-57), or metaphorical language for all kinds of threats and dangers (Tate, *Psalms 51–100*, 454). Although these explanations are not totally misplaced, recognizing the connection with the covenant blessings and curses gives another dimension to the promises in 91:3-13.

[88]The change of person in verses 1-13 has produced discussion concerning the origin of the psalm. McCann ('Psalms,' 4:1046) lists the following possibilities: testimony from a person who sought refuge in the temple or from someone who has recovered from illness, a liturgy for entrance into the temple, or of a king before battle. The reason for the change of person is also debated. Are different people speaking (Delitzsch, 'Psalms,' 60-62) or is the psalmist addressing himself (Calvin, 'Psalms,' 5:479)? It is impossible to be sure of the setting of Psalm 91.

[89]For discussions of the kingdom, see George Ladd, *The Gospel of the Kingdom* (Eerdmans, 1959), Ridderbos, *The Coming of the Kingdom* (The Presbyterian and Reformed Publishing Co., 1975), and Gerhardus Vos, *The Teaching of Jesus concerning the Kingdom of God and the Church* (Presbyterian and Reformed Publishing Co., 1972).

[90]Brueggemann (*The Message of the Psalms*, 201) quotes Fretheim that Psalm 91 is a statement of a theology of glory.

[91]Delitzsch ('Psalms,' 5:65) comments that the animals mentioned in 91:13 refer to all kinds of destructive powers, including spiritual powers. Although 'treading on' and 'trampling underfoot' does not fit the lion as well as the serpent, Tate (*Psalms 51–100*, 457) argues for the legitimacy of this concept.

[92]Although Psalm 46 does praise God it is not a hymn in the formal sense because it lacks an introductory call to praise (Craigie, *Psalms 1–50*, 342). The emphasis on the city of God has led some to classify it as a Song of Zion (see Kraus, *Psalms 1–150*, 1:459-63 who lists extensive evidence that Psalm 46 is a Song of Zion), but not all are convinced of this classification (see Craigie, *Psalms 1–50*, 342 for problems with this view). The strong theme of trust helps identify it as a psalm of confidence (Craigie, 342; Kraus, 1:459; Wilson, *Psalms Volume 1*, 714).

[93]Psalm 46 has several metaphors to describe the protection God offers his people, particularly refuge, strength, and fortress, which describe places of isolation or elevation that give protection (VanGemeren, 'Psalms,' 5:351). Such use of metaphors is a mark of a psalm of confidence. McCann ('Psalms,' 4:864) also points out how 'refuge' is a major theme of Books I–II of the Psalter.

[94]Mays, *Psalms*, 183.

[95]McCann, 'Psalms,' 4:865.

[96]John Calvin, *Psalms 36-92* (Calvin's Commentaries; trans. Henry Beveridge; 22 vols; Baker, 1996 reprint), 5:196.

[97]Schaefer, *Psalms*, 117.

[98]Wilson, *Psalms Volume 1*, 716. He also notes that in the Mesopotamian flood story the gods cower in fear behind the walls of their heavenly abode as the chaotic waters threaten to destroy the gods as well. Of course Yahweh is always in complete control.

[99]Anderson, *Psalms*, 1:356.

[100]The same verb *mwṭ* (מוט) is used of the mountains (v. 2), the kingdoms (v. 6), and the city (v. 5) to show the contrast between the instability of the world and the stability of the city.

[101]Although older commentators (Calvin, *Psalms 36–92*, 5:194-95 and Delitzsch, 'Psalms,' 5:91-92) tend to look for some historical setting as the background to Psalm 46, such as 2 Chronicles 20 or the Sennacherib invasion, the psalm transcends any known historical situation (Anderson, 'Psalms,' 1:355; VanGemeren, 'Psalms,' 5:350). It is also not necessary to find the setting for the psalm in a specific festival of Israel, whether a Great Autumn Festival (Anderson, 'Psalms,' 1:355), an annual Zion festival (Kraus, *Psalms 1–150*, 1:461), or the event of the establishment of David's royal cult in Jerusalem (Craigie, *Psalms 1–50*, 344).

[102]Although it is possible that the psalm has in view the tunnel of Hezekiah or the spring of Gihon, it is not necessary that the reference to a river is literal. The river may be symbolical of God's presence referring back to the presence of God in the Garden of Eden, representing the restoration of the blessings of paradise in the city of God (Anderson, Psalms,' 1:357; VanGemeren, 'Psalms,' 5:352). It is also interesting that a stream flowed from the cosmic mountain where the gods dwelt (Mays, *Psalms*, 185), a false picture of blessing and a false identification of the true center of the universe, which remains with Yahweh and his presence. For a discussion of the correspondences between Eden, Zion, and the Temple, see Warren Austin Gage, *The Gospel of Genesis* (Eisenbrauns, 1984), 49-58.

[103]Craigie, *Psalms 1–50*, 345.

[104]Yahweh as a divine warrior who delivers and fights for his people becomes prominent in the Exodus from Egypt (Exod. 15:1-3), and is a theme that is significant throughout Scripture. For a development of this theme, see Tremper Longman III and Daniel G. Reid, *God Is a Warrior* (Zondervan, 1995).

[105]Wilson (*Psalms Volume 1*,718) comments that the noun 'hosts' (ṣābāh; the plural form is Sabaoth, which is used in some hymns) comes from the verb that means 'to go to war' or 'serve as a soldier.' The noun refers to soldiers who serve in the army, and in relationship to Yahweh, probably refers to the heavenly armies.

[106]McCann, 'Psalms,' 4:865.

[107]The Hebrew reads 'God is for us a refuge and strength' which is translated 'God is our refuge and strength.'

[108]Mays, *Psalms*, 185.

[109]See Edmund P. Clowney, 'The Final Temple,' *WTJ* 35 (1973): 156-89.

[110]There is debate whether in John 7 the phrase 'out of his heart shall flow rivers of living water' refers to Jesus or the individual believer. D. A. Carson (*The Gospel According to John* [PNTC; Eerdmans, 1991], 321-28) reviews the evidence for both views and acknowledges how much both views have in common, especially if the individual believer is not seen as the source of the living water. He, along with Herman Ridderbos (*The Gospel of John: A Theological Commentary* [Eerdmans, 1997], 272-75), opts for the individual believer, partly on the basis of grammar and partly on the basis of John 4:13-14. There is also debate as to which Scripture is being cited in 7:38. Carson thinks Jesus draws from Nehemiah 9 and the reference there to the provision of water from the rock, with the connection Nehemiah draws between the water/manna and the law/Spirit. These connections have merit, as well as the picture of water that flows from the place of God's presence (Gen. 2:10; Ezek 47:1-12). If Jesus is the locus of God's presence, then the blessings of living water flow from him, but they can also flow from the believer, because the one who believes is also the locus of God's presence, with Jesus being the source of the living water.

[111]One of the results of God's coming (theophany) is the upheaval of creation, seen in Exodus 19:16-21 on Mt. Sinai and throughout the Old Testament whenever God comes in judgment (Hab. 3:8-13; Nahum 1). The upheavals in Psalm 46 could be connected with God's coming. It is interesting that Haggai 2 states twice that the nations will be shaken, once in reference to the temple (2:6-9) and once in reference to the Davidic line (2:20-23). Hebrews 12:27-29 picks up on this shaking 'of things that have been made' leaving the one thing that cannot be shaken – the kingdom of God. When God comes in judgment those who are a part of his kingdom will have nothing to fear.

Chapter 5: Indirect Messianic Psalms: Psalms of Disorientation

[1]Claus Westermann (*Praise and Lament in the Psalms* [John Knox Press, 1981], 31) demonstrates that praise and lament are not just two literary categories among others, rather they encompass the whole reality of human existence. They represent the two poles of human life.

[2]For discussions on the importance of lament for the Christian life and the problems that arise when lament is lost, see Walter Brueggemann, 'The Costly Loss of Lament,' *JSOT* 36 (1986): 57-71 and Claus Westermann, 'The Role of the Lament in the Theology of the Old Testament,' *Int* 28 (1974): 20-38, which is also found as the last chapter in the book *Praise and Lament in the Psalms*.

[3]Tremper Longman, III, *How To Read the Psalms* (InterVarsity Press, 1988), 45. C. Hassell Bullock (*Encountering the Book of Psalms* [Baker, 2001], 139) points out that the individual psalms of lament mostly occur in Book I, with community psalms of lament being scattered throughout Books II–V. However, there does seem to be a movement in the Psalter toward praise (Westermann, *Praise and Lament*, 257), a movement which is also seen in the lament psalms themselves (see below).

[4]James Mays, *The Lord Reigns: A Theological Handbook to the Psalms* (Westminster John Knox Press, 1994), 26 and Patrick D. Miller, *Interpreting the Psalms* (Fortress Press, 1986), 4.

[5]Noted in both Herman Gunkel (*Introduction to the Psalms: The Genres of the Religious Lyric of Israel* [trans. James D. Nogalski; Mercer University Press, 1998], 122-23) and J. Day, *Psalms* (OT Guides; Sheffield Academic Press, 1999), 21. Although the 'I' in some situations could be a personification of the nation, as in Psalm 129:1, it is better to take the 'I' as an individual unless there are clear indicators to the contrary, partly because the statements are so personal (Gunkel lists other reasons why the 'I' cannot be the nation in most psalms).

[6]Sigmund Mowinckel, *The Psalms in Israel's Worship* (Abingdon, 1962), 225. Hans-Joachim Kraus (*A Theology of the Psalms* [trans. Keith Crim; Fortress Press, 1992], 107) argues against this view partly because it expands the definition of the royal psalms to psalms that contain no royal motifs. The question of the identification of the enemies also has implications for the view of the king as representative of the people (see below).

[7]Mowinckel (*The Psalms in Israel's Worship*, 194-95) understands these psalms in the context of an annual New Year Festival, and Artur Weiser (*The Psalms: A Commentary* [OTL; Westminster Press, 1962], 52) in the context of an annual Covenant Renewal Festival.

[8]See the summary of K. Seybold's criteria for distinguishing psalms that arise out of illness in Day, *Psalms*, 26-27. Others who accept a category of psalms of sickness are Bullock (*Encountering the Psalms*, 139), Gunkel (*Psalms*, 135), and Hans-Joachim Kraus (*Psalms 1–150* [2 vols; Continental Commentary; Fortress Press, 1993], 1:53). Kraus places Psalms 6, 13, 22, (31), 38, 41, 69, 71, 88, 102, and 103 in this category. Bullock places Psalms 38, 41, and 88 in the category of psalms of illness, but he has another category, psalms of illness and anguish, where the distinction between illness and spiritual anguish disappears.

Psalms in this latter category include 6, 13, 22, 30, 31, 32, 35, 39, 51, 69, 71, 91, 102, 103, and 130.

[9]See Miller (*Interpreting the Psalms*, 5) and Day (*Psalms*, 27-29) for a discussion and critique of these views.

[10]H. Birkeland, *The Evildoers in the Book of Psalms* (Dybwad, 1955). See Day (*Psalms*, 23-25) for a critique of this view.

[11]Miller (*Interpreting the Psalms*, 8) comments that the search for a readily identifiable situation may be illusory or unnecessary because the stereotypical and generalized style of the psalms is open-ended; thus, they can be adapted to a variety of circumstances. Mays (*The Lord Reigns*, 36-37) notes that the prayers in the Psalter have been dissociated from their actual circumstances for which they were originally written. Three traditional sets of metaphors for the enemies are used: warfare (the enemies are at war with the psalmist), hunting and fishing (they pursue the psalmist), and beasts. The purpose of the descriptions is to transcend the personal and evoke its existential and religious dimensions.

[12]The plea for help, also called the petition, can occur in a number of places in a psalm of lament. Some discuss it under the complaint section of the psalm (Gunkel, *Psalms*, 160-63, and James L. Mays, *Psalms* [Interpretation; John Knox Press, 1994], 21), while others place it after the confidence of being heard (B. W. Anderson, *Out of the Depths: The Psalms Speak For Us Today* [rev.; Westminster Press, 1983], 77 and Westermann, *Praise and Lament*, 64). This demonstrates the fluid nature of the psalms of lament.

[13]Longman, *How To Read the Psalms*, 27. Psalm 13:1-2 has all three elements.

[14]Anderson (*Out of the Depths*, 77) notes that many times this move toward confidence is introduced by the word 'but.' There is some discussion concerning what has caused this movement in the psalm from complaint to trust. Some advocate an 'oracle of salvation' pronounced by a member of the community, perhaps a priest at the temple, as the basis for moving toward confidence that God has heard (Walter Brueggemann, *The Message of the Psalms* [Augsburg Publishing House, 1984], 57 and Gunkel, *Psalms*, 182). However, the fact that there is no example in the Psalter of such an oracle at the appropriate place in a lament psalm argues against this view, and leads Day (*Psalms*, 32) to attribute this move to confidence to an inner change that takes place in the person who is praying.

[15]A vow of praise, a vow to testify before the community what God has done, is included by many as part of the structure of a lament psalm (Anderson, *Out of the Depths*, 77; Bullock, *Encountering the Psalms*, 143; and Westermann, *Praise and Lament*, 64).

[16]Kraus, *Psalms 1–150*, 1:48.

[17]Ibid, 1:47.

[18]Brueggemann, *The Message of the Psalms*, 67 and Gunkel, *Psalms*, 82.

[19]Claus Westermann, *The Psalms: Structure, Content, and Message* (Augsburg Publishing House, 1980), 39.

[20]Kraus, *Psalms 1–150*, 1:50.

[21]Gunkel, *Psalms*, 82.

[22]J. Clinton McCann, Jr., 'Psalms,' in *New Interpreter's Bible* (Abingdon Press, 1996), 4:995.

[23]Mays, *Psalms*, 261.

[24]Not being buried was considered a horrible fate in the ANE (Willem VanGemeren, 'Psalms,' in *The Expositor's Bible Commentary* [12 vols.; Zondervan, 1991], 5:520) and it also contributed to the defilement of the city of Jerusalem and temple (Marvin E. Tate, *Psalms 51–100* [WBC; Word Books, 1990], 300).

[25]McCann, 'Psalms,' 4:995.

[26]Kraus, *Psalms*, 2:136.

[27]Franz Delitzsch ('Psalms,' in *Commentary on the Old Testament* [10 vols.; Eerdmans, 1978], 5:23) believes leprosy is in view, but Kraus (*Psalms 1–150*, 2:192) understands the psalm to be talking about a very sick person near death.

[28]McCann, 'Psalms,' 4:1027 and Tate, *Psalms 51–100*, 400-01.

[29]McCann, 'Psalms,' 4:1027.

[30]Ibid., 4:1028.

[31]VanGemeren, 'Psalms,' 5:608 and McCann, 'Psalms,' 4:1028.

[32]Erhard S. Gerstenberger, *Psalms, Part 2, and Lamentations* (FOTL; Eerdmans, 2001), 145.

[33]For a discussion of the meaning of 'Sheol', see Desmond Alexander, 'The Old Testament View of Life after Death,' *Themelios* 11 (1986): 41-46.

[34]VanGemeren, 'Psalms,' 5:570 and Kraus, *Psalms 1–150*, 2:194.

[35]Obviously there is more to the Mosaic covenant than material blessings, but God does promise that if Israel would be obedient to the covenant, they would experience these blessings in the land that he was giving them. Israel's failure does not negate the promise of material

blessings, for they will be fulfilled in the new heavens and new earth for God's people.

[36]This is stated in the author's preface to the psalms (Calvin, *Psalms 1-35*, 5:xxxvi). He goes on to say 'there is not an emotion of which any one can be conscious that is not here represented as in a mirror,' and then also, 'the Holy Spirit has here drawn to the life all the griefs, sorrows, fears, doubts, hopes, cares, perplexities, in short, all the distracting emotions with which the minds of men are wont to be agitated.'

[37]It is not necessary to argue that the sentiments expressed in this psalm are 'confused conceptions' or 'unadvised words' in the midst of affliction (surprisingly, argued by Calvin, *Psalms 36-92*, 5:410). They are appropriate prayer in a difficult, unresolved situation. It is interesting that Calvin also notes that the lamentations in verse 14 are tacit prayers and can be seen as a part of the unutterable groanings of the Holy Spirit mentioned in Romans 8:26 (pp. 415-16).

[38]Longman, *How to Read the Psalms*, 45.

[39]Not every expression in every psalm has to apply to what we are experiencing for us to use the psalm with benefit. The same would be true in Jesus' use of the psalms. But even the expression in Psalm 88:15, 'close to death from my youth up,' could refer to Jesus as he would have had a sense early on that his life was going to end prematurely in death on a cross (see Jesus' comment in Luke 12:50).

[40]Both VanGemeren ('Psalms,' 5:564) and A. A. Anderson (*The Book of Psalms* [NCB; 2 vols.; Eerdmans, 1972], 2:622) mention the connection of Psalm 88 with the events of Good Friday.

[41]The word for 'terrors' in Psalm 88:15 is used in other places of the Old Testament to refer to the dread which God sends upon his enemies (Exod. 15:16; 23:27). Jesus experiences that terror in the prospect of bearing the judgment of God for our sin.

[42]Jesus' death on the cross, followed by the resurrection and ascension, gives new meaning to suffering. As we take up the cross and follow Jesus we are promised that we will be persecuted and suffer for his name's sake.

[43]The traditional term for these psalms is imprecatory psalms, but Bullock (*Encountering the Psalms*, 228) prefers the terminology psalms of anger or wrath.

[44]Anderson (*Out of the Depths*, 77) lists 35, 59, 69, 70, 109, 137, and 140 as imprecatory psalms, while Bullock (*Encountering the Psalms*, 228) lists 35, 55, 59, 69, 79, 109, and 137. Sometimes it is a judgment call as to how much the curse dominates the psalm.

[45]See footnote 55 for articles dealing with the imprecatory psalms. See also James E. Adams, *War Psalms of the Prince of Peace* (Phillipsburg: Presbyterian and Reformed Publishing, 1991) and John N. Day, *Crying for Justice* (Grand Rapids: Kregel, 2005).

[46]The use of perfect verbs (completed action) along with the adverb 'there' (v. 3) gives the sense of looking back on the situation from a distance (Leslie Allen, *Psalms 101–150* [WBC; Word Books, 1983], 239). Some place the psalm during the early years of the return from exile between 537 and 515 (Anderson, *Psalms*, 2:897 and VanGemeren, 'Psalms,' 5:826), perhaps used in a service of lamentation for the destruction of Jerusalem and the temple (Gerstenberger, *Psalms, Part 2*, 395 and Kraus, *Psalms 1–150*, 2:502). Mays (*Psalms*, 421) argues that the memories of humiliation are fresh and the account with Edom is unsettled.

[47]McCann, 'Psalms,' 4:1227 and VanGemeren, 'Psalms,' 5:826.

[48]Although some argue that the setting for Psalm 109 is a courtroom where false accusations are being brought against the psalmist (Allen, *Psalms*, 101-150, 76; Anderson, *Psalms*, 2:759; and Mays, *Psalms*, 349), it is possible to take the statements in this psalm as metaphorical (mentioned by McCann ['Psalms,' 4:1125]) for a situation of betrayal.

[49]One of the major problems of Psalm 109 is whether or not the curses of verses 6-20 are quotations of curses spoken against the psalmist, or whether the psalmist is himself cursing an enemy. Kraus (*Psalms 1–150*, 2:338) presents an extensive argument that the curses are quotations of an enemy based partly on the switch from the plural to the singular in verse 6 and the fact that the psalm specifically mentions that the enemy curses. Against this view is the fact that there is nothing in the text to designate that there is a different speaker in verse 6 (McCann, 'Psalms,' 4:1125). Gerstenberger (*Psalms, Part 2*, 259) shows that enemy quotations in the psalms are carefully identified (Psalms 2:1-3; 10:6, 11; 22:7-8) and that it would be a liturgical disaster to quote extensively the words of a hateful opponent. If one is concerned about the problem of cursing in the psalms, making verses 6-20 as the words of an enemy of the psalmist does not remove the problem, for the psalmist in verse 20 prays that the curses would fall on the accuser (Mays, *Psalms*, 349).

[50]Weiser (*Psalms*, 432) sees these psalms as inferior to the Christian ethic when he comments that they are 'dangerous poisonous blossoms... that show the limits set to the OT religion.' Brueggemann (*The Message of the Psalms*, 81) calls the curses undisciplined, unrestrained, hateful speech that is not shaped by the covenant or focused on Yahweh, which

he contrasts with the other parts of Psalm 109 that he sees as faithful, disciplined covenant speech. These dichotomies are not necessary, but are even found among those who are evangelical. Delitzsch ('Psalms,' 5:177) contrasts the wrathful spirit of Sinai with the spirit of Zion and the New Testament, which is the spirit of love. Peter C. Craigie (*Psalms 1–50* [WBC; Waco: Word Books, 1983], 41) states that these psalms are not the oracles of God and the sentiments are in themselves evil, and C.S. Lewis (*Reflections on the Psalms* [Harcourt Brace Jovanovich, 1958], 25) calls them 'devilish'. Even though many Bible-believing people would not be comfortable with such negative characterizations of these psalms, in practice the imprecatory psalms have been excised from our public use because most hymnals containing responsive readings omit the difficult sections of imprecation.

[51]D. Martyn Lloyd-Jones, *Studies in the Sermon on the Mount* (2 vols.; Eerdmans, 1971), 1:301-02 and D. A. Carson, *The Sermon on the Mount* (Baker, 1978), 50-51.

[52]Paul argues against personal revenge in Romans 12:14-21 and exhorts the people to leave vengeance in the hands of God (v. 19). He goes on in Romans 13 to show that government is one way that God establishes justice and avenges wrongs. But not all governmental expressions of power are just. Revelation 13 shows the other side of government when it is used for evil purposes to persecute God's people.

[53]The Hebrew has the personal pronoun 'I' followed by the noun prayer, which can be translated 'I am prayer.' In context it makes better sense to see the psalmist breaking off his thought and turning to God in prayer, 'but I – prayer.'

[54]Many who do not want to reject the imprecatory psalms try to find some benefit in them as a human response that defuses anger (see Eric Zenger, *A God of Vengeance?* [trans. Linda M. Maloney; Westminster John Knox Press, 1996], 87-88). Certainly there is truth in recognizing that taking our anger to God in prayer does benefit us, but to limit the scope of the imprecatory psalms to what they teach us about ourselves, or to view them as just a way to vent anger is to seriously underestimate what we can learn from them.

[55]Approaches that emphasize the relationship of the imprecatory psalms to covenant curse include E. Calvin Beisner, *Psalms of Promise* (2nd ed.; P & R Publishing, 1994), 171; John Day, 'The Imprecatory Psalms and Christian Ethics,' *BibSac* 159 (2002), 166-86; Allan

Harman, 'The Continuity of the Covenant Curses in the Imprecations of the Psalms,' *RTR* 54.2 (1995), 65-72; and Alex Luc, 'Interpreting the Curses in the Psalms, *JETS* 42.3 (1999), 395-410.

[56]The phrase 'in return for my love they accuse me' (v. 4) might refer to a situation of friendship (VanGemeren, 'Psalms,' 5:690) or a betrayal of a close associate (Beisner, *Psalms of Promise*, 167).

[57]Beisner (*Psalms of Promise*, 184) notes that leaders of the church who confront unrepentant heresy or apostasy, or unrepentant sin among church members, can pray the imprecatory psalms.

[58]Beisner (*Psalms of Promise*, 179, 181, 184) notes that those who are suffering persecution for the sake of the gospel might use imprecatory psalms but only after long struggles in prayer and when the enemy seems hardened beyond repentance. Such prayers should not be for personal revenge but for the sake of the cause of Christ. Although Beisner recognizes that believers can pray such prayers, he also sets limits to their use (they must be rooted in God's righteousness, they must be for God's glory, and they must be offered in utter humility). We should always pray for the conversion of our enemies.

[59]Mays, *Psalms*, 197-98.

[60]Psalm 32 has historically been listed with the penitential psalms, but it is really a psalm of thanksgiving.

[61]Tate, *Psalms 51–100*, 8.

[62]Ibid., 12. Konrad Schaefer (*Psalms* [Berit Olam; The Liturgical Press, 2001], 129) has the simplest structure based on a literary analysis and the occurrence of key words that frame the individual units. He divides the psalm into three movements: request for personal cleansing (vv. 1-9), request for personal renewal and right sacrifice (vv. 10-17), and restoring the city and the liturgy (vv. 18-19). Others, like Gerald H. Wilson (*Psalms Volume 1* [NIVAC; Zondervan, 2002], 773), have a more detailed outline of Psalm 51. He divides the psalm into six parts: an opening plea for forgiveness (1-2), a confession of sin (3-6), a plea for cleansing from sin (7-9), a plea for spiritual restoration (10-12), a vow of praise and public contrition (13-17), and a concluding plea for the restoration of Jerusalem and righteous sacrifice (18-19).

[63]Many who do not accept the Davidic authorship of Psalm 51 are willing to recognize that the historical situation of David and Bathsheba is an appropriate setting for this psalm (Tate, *Psalms 51–100*, 8–9). Kraus (*Psalms 1–150*, 1:501) does not believe the title corresponds to historical fact, but he also does not think it should be ignored because it

is living proof of how the community heard and understood the psalm. Mays (*Psalms*, 198-99) sees a verbal connection between Psalm 51:4 and the historical narrative in 2 Samuel 11:27 and 12:13, but thinks the historical setting is in tension with the liturgical use of the psalm. However, such a dichotomy is unwarranted if many of the psalms arose in a variety of life experiences. Although the last two verses of Psalm 51 may have been an addition by a scribe during the exile (yet see Delitzsch, 'Psalms,' 5:142-43, who argues that 51:18-19 [20-21] could come from David), the rest of the psalm comes from David.

[64]Alex Luc, 'חטא (*ḥṭ'*),' *NIDOTTE* (ed. Willem VanGemeren; 5 vols.; Zondervan, 1997), 2:87-88.

[65]Tate, *Psalms 51–100*, 15, quotes E. R. Dalglish, *Psalm 51 in the Light of Ancient Near Eastern Patternism* (Leiden: Brill, 1962), 88.

[66]This is Tate's translation (*Psalms 51–100*, 3).

[67]Luc, 'עוֹן (*'āwon*)' *NIDOTTE*, 3:351.

[68]VanGemeren, 'Psalms,' 5:380 and Wilson, *Psalms Volume 1*, 774.

[69]Psalm 51:5 is not just a statement of 'liturgical hyperbole' (Brueggemann, *The Message of the Psalms*, 99), nor is it a statement of exaggeration with little dogmatic implications (Erhard S. Gerstenberger, *Psalms Part 1* [FOTL; Eerdmans, 1988], 214), but is relevant to the doctrine of original sin, which emphasizes that sin is hereditary (Delitzsch, 'Psalms,' 5:136) and that guilt is the determining force under which life began (Kraus, *Psalms 1–150*, 1:503). For a discussion of original sin, see L. Berkhof, *Systematic Theology* (Eerdmans, 1941), 244-49 and Francis Turretin, *Institutes of Elenctic Theology* (3 vols.; P & R Publishing, 1992), 1:629-43.

[70]When David was confronted with his sin by Nathan he declared, 'I have sinned against Yahweh' (2 Sam. 12:13).

[71]Mays, *Psalms*, 200. See Beisner (*Psalms of Promise*, 103) for a thorough explanation of the statement in verse 4, 'Against you, you only, have I sinned.'

[72]Tate, *Psalms 51–100*, 14 and Wilson, *Psalms Volume 1*, 773.

[73]Tate, *Psalms 51–100*, 14-15.

[74]Ibid., 22-23.

[75]Ibid., 22.

[76]There is debate about the role of the Holy Spirit in the Old Testament (for a discussion of the various views, see James M. Hamilton, 'Old Covenant Believers and the Indwelling Spirit: A Survey of the Spectrum of Opinion,' *TrinJ* 24ns [2003]: 37-54). It is imperative to affirm that

the basis of salvation in the Old Testament is by grace through faith (Gen. 15:6) and that the Old Testament saints were regenerated by the Holy Spirit and gave evidence of a changed life (Gen. 26:5). The sticking point is whether the believers in the Old Testament were indwelt by the Spirit, or whether that comes at Pentecost. For the argument that believers were not indwelt by the Spirit but that God did operate on them inwardly, see James M. Hamilton, 'God With Men in the Torah,' *WTJ* 65 (2003), 113-33. Hamilton argues that in the Old Testament God's presence was manifested in the temple and that believers were not indwelt by the Spirit. For the view that believers in the Old Testament were indwelt by the Spirit, but not at the same level as the New Testament, see B. B. Warfield, 'The Spirit of God in the Old Testament,' *Biblical and Theological Studies* (The Presbyterian and Reformed Publishing Co., 1968), 137-56 (also reprinted in *The Person and Work of the Holy Spirit* [Calvary Press, 1997], 119-42) and Leon J. Wood, *The Holy Spirit in the Old Testament* (Zondervan, 1976). Although it is possible to argue that David's prayer that God would not take the Holy Spirit from him refers to the Spirit that comes on the anointed king to help him fulfill his duties, the fact that this psalm would have been sung and prayed by God's people is significant. Not only is it a prayer of the king, but it is the prayer of a believer that God not remove the Holy Spirit from him. The issues in Psalm 51 focus on the psalmist's relationship to God in terms of sanctification and restoration, which are relevant to all believers, even in the Old Testament. Sin disrupts our relationship with God so that we need to confess our sin regularly and seek forgiveness and renewal. Although Pentecost brings significant changes in terms of the role of the Spirit (an inclusiveness in relationship to the nations, a fuller manifestation of power in the believer's life, and kingdom gifts are given to all, not just leaders), one must recognize that the Holy Spirit in the Old Testament is involved in the individual life of believers, not just on the level of justification, but on the level of sanctification.

[77]Mays, *Psalms*, 201 and McCann, 'Psalms,' 4:887.

[78]VanGemeren, 'Psalms,' 5:383.

[79]Schaefer, *Psalms*, 129.

[80]Mays, *Psalms*, 204.

[81]For example, see Charles Hodge, *Systematic Theology* (3 vols.; Eerdmans, 1952), 2:496.

[82]Although the prayer of Jesus in Luke 23:34, 'Father, forgive them, for they know not what they do,' is definitely related to Isaiah 53:12 (see

A. W. Pink, *The Seven Sayings of the Saviour on the Cross* [Baker, 1958], 11-12), it is Jesus' prayer for his enemies in the specific act of crucifixion and demonstrates his faithfulness to his own teaching (Matt. 5:43-45).

[83]The phrase 'answerable for our guilt' comes from Calvin, *Isaiah 33–66* (Calvin's Commentaries; 22 vols.; Baker Books, 1996), 8:119.

[84]Thornwell, 'The Priesthood of Christ,' *Collected Writings* (3 vols.; The Banner of Truth Trust, 1974), 2:279, 284.

[85]The most difficult part of Psalm 51 to relate to Christ is verse 5, 'in sin did my mother conceive me.' Even though Christ is sinless, he is our covenant representative and takes upon himself our problem of original sin. He identifies with all aspects of our sin and bears its curse that we might one day even be free from the taint of original sin.

[86]Gunkel categorizes Psalm 26 as a lament psalm under the subcategory psalm of innocence. He sees it as the prayer of a sick man; however, there is no clear reference to sickness in the psalm (Craigie, *Psalms 1–50*, 224). Some have questioned whether the term 'lament' is appropriate for this psalm because the description of distress is missing from the psalm (noted by Anderson, *Psalms*, 1:213). Kraus (*Psalms 1–150*, 1:325) abandons the category of lament for the broad title song of prayer. Yet, Gerstenberger (*Psalms Part 1*, 123-124) shows how the category 'complaint' (lament) does fit this psalm because its urgent petitions, its fervent confessions of trust, and its insistence on justice presuppose imminent disaster. Bullock (*Encountering the Psalms*, 144-45) calls this category 'psalms of the persecuted and accused' and he includes Psalms 3, 4, 5, 7, 11, 17, 23, 27, 57, and 63 in this category.

[87]Delitzsch ('Psalms,' 5:349) thinks the psalm fits the historical situation of Absalom, who had stolen the hearts of the men of Israel and forced David to flee Jerusalem.

[88]Kraus (*Psalms 1–150*, 1:325-26) lays out the whole procedure that one must go through for such a trial at the temple; however there is no evidence of an institution of divine jurisdiction in the temple (Day, *Psalms*, 29).

[89]Craigie, *Psalms 1–50*, 224.

[90]Mays (*Psalms*, 127-28) argues that the language is formulaic and traditional, which means it is open to a variety of situations.

[91]Calvin, *Psalms 1–35*, 4:437.

[92]For different ways to state the chiastic structure of the psalm, see McCann, 'Psalms,' 4:782; Schaefer, *Psalms*, 64, and VanGemeren, 'Psalms,' 5:238.

[93]Craigie, *Psalms 1–50*, 225; Mays, *Psalms*, 129; and Wilson, *Psalms Volume 1*, 472.

[94]McCann, 'Psalms,' 4:783.

[95]Ibid., 4:782.

[96]Wilson, *Psalms Volume 1*, 473.

[97]Ibid., 477-78.

[98]Allan Harman, *A Commentary on the Psalms* (Christian Focus, 1988), 131.

[99]Psalm 26:2 mentions both heart and kidney. Wilson (*Psalms Volume 1*, 471, n 10) notes that because of their inaccessibility deep in the inner recesses of the abdominal cavity, they provided an apt metaphor for the deep inward recesses where humans sought to hide their sin.

[100]Anderson (*Psalms*, 1:215) sees in verses 4-5 a connection to the false charges that were being brought against the psalmist.

[101]VanGemeren, 'Psalms,' 5:239.

[102]McCann, 'Psalms,' 4:783.

[103]The translation 'I will not slip' (NKJV) is a literal translation of the Hebrew. The ESV has 'without wavering,' which VanGemeren ('Psalms,' 5:239) explains as a circumstantial clause that describes the kind of trust the psalmist has in God. The translation 'I will not slip' provides a better parallel with verse 12: 'my foot stands on level ground.'

[104]Craigie, *Psalms 1–50*, 227; Harman, *Psalms*, 132; and Anderson, *Psalms*, 1:218, see both meanings in view.

[105]See the discussion of wisdom psalms in Chapter 4. Mays (*Psalms*, 28-29) notes that the contrast between the righteous and the wicked is fairly pervasive in the psalms, even if the contrast does not dominate a particular psalm. He lists the following psalms that mention this contrast: 1, 9-10, 11, 12, 14, 32, 34, 37, 49, 52, 58, 73, 75, 91, 92, 94, 111-112, and 119.

[106]Brueggemann (*Message of the Psalms*, 106) comments that these psalms are more reflective statements removed from the intensity of the first shock of disorientation. They have come to terms with the reality of the situation, but there is a confident restlessness that affirms that God will triumph.

[107]For a discussion of the various possibilities of the genre of Psalm 73 and the difficulties involved, see Tate (*Psalms 51–100*, 231-232), who mentions wisdom psalm, individual psalm of lament, an individual song of thanksgiving, and a psalm of confidence as various possibilities. He finally calls it a reflective testimony.

[108]Mays, *Psalms*, 240. VanGemeren ('Psalms,' 5:475) calls it an autobiographical reflection.

[109]These parallels include not only subject matter and first person reflection, but also an intense struggle based on what is observed, the inability to understand rationally how everything fits together, the infrequent use of the name Yahweh, the comparison of humans to beasts, and finally some breakthrough to a resolution (see Richard P. Belcher, Jr., *Divine Retribution in Ecclesiastes* [PhD diss,, Westminster Theological Seminary, 2000], 256-57).

[110]McCann ('Psalms,' 4:968) lays out this basic structure.

[111]Tate, *Psalms 51–100*, 227, 235.

[112]Not only is this movement seen within Psalm 73, but many believe that Psalm 73 is pivotal in the structure of the book of Psalms. McCann ('Psalms,' 4:968) makes connections between Psalms 1–2 and Psalm 73 and sees Psalm 73 as a summary of what the reader would have learned after reading Psalms 1-72.

[113]Kraus, *Psalms 1–150*, 2:87.

[114]McCann ('Psalms,' 4:969) sees verse 15 as just as much a turning point as verse 17 because for the first time the psalmist addresses God and understands clearly his relationship to the community. What brings the psalmist through the crisis is his identity as a member of God's people, which comes before the visit to the temple.

[115]The Hebrew word for temple is plural. A variety of explanations have been given for the plural, such as it refers to the heavenly temple (Dahood cited by VanGemeren, 'Psalms,' 5:480), or the celestial doctrine learned from God's word (Calvin, *Psalms 36-92*, 5:142), or even that it refers to pagan shrines (Schaefer, *Psalms*, 179). However, it is better to see the word as referring to the temple, and to understand the plural as an intensive plural referring to the temple as great (VanGemeren, 'Psalms,' 5:480) or as referring to the sanctuary with its various buildings (Kraus, *Psalms 1–150*, 2:84).

[116]Kraus (*Psalms 1–150*, 2:89) comments that 'the end' refers to the final outcome, the final event that explains everything, and Calvin (*Psalms 36–92*, 5:143) sees this as a reference to the final judgment of God.

[117]Brueggemann, *Message of the Psalms*, 118-19.

[118]McCann, 'Psalms,' 4:969.

[119]Ibid., 4:970.

[120]Commentators are divided over whether this phrase refers to this life or life after death. Many argue that a developed view of the afterlife

did not fully arrive until later in the Old Testament (see the discussion in Anderson, *Psalms*, 2:535). Tate (*Psalms 51–100*, 236) comments that the glory refers to a life guided by God and ends with a glory that testifies to its worth and fulfillment. However, it is hard to limit the ideas expressed in verse 24 to this life, so some are willing to recognize that this psalm pushes the boundaries of Israel's usual conception of life and death (Anderson, *Psalms*, 2:535 and McCann, 'Psalms,' 4:970). Although the New Testament is much clearer in its views on life after death, the reality of life with God after death is taught in the Old Testament (Harman, *Psalms*, 258).

[121]VanGemeren, 'Psalms,' 5:483.

Chapter 6. Indirect Messianic Psalms: Psalms of New Orientation

[1]Walter Brueggemann (*The Message of the Psalms* [Augsburg Publishing House, 1984], 124) notes that new orientation is not just a return to the earlier situation of orientation. A person who goes through a period of difficulty usually experiences growth in his relationship with God so that he is not exactly the same person after the trial.

[2]Brueggemann (*Message of the Psalms*, 124-26) acknowledges that it is not always clear whether a psalm speaks of old or new orientation, whether a psalm articulates the surprise of new grace or whether it speaks of the enduring graciousness of God. In his discussion of psalms under New Orientation he discusses thanksgiving songs, but he also includes enthronement psalms, which speak of the new kingship of Yahweh based on his victory over Israel's enemies (29, 93, 96, 97, 97, 99, 114), psalms of confidence (23, 27, 91), and hymns of praise that are exuberant in their praise (100, 103, 113, 117, 135, 146–150).

[3]Claus Westermann (*Praise and Lament in the Psalms* [John Knox Press, 1981], 17-26) considers the songs of thanksgiving as psalms of praise. He calls the psalms of thanksgiving declarative songs of praise and the hymns he designates as descriptive psalms of praise. He argues that there is no word in Hebrew for 'thanks' so that in the Old Testament to give thanks is a way to give praise. However, most scholars prefer to use the old terminology, with many arguing for a separate genre category for the psalms of thanksgiving (see the discussion in J. Day, *Psalms* [OT Guides; Sheffield Academic Press, 1999], 44-46).

[4]Tremper Longman (*How To Read the Psalms* [InterVarsity Press, 1988], 30) calls them a response to an answered lament.

[5]B. W. Anderson, *Out of the Depths: The Psalms Speak For Us Today* (rev.; Westminster Press, 1983), 114-15 and C. Hassell Bullock, *Encountering the Book of Psalms* (Baker, 2001), 152-53.

[6]The psalms included in a list of individual psalms of thanksgiving vary greatly from one person to the next. Bullock (*Encountering the Psalms*, 154) notes that the lists of Gunkel, Mowinckel, Westermann, and Kraus have only three psalms in common (30, 40:2-12, and 116). If one leaves out Mowinckel, then there are six psalms in common (18, 30, 40:2-12, 66, 116, and 118). Bullock's own list includes 18, 30, 31, 32, 40, 66, 92, 116, 118, and 120.

[7]The community psalms of thanksgiving seem to be very nebulous, as can be seen by the few psalms in this category: Gunkel lists 66:8-12; 67, 124, and 129; Westermann lists 124 and 129; and Weiser has only 124 in this category. Crüsemann denies the existence of the category altogether (see the discussion in Day, *Psalms*, 48-49). Part of the problem is that the communal nature of these psalms make them close to hymns (Anderson, *Out of the Depths*, 111). However, if one keeps in mind that the thanksgiving song is a thanksgiving for a specific act of God in response to a particular situation, then there is a distinction between the community psalm of thanksgiving and the hymn (Brueggemann, *Message of the Psalms*, 134; Day, *Psalms*, 49; and Erhard S. Gerstenberger, *Psalms Part 1* [FOTL; Eerdmans, 1988], 16).

[8]Bullock, *Encountering the Psalms*, 159

[9]Those who classify Psalm 32 as an individual psalm of thanksgiving are Gerstenberger (*Psalms Part 1*, 143) and Gerald H. Wilson (*Psalms Volume 1* [NIVAC; Zondervan, 2002], 544). Peter C. Craigie (*Psalms 1–50* [WBC; Word Books, 1983], 265) and Willem VanGemeren ('Psalms,' in *The Expositor's Bible Commentary* [12 vols.; Zondervan, 1991], 5:270) call it a thanksgiving psalm that has been adapted to the wisdom tradition because of the strong instructional component in the psalm.

[10]Brueggemann, *Message of the Psalms*, 96.

[11]The structure used here adapts the structure in Wilson, *Psalms Volume 1*, 544.

[12]Konrad Schaefer, *Psalms* (Berit Olam; The Liturgical Press, 2001), 81.

[13]See J. Clinton McCann, Jr. ('Psalms,' in *New Interpreter's Bible* [Abingdon Press, 1996], 4:805) for other connections between Psalm 1 and 32.

[14]Craigie, *Psalms 1–50*, 266.

[15]This sentence tries to bring out the different words for sin and the different actions of God against sin as represented in Psalm 32.

[16]Craigie, *Psalms 1–50*, 267.

[17]Brueggemann (*Message of the Psalms*, 158) notes that the body sometimes pays for covenantal disturbances.

[18]The 'rush of great waters' in verse 6 probably refers to dry wadis that can become full of raging torrents in a few moments in a downpour of rain (Anderson, *Psalms*, 1:258). The 'trouble' mentioned in verse 7 refers to any kind of distress.

[19]This traditionally has been called the passive obedience of Christ. Although there is debate about the usefulness of the term 'passive' to refer to this aspect of Christ's work because all that Christ did he did with full willingness on his part (Robert Reymond, *A New Systematic Theology of the Christian Faith* [Thomas Nelson, 1998], 631), this aspect of Christ's work is his willing obedience to bear all the sanctions imposed by the law against his people because of their transgressions (see Reymond, *Systematic Theology*, 631 and L. Berkhof, *Systematic Theology* (Eerdmans, 1941), 379-81.

[20]Some think that a priest or temple servant is speaking in verses 8-10 (Craigie 267, Wilson 548), while others argue that the speaker is Yahweh (Hans-Joachim Kraus (*Psalms 1–150* [2 vols; Continental Commentary; Fortress Press, 1993], 1:371). Some believe the speaker is the psalmist (Franz Delitzsch, 'Psalms,' in *Commentary on the Old Testament* [10 vols.; Eerdmans, 1978], 5:398; McCann, 'Psalms,' 4:806), with Allan Harman specifying David as the psalmist (*A Commentary on the Psalms* [Christian Focus, 1988], 147). VanGemeren ('Psalms,' 5:274) argues it is the psalmist quoting Yahweh! Whoever the speaker is in Psalm 32, there is no problem as seeing these words as the words of Christ.

[21]Leslie Allen, *Psalms 101–150* (WBC; Waco: Word Books, 1983), 63; Anderson, *Psalms*, 2:749; Kraus, *Psalms 1–150*, 2:325; and McCann, 'Psalms,' 4:1117.

[22]Anderson, *Psalms*, 2:749.

[23]VanGemeren, 'Psalms,' 5:681.

[24]McCann, 'Psalms,' 4:1116-17. Both McCann and Delitzsch show the numerous connections between Psalm 106 and 107.

[25]Allen, *Psalms 101–150*, 63.

[26]James L. Mays, *Psalms* (Interpretation; John Knox Press, 1994), 344.

[27]Allen, *Psalms 101–150*, 58. The redeemed are identified as the returned exiles in Isaiah 62:12.

[28]McCann, 'Psalms,' 4:1119.

[29]Allen (*Psalms 101–150*, 63) calls verses 33-43 a didactic meditation and Schaefer (*Psalms*, 267) terms it a meditation with wisdom motifs. Anderson (*Psalms*, 2:749) stresses the theme of the providence of God.

[30]John Calvin, *Psalms 93-150* (Calvin's Commentaries; 22 vols.; Baker Books, 1996), 6:265.

[31]McCann, 'Psalms,' 4:1119.

[32]Longman (*How To Read the Psalms*, 32) terms these psalms as psalms of remembrance. They are also called story-telling psalms (Anderson, *Out of the Depths*, 53) and historical psalms (Day, *Psalms*, 58).

[33]Many deal with the psalms of remembrance under the genre of hymn, because part of the purpose of these psalms is to praise God (Gerstenberger, *Psalms Part 1*, 18; Herman Gunkel, *Introduction to the Psalms: The Genres of the Religious Lyric of Israel* [trans. James D. Nogalski; Macon: Mercer University Press, 1998], 22; and Westermann, *Praise and Lament*, 116). Kraus (*Psalms 1–150*, 1:59) calls them historical hymns and James Mays (*The Lord Reigns: A Theological Handbook to the Psalms* [Westminster John Knox Press, 1994], 133) calls them narrative hymns. However, Longman (*How To Read the Psalms*, 32), Anderson (*Out of the Depths*, 53), and Day (*Psalms*, 58) place these psalms in their own genre category. Brueggemann (*Message of the Psalms*, 158) discusses whether the hymns of praise should be placed in Orientation or New Orientation, and concludes that the more a hymn is decisively declarative and the more a hymn focuses on historical liberation the more it is about new orientation. He notes that we are closing the circle, for the new, new song is becoming the old, old story. These psalms also seem to have some relationship to the declarative praise in the individual songs of thanksgiving (Gunkel, *Psalms*, 246 and Westermann, *Praise and Lament*, 141-42), which would support a new orientation outlook.

[34]Longman, *How To Read the Psalms*, 32, and Day, *Psalms*, 58.

[35]The dominant praise element at the beginning of Psalm 105 has led many to call this psalm a hymn (Mays, *Psalms*, 338). Allen (*Psalms 101–150*, 40) calls it an expanded hymn of the imperative type. Yet the psalm does not have further exhortations to praise near the end but stresses the purpose for God's actions. The historical element dominates. Kraus (*Psalms 1–150*, 2:308-09) sees an interlocking of hymn and historical summary and calls it a historical psalm in hymnic style.

[36]The structure of this psalm is adapted from Allen (*Psalms 101–150*, 40, 42).

[37]E. Calvin Beisner, *Psalms of Promise* (2nd ed.; P & R, 1994), 218.

[38]Harman, *Psalms*, 345.

[39]Anderson, *Psalms*, 2:729.

[40]The order of the plagues in Psalm 105 does not follow the order of the narrative of Exodus. The fifth and sixth plagues are omitted, and the first plague recounted is the plague of darkness. The poet starts with the plague of darkness because this plague demonstrates the power and sovereignty of God (see VanGemeren, 'Psalms,' 5:670 for a comparison of the order of the plagues).

[41]McCann, 'Psalms,' 4:1104.

[42]Beisner (*Psalms of Promise*, 224, 226) specifically reflects on the meaning of Psalm 105 to the exilic community.

[43]VanGemeren, 'Psalms,' 5:673.

[44]Allen, *Psalms 101–150*, 47.

[45]Anderson, *Psalms*, 2:737-38.

[46]Mays, *Psalms*, 341.

[47]The emphasis on confession has led Allen (*Psalms 101–150*, 49-50) to identify Psalm 106 as a communal complaint strongly marked by hymnic features. He discusses the relationship between the elements of complaint and praise. VanGemeren ('Psalms,' 5:672) and Kraus (*Psalms 1–150*, 2:317) emphasize more the hymnic elements of the psalm. Historical review, however, dominates the psalm.

[48]McCann ('Psalms,' 4:1110) notes that the psalm seeks to actualize the experience of God's people in history for the exilic community.

[49]The verb translated 'consider' (*śkl*) in verse 7 can mean 'wisdom' (McCann, 'Psalms,' 4:1111). It may relate to their inability to evaluate the difficulties of life on the basis of the character and the wondrous works of God.

[50]Anderson (*Psalms*, 2:740) notes Spurgeon's comment that between Israel's singing and Israel's sinning there is scarce a step.

[51]In theological terms this is called the second use of the law. When we realize that we are not able to keep the law and stand under the judgment of God, we see more clearly our need of Christ who did keep the law and bore the judgment of God on our behalf on the cross. We are justified through faith in what Christ has accomplished for us.

[52]In this way Phinehas may be seen as a type of Christ, whose whole life, not just one act, was lived in obedience to the law.

[53]Mays (*Psalms*, 342) also notes that Paul draws broadly on the language of Psalm 106 in his depiction of universal human sin in Romans 1:18-32.

[54]The apostle Paul (1 Cor. 10:1-6) and the author of Hebrews (Heb. 3:7–4:11) use the example of Israel as a warning for God's people not to be disobedient to God.

[55]The use of the law as a guide for how the believer should live his life is called the third use of the law, which deals more with sanctification.

Chapter 7. The Royal Psalms

[1]C. Hassell Bullock, *Encountering the Book of Psalms* (Baker, 2001), 178.

[2]*Ibid.*

[3]James Mays, *The Lord Reigns: A Theological Handbook to the Psalms* (Westminster John Knox Press, 1994), 7-20.

[4]Bullock, *Encountering the Psalms*, 178.

[5]*Ibid.*, 182; see also Bernhard W. Anderson, *Out of the Depths: The Psalms Speak For Us Today* (rev.; Westminster Press, 1983), 192; J. Day, *Psalms* (OT Guides; Sheffield Academic Press, 1999), 97; Hans-Joachim Krauss, *A Theology of the Psalms* (trans. Keith Crim; Fortress Press, 1992), 123; and Claus Westermann (*The Psalms: Structure, Content, and Message* [Augsburg Publishing House, 1980], 106. The place of the royal psalms in the editorial shaping of the book of Psalms also demonstrates the continuing hope related to kingship (see Chapter 1).

[6]The problem of identifying the royal psalms as a separate genre is that they at times fit the other genre categories of complaint, thanksgiving, and hymn (Herman Gunkel, *Introduction to the Psalms: The Genres of the Religious Lyric of Israel* [trans. James D. Nogalski; Mercer University Press, 1998 and Erhard S. Gerstenberger, *Psalms Part 1* [FOTL; Eerdmans, 1988], 19). The same problem is seen where the 'enthronement psalms' (47, 93, 96–99) and the 'songs of Zion' (46, 48, 76, 84, 87, 122, 132, 147) are covered. They are hymns, but some discuss them under kingship, the former dealing with the reign of Yahweh and the latter with the special place God has chosen.

[7]There has been a tendency among some scholars to expand the definition and number of royal psalms. J. H. Eaton (*Kingship and the Psalms* [SCM Press Ltd, 1976]) argues that more psalms should be understood as royal on the basis of the role of the psalms in a New Year's festival with the individual in the psalm understood as the king. Others acknowledge

the possibility of more royal psalms on the basis of an identification of the enemy in the psalm as a foreign nation (see the discussion in Day, *Psalms*, 89). However, Hans-Joachim Kraus (*A Theology of the Psalms* [trans. Keith Crim; Fortress Press, 1992], 107) argues that it is not legitimate to extend the concept of 'royal songs' to psalms that contain no royal motifs, or only contain weak allusions to such a motif.

[8]Tremper Longman (*How To Read the Psalms* [InterVarsity Press, 1988], 34) calls these psalms kingship psalms.

[9]Bullock, *Encountering the Psalms*, 178.

[10]Day, *Psalms*, 92-95.

[11]J. Clinton McCann, Jr. ('Psalms,' in *New Interpreter's Bible* [Abingdon Press, 1996], 4:691) states, 'It is the disparity between the proclamations and promises of Psalm 2 and historical actualities that present us with the crucial interpretive issue.'

[12]A. A. Anderson (*The Book of Psalms* [NCB; 2 vols.; Eerdmans, 1972], 1:64) and Hans-Joachim Kraus (*Psalms 1–150* [2 vols; Continental Commentary; Fortress Press, 1993], 1:127) discuss this possibility.

[13]Kraus, *Psalms 1–150*, 1:127-28.

[14]Peter C. Craigie, *Psalms 1–50* (WBC; Word Books, 1983), 68.

[15]Craigie has a tendency to say that the later Messianic meaning was not a part of the original meaning of the psalm (see his comments in *Psalms 1–50* on Psalm 2 [p. 68], 16 [p. 158], and 22 [p. 202]). Also, the literary critical approach (see Chapter 2) leans heavily in this direction.

[16]See the discussion of J. H. Charlesworth, 'From Messianology to Christology: Problems and Prospects,' in *The Messiah* (ed. J. H. Charlesworth; Fortress Press, 1992), 3-35.

[17]Even Walter Kaiser, who limits meaning to the human author, sees the importance of the divine intent in understanding typology (*The Uses of the Old Testament in the New* [Moody Press, 1985], 102-03).

[18]Dan McCartney and Charles Clayton, *Let the Reader Understand* (Victor Books, 1994), 153-55.

[19]Typology should be distinguished from allegory, which does not have the same restrictions on the meaning of the text as typology does. Typology is dependent on the unity of patterns and the development of history in the progress of revelation, which is dependent on the role of the divine author.

[20]Willem VanGemeren, 'Psalms,' in *The Expositor's Bible Commentary* (12 vols.; Zondervan, 1991), 5:66; see also Gerard Van Groningen, *Messianic Revelation in the Old Testament* (Baker, 1990), 338.

[21]John Calvin, *Joshua; Psalms 1-35* (Calvin's Commentaries; 22 vols.; Baker Books, 1996), 4:9, 11.

[22]E. W. Hengstenberg, *The Christology of the Old Testament* (Kregel Publications, 1970), 44-46.

[23]Walter Kaiser, *The Messiah in the Old Testament* (Zondervan, 1995), 99, and Robert L. Reymond, *Jesus, Divine Messiah* (Christian Focus, 2003), 78. It is interesting that both Hengstenberg and Kaiser argue for the Davidic authorship of Psalm 2.

[24]Avraham Gileadi, 'The Davidic Covenant: A Theological Basis for Corporate Protection,' in *Israel's Apostasy and Restoration* (ed. Avraham Gileadi; Baker, 1988), 158; see also Moshe Weinfeld, 'The Covenant Grant in the Old Testament and in the Ancient Near East,' *JAOS* 90 (1970): 184-203.

[25]The promises of the Davidic covenant cannot be separated from the Abrahamic and Mosaic covenants. 2 Samuel 7 reflects the contents of those covenants, especially making your name great (Gen. 12:3), being planted securely in the land (Gen. 12:3; 15:18; Deut. 11:24-25), and being given rest from enemies (Deut. 12:9; Joshua 21:44-45). For an analysis of the relationship between the covenants, see O. Palmer Robertson, *Christ of the Covenants* (P & R, 1980), 27-66.

[26]Jinkyu Kim, *Psalm 110 in Its Literary and Generic Contexts: An Eschatological Interpretation* (PhD diss., Westminster Theological Seminary, 2003), 135.

[27]Typology deals with events, persons, or institutions and 'fuller meaning' deals with concepts and words (Douglas J. Moo, 'The Problem of Sensus Plenior,' in *Hermeneutics, Authority, and Canon* (eds. D. A. Carson and John D. Woodbridge; Zondervan, 1986), 202.

[28]Both Calvin (*Psalms 1-35*, 9) and Kaiser (*Messiah*, 97) assign the psalm to the period of David when he was challenged by the nations surrounding him. Franz Delitzsch ('Psalms,' in *Commentary on the Old Testament* [10 vols.; Eerdmans, 1978], 5:90) argues that the setting might be David in light of 2 Samuel 10:6, but a better option would be Hezekiah or Uzziah. Although the rebellion of the nations would fit the reaction of nations when a new king comes to the throne, there is not enough specific information in Psalm 2 to be definitive of any historical situation.

[29]This view is mentioned by Anderson (*Psalms*, 1:63) and James L. Mays (*Psalms* [Interpretation; John Knox Press, 1994], 45) with Kraus (*Psalms 1–150*, 1:126) arguing for an annual enthronement festival that has parallels with the Egyptian *Sed* festival.

[30]Van Groningen, *Messianic Revelation*, 33, n 27.

[31]VanGemeren, 'Psalms,' 5:64.

[32]Mays, *Psalms*, 46-47.

[33]Mays, *Psalms*, 48; McCann, 'Psalms,' 4:689; and Wilson, *Psalms Volume 1*, 107-08.

[34]VanGemeren, 'Psalms,' 5:66.

[35]McCann, 'Psalms,' 4:689.

[36]Although there is some debate about the specifics of this decree most connect it in some way to the Davidic covenant or some aspect of kingship. Craigie (*Psalms 1–50*, 67) connects the decree to a personal document given to the king renewing God's covenant, and Kraus (*Psalms 1–150*, 1:130) connects it with a royal protocol proclaiming the legitimacy of the king. VanGemeren ('Psalms,' 5:69), however, is skeptical of such specifics related to the decree.

[37]Kraus, *Psalms 1–150*, 1:130-31.

[38]VanGemeren, 'Psalms,' 5:70. Kraus (1:130-31) notes that the Israelite concept is much closer to the Mesopotamian idea, where the king becomes 'son of God' through the call and the announced installation rather than the Egyptian concept where the king is considered deity.

[39]The 'today' of Psalm 2:7 is taken by some to be connected to the ritual of coronation or the day of a king's enthronement (Craigie, *Psalms 1–50*, 67; Kraus, *Psalms 1–150*, 1:132; and McCann, 'Psalms,' 4:689). Van Groningen (*Messianic Revelation*, 336), however, connects 'today' to Yahweh's covenanting act with David when promises were made to David and the father-son relationship was established.

[40]Many times in Joshua it states that Yahweh gave the enemy into the hand of Israel (6:2; 8:1; 10:19; 11:8) and there are statements that Yahweh fought for Israel (Exod. 14:25; Joshua 10:14).

[41]Mays, *Psalms*, 51.

[42]Craigie, *Psalms 1–50*, 69.

[43]H. N. Ridderbos (*Matthew* [Bible Student's Commentary; Zondervan, 1987], 61) argues that at the baptism 'son' does not necessarily refer to the divine nature of Jesus but is an official title referring to the unique relationship he has with God by virtue of the messianic office. William L. Lane (*The Gospel According to Mark* [NICNT; Eerdmans, 1974], 57-58), on the other hand, argues that 'son' at the baptism of Jesus goes beyond the Messianic connotation and refers to his divine status. Both are in view, with the divine status of Jesus becoming clearer as his ministry unfolds.

[44]Norval Geldenhuys, *Commentary on the Gospel of Luke* (NICNT; Eerdmans, 1977), 146-47.

[45]Ridderbos, *Matthew*, 60.

[46]Wilson, *Psalms Volume 1*, 107.

[47]It is suggested by Lane (*Mark*, 319) that Peter is seeking to erect tents of meeting where God can communicate with them, perhaps as fulfillment of the promised glory apart from the suffering for which Jesus has been preparing them.

[48]John Murray (*The Epistle to the Romans* [Eerdmans, 1965], 9–11) shows that the concept of 'son' in Paul can refer to his eternal preexistence and his eternal relationship to the father (Rom. 9:5; Phil. 2:6; Col. 1:19, and 2:9). The use of the phrase in Romans 1:4 refers to the new phase of his messianic lordship in his resurrection.

[49]This view is mentioned by Kraus, *Psalms 1–150*, 1:134.

[50]Those who take Psalm 2:7 as a direct prediction of Christ are Hengstenberg, *Christology*, 44; Kaiser, *Messiah*, 99; and Reymond, *Divine Messiah*, 78.

[51]Calvin, *Psalms 1-35*, 4:9, 11; see also VanGemeren, 'Psalms,' 5:66.

[52]Gerard Van Groningen, *Messianic Revelation in the Old Testament* (Baker, 1990), 338.

[53]Anderson, *Psalms*, 1:346.

[54]Wilson (*Psalms Volume 1*, 702) understands the phrase 'grace is poured upon your lips' as referring to a gifted ability of graceful speech.

[55]The Hebrew literally reads 'daughter of Tyre,' but 'daughter' may signify a member of a group, which is supported by the parallel 'the richest of the people' (VanGemeren, 'Psalms,' 5:348).

[56]There is no consensus concerning which king's wedding was the origin of Psalm 45, whether Solomon's marriage to the Egyptian princess (Calvin, *Psalms 1-35*, 173) or Joram of Judah's marriage to Athaliah (Delitzsch, 'Psalms,' 5:74). The reuse of psalms makes it difficult to find the original wedding.

[57]Kraus, *Psalms 1–150*, 1:452-55.

[58]Murray J. Harris ('The Translation of *Elohim* in Psalm 45:7-8,' *TynBul* 35 [1984]: 71-72, 75-77) points out the syntactical difficulties with these two translations.

[59]Craigie, *Psalms 1–50*, 337.

[60]Craigie (*Psalms 1–50*, 337) comments that this translation follows the punctuation and obvious syntax of the Hebrew text.

[61]Anderson, *Psalms*, 1:349.

[62]McCann, *Psalms*, 4:862.

[63]Delitzsch, 'Psalms,' 5:83.

[64]Mays, *Psalms*, 181.

[65]Van Groningen, *Messianic Revelation*, 367. He also comments that the king is not God but is the symbol by and through which God is present (p. 370).

[66]Delitzsch, 'Psalms,' 5:83; Mays, *Psalms*, 181; and McCann, 'Psalms,' 4:862.

[67]Delitzsch, 'Psalms,' 5:73.

[68]Craigie, *Psalms 1–50*, 340.

[69]Van Groningen, *Messianic Revelation*, 367. But he does view the psalm as having a typological relationship to Christ.

[70]Delitzsch, 'Psalms,' 5:74.

[71]McCann, 'Psalms,' 4:863 and Wilson, *Psalms Volume 1*, 710-12.

[72]Calvin, *Psalms 36-92*, 180-81.

[73]Kaiser, *Messiah*, 127 and Hengstenberg, *Christology*, 50-51.

[74]Allan M. Harman, 'The Syntax and Interpretation of Psalm 45:7,' in *The Law and the Prophets* (ed. John H. Skilton; Presbyterian and Reformed, 1974), 186-87.

[75]Wilson, *Psalms Volume 1*, 702-03.

[76]Wilson (*Psalms Volume 1*, 702-03) comments that the ambiguity related to who is addressed in the actions in Psalm 45 leads to an exploitation of meaning in a messianic direction, but it is better to say that there is a development of the original meaning toward a Messianic meaning. The human author would understand verse 6 as an address to God, but the divine author knows that one day a king will arise who would be divine and rightly called God.

[77]Ridderbos, *Matthew*, 185.

[78]See Hendriksen, *Matthew*, 797-98 for the argument that a wedding robe had been given to each guest.

[79]Ridderbos, *Matthew*, 406.

[80]Mays, *Psalms*, 236.

[81]It is possible this title means that Solomon wrote Psalm 72 because the same title used with 'David' refers to Davidic authorship (Delitzsch, 'Psalms,' 5:298-299). The postscript (72:20) noting that the prayers of David are ended seems to argue against Solomonic authorship (Tate, *Psalms 51–100*, 222), making it possible that David wrote this psalm for Solomon. Calvin (*Psalms 36-92*, 99-100) sets forth the interesting

view that David wrote the psalm for Solomon, but then Solomon put the prayer of his father into the poetry of this psalm.

[82]Tate (*Psalms 51–100*, 222) notes that this postscript may have concluded an earlier collection of Davidic psalms, which was later incorporated into a larger collection of psalms.

[83]Although Psalm 72 was composed by David for Solomon it was probably reused in the inauguration of other Davidic kings (Mays, *Psalms*, 236).

[84]Erhard S. Gerstenberger (*Psalms, Part 2, and Lamentations* [FOTL; Eerdmans, 2001], 64-65) comments that the psalm is not very well organized and that many commentators do not try to find a convincing structure.

[85]Kaiser, *Messiah*, 134. Some remove verses 18-20 from the structure of the psalm (McCann, 'Psalms,' 4:963).

[86]This structure is adapted from Knut Heim, 'The Perfect King of Psalm 72: An Intertextual Inquiry,' in *The Lord's Anointed* (eds. Philip E. Satterthwaite, Richard S. Hess, and Gordon J. Wenham), 228.

[87]Wilson (*Psalms Volume 1*, 985, n 5, and 993) points out that verse 1 contains the only imperative in Psalm 72. The rest of the petitions are probably to be taken as jussives ('may he') rather than imperfects ('he will'). Imperfects would be indicative statements of what will happen, as in the NIV. Part of the problem is that some forms of the imperfect can also be jussive in meaning. Where a distinct form of jussive can be used, Psalm 72 uses it (vv. 15-17), which probably means the other imperfects should be taken as jussives in the original context. However, in light of the meaning of this psalm in reference to Christ, the imperfects can be taken as indicative statements of what Christ will do.

[88]McCann, 'Psalms,' 4:963.

[89]Calvin, *Psalms 36-92*, 103-04.

[90]Tate, *Psalms 51–100*, 223-24.

[91]The plural verb at the beginning of 72:5 is seen by many to be problematic, leading to the suggested emendation 'may he continue' (Tate, *Psalms 51–100*, 220), but see Heim ('Perfect King of Psalm 72,' 238-39) for a solid defense of the third plural verb in the Hebrew text.

[92]Anderson, *Psalms*, 1:521.

[93]Tate, *Psalms 51–100*, 225.

[94]This is argued by Harman (*Commentary on the Psalms* [Christian Focus, 1998], 251-52); Hengstenberg (*Christology*, 57-62); and Kaiser (*Messiah*, 133-34) based on the testimony of tradition and that the

promises in Psalm 72 go far beyond anything that could be promised to an ordinary descendant of David.

[95]Calvin (*Psalms 36-92*, 100) comments that those who take this psalm as a prophecy of the kingdom of Christ seem to put a construction on the words that does violence to them and gives the Jews an occasion for outcry by applying things to Christ that do not directly apply to him.

[96]Mays, *Psalms*, 238.

[97]Heim ('Perfect King of Psalm 72,' 245) argues that the ambiguity of 72:8 lends itself to a more universal meaning.

[98]Kim, *Psalm 110*, 109-10.

[99]Verse 19 begins with *'az* ('then' in NKJV, 'once' in NIV) and verse 38 begins with *uᵉ'attâh* ('but now you' in the ESV and 'but you' in the NKJV and NIV).

[100]VanGemeren, 'Psalms,' 5:575.

[101]There are a number of suggestions concerning the setting of Psalm 89. It is difficult to set this psalm into some kind of festival because of the humiliation of the king, unless it is a festival similar to the Babylonian festival of the dying and rising ritual of a king (see Tate, *Psalms 51–100*, 415 for arguments against this view). Even Kraus (*Psalms 1–150*, 2:203) rejects a connection of this psalm to a festival and argues for a preexilic date of the psalm based on the fact that a king has lost a battle and that no hint of the exile is present in the psalm. Several possible kings have been suggested for the setting of Psalm 89. Calvin (*Psalms 36-92*, 418) and Delitzsch ('Psalms,' 5:33-34) suggest Rehoboam, the latter particularly stresses Shishak's invasion. Kraus (*Psalms 1–150*, 2:203) thinks the psalm refers to a successor of Josiah, who died in 609BC, and Harman (*Psalms*, 306) relates it to Jehoiachin based partly on the reference in verse 45 of cutting short the days of his youth (597BC). Although McCann ('Psalms,' 4:1034) thinks the origin of the psalm is elusive, he suggests the destruction of Jerusalem in 587BC. Finally, Tate (p. 417) places the psalm in the exilic or postexilic situation during the collapse of the expectations surrounding the monarchy under Zerubbabel, leading to a crisis of faith as expressed in Psalm 89. Because psalms were reused in similar situations it is sometimes hard to nail down a specific date for the psalms.

[102]The word *ḥesed* in verse 1 is in the plural, which refers to deeds of Yahweh in which he demonstrates his covenant obligations to Israel (Tate, *Psalms 51–100*, 419).

[103]McCann, 'Psalms,' 4:1034. Although 'steadfast love' and 'faithfulness' are not used in verse 3 in connection to the covenant with David, the use of the same verbs in vv. 2-3 in a chiastic arrangement (build – establish – establish – build) ties these terms to the covenant with David.

[104]Tate (*Psalms 51–100*, 423) lists the connections between Yahweh and David.

[105]Tate, 425. Delitzsch ('Psalms,' 5:40) notes that God takes the last born and makes him the first born and the most-favored.

[106]There is debate about whether the references to the sea and the rivers are a geographical reference, describing the boundaries of the kingdom of David, or whether they are mythological references. The point is that the reign of the king will be universal over everything (Tate, *Psalms 51–100*, 423).

[107]VanGemeren, 'Psalms,' 5:633 and Kraus, *Psalms 1–150*, 2:209.

[108]Tate, *Psalms 51–100*, 424.

[109]McCann, 'Psalms,' 4:1034.

[110]David M. Howard, *The Structure of Psalms 93-100* (Eisenbrauns, 1997).

[111]Kim, *Psalm 110*, 117.

[112]Kim, *Psalm 110*, 117.

[113]See Kraus, *Psalms 1–150*, 2:345 and Allen, *Psalms 101–150*, 83.

[114]It needs to be pointed out that even when there is agreement on a particular setting of Psalm 110 there may not be agreement on the details of how certain verses or phrases are understood.

[115]McCann ('Psalms,' 4:1130) points out that the discernment of the structure of Psalm 110 is hindered by the difficulty of understanding verses 3 and 7. Kraus (*Psalms 1–150*, 2:346) is one of the few who sees three oracles in Psalm 110 (vv. 1, 3, 4).

[116]The chart is adapted from Van Groningen, *Messianic Revelation*, 392, and Harman, *Psalms*, 361.

[117]Because the second oracle relates to the priesthood, some think that the setting for Psalm 110 is the coronation of a high priest, such as Zadok (Anderson, *Psalms*, 2:771) or Joshua (Gerstenberger, *Psalms, Part 2*, 266-67).

[118]Allen, *Psalms 101–150*, 83.

[119]Allen (*Psalms 101–150*, 84) recognizes the danger of forcing the content of the psalm to fit a royal coronation and believes the psalm may only be an echo of a coronation ceremony. Kraus (*Psalms 1–150*, 2:347)

is more confident, connecting the psalm to a yearly enthronement festival of Yahweh where these oracles concerning the king are uttered.

[120]Allen (*Psalms 101–150*, 79, 86) notes the possibility that this psalm originated in the time of David, celebrating the capture of Jerusalem and his succession to the Jebusite throne.

[121]Allen, *Psalms 101–150*, 79 and Kraus, *Psalms 1–150*, 2:346.

[122]Kraus, *Psalms 1–150*, 2:353. Allen (*Psalms 101–150*, 86) takes 'sit at my right hand' metaphorically, showing that God is the real king and that the human king derives his authority from God.

[123]Kraus, *Psalms 1–150*, 2:349.

[124]Allen (*Psalms 101–150*, 80) takes the imperative 'rule' as expressing a certain consequence.

[125]Kraus, *Psalms 1–150*, 2:350. He accepts the emendation of the Hebrew text at the end of verse 3. Instead of 'your youth' he takes it as 'I have begotten you', in parallel with Psalm 2:7. He also understands the dew as referring to the quickening strength the king brings with him.

[126]Allen, *Psalms 101–150*, 86. Allen rejects the emendation at the end of verse 3, 'I have begotten you.' He does not believe there is a real parallel with Psalm 2 if the structure of Psalm 110 is examined closely. Plus, there is a problem going from a third person reference to Yahweh to a first person reference at the end of the verse.

[127]Allen, *Psalms 101–150*, 87.

[128]Kraus, *Psalms 1–150*, 2:351.

[129]Allen, *Psalms 101–150*, 87 and Kraus, *Psalms 1–150*, 2:352.

[130]Ibid. Neither Allen nor Kraus believe that the original meaning of the psalm is Messianic. It refers only to the ruling historical king. The Messianic meaning only developed later.

[131]Kaiser, *Messiah*, 96.

[132]Delitzsch, 'Psalms,' 5:187.

[133]See Allen, *Psalms 101–150*, 83.

[134]Kaiser, *Messiah*, 95.

[135]This view understands the divine oracle to be a direct reference to Christ and not something said about the historical king (Kaiser, *Messiah*, 95; Delitzsch, 'Psalms,' 5:189; and Van Groningen, *Messianic Revelation*, 392).

[136]Kaiser, *Messiah*, 95.

[137]Delitzsch, 'Psalms,' 5:191.

[138]Kaiser, *Messiah*, 95 and Delitzsch, 'Psalms,' 5:191-92.

[139]Delizsch, 'Psalms,' 5:191.

[140]Van Groningen, *Messianic Revelation*, 394. Delitzsch ('Psalms,' 5:192) asks, 'How could David claim this when he had no claim on the tithes of priests and to whom was denied the authority to offer sacrifices?'

[141]Van Groningen, *Messianic Revelation*, 395.

[142]Delitzsch, 'Psalms,' 5:194.

[143]Kaiser, *Messiah*, 95 and Van Groningen, *Messianic Revelation*, 395-96.

[144]Delitzsch, 'Psalms,' 5:194-95.

[145]Delitzsch, 'Psalms,' 5:196 and Van Groningen, *Messianic Revelation*, 396. Kaiser (*Messiah*, 96) understands verse 7 to refer to David, who pauses to refresh himself both physically, with cool water, and spiritually, by reflecting on what God had done in a similar situation with Abraham (Gen. 14:18-20).

[146]Gerald H. Wilson, *The Editing of the Hebrew Psalter* (Scholars Press, 1985).

[147]Wilson demonstrated that the placement of royal psalms at the seams of Books I–III was significant, and that each of these royal psalms was followed by a concluding doxology. Kim (*Psalm 110*, 88, 93–94) attempts to show that the same pattern is basically followed in Books IV–V of the Psalter in relation to key royal psalms. He argues that royal psalms are positioned at or near the end of a group and are followed by a doxology or doxologies. Thus Psalm 110 is placed at the end of a group (90–110) and is followed by a collection of doxological psalms (111–118). Whether or not one is convinced by Kim's overall proposal, he makes some significant contributions concerning the relationship of royal psalms in the Psalter and how they show the development of the Davidic covenant.

[148]Kim (*Psalm 110*, 312) believes the original setting of the psalm was related to a festal ceremony to celebrate David's conquest of Jerusalem and succession to the Jebusite kingship. The psalm was then reused by later kings.

[149]Kim, *Psalm 110*, 126, 275, 294.

[150]Kim, *Psalm 110*, 303, 315, 351. Although the speaker in the literary, final form of the Psalter is identified as David, Kim believes the speaker in the original, historical context of the psalm could have been a court prophet who delivered Yahweh's oracle to the Davidic king. Thus the psalm was not originally Davidic, nor was it originally eschatological. But this seems to set up a disjunction between the original meaning of

the psalm and its later eschatological meaning. It would be helpful for Kim to show how that gap can be bridged and what the implications are for the statement of Jesus that David spoke this oracle through the Holy Spirit (Matt. 22:41-46).

[151]Kim, *Psalm 110*, 317, 322.

[152]Ibid., 329-30. Instead of 'holy garments' (*hdr*, הדר) Kim reads 'holy mountains' (*hrr*, הרר) in verse 3 because mountains more than garments are common in eschatological settings. Zion is called the holy mountain (Ps. 2:6) and in Psalm 110 Zion is linked to holy mountains where the eschatological battle takes place on the Day of Yahweh.

[153]Kim, *Psalm 110*, 336, 339, 346-49.

[154]Allen, *Psalms 101–150*, 85.

[155]Kraus, *Psalms 1–150*, 2:348 and Delitzsch, 'Psalms,' 5:189. The phrase is *yhwh ne'um*, נאם יהוה.

[156]Kim, *Psalm 110*, 296.

[157]Ibid., 355.

[158]There is no need to try to find an exact parallel with Christ concerning the concept in verse 7 of drinking from a brook. It may refer in context to refreshment or strength in order to finish the pursuit of the enemies. In light of the end of the verse, total victory is in view.

[159]Many recognize that Psalm 132 has both royal and songs of Zion emphases (Allen, *Psalm 101-150*, 206; Kraus, *Psalms 1–150*, 2:474; McCann, 'Psalms,' 4:1213; and VanGemeren, 'Psalms,' 5:804).

[160]See Mays, *Psalms*, 409-10.

[161]The analysis of the structure of Psalm 132 and the relationship of the parts to each other is heavily indebted to Allen, *Psalms 101–150*, 204-06; Mays, *Psalms*, 412; and McCann, 'Psalms,' 4:1211.

[162]VanGemeren, 'Psalms,' 5:807.

[163]Harman, *Psalms*, 417-18.

[164]Allen, *Psalms 101–150*, 205.

[165]The verb 'desire' (*'wh*, אוה) expresses an intensely personal attitude showing God's enthusiastic fervor for Jerusalem (Allen, *Psalms 101–150*, 203, 210).

[166]Allen, *Psalms 101–150*, 206.

[167]Both horn and lamp may refer to the permanence of the Davidic dynasty (VanGemeren, 'Psalms,' 5:809).

[168]Many argue for a preexilic setting for Psalm 132, believing that it presupposes the existence of the Davidic monarchy and gives no hint that Jerusalem has suffered exile (Allen, *Psalms 101–150*, 207).

Calvin (*Psalms 93-150*, 143) and Delitzsch ('Psalms,' 5:309) believe the psalm comes from the time of David or Solomon, perhaps composed when the ark was moved by Solomon into the temple, as is reflected in 2 Chronicles 6:41-42. Allen (*Psalms 101–150*, 209) believes the psalm is no later than the time of Josiah and was used in a ceremony that re-enacted David bringing the ark to Jerusalem. Kraus (*Psalms 1–150*, 2:477) connects the psalm to an annual royal festival. Others argue for a postexilic origin for Psalm 132 because it reflects a postexilic situation, based on its placement in Book V of the Psalter (McCann, 'Psalms,' 4:1211). Others stress traces of late community organization and Messianic hopes for the restoration of the Davidic monarchy (Gerstenberger, *Psalms, Part 2*, 369). It is hard to come to a firm conclusion. The first part of the psalm seems to presuppose the Davidic monarchy, but verse 17 seems to imply there is no Davidic king. A firm conclusion is not absolutely necessary to understand the meaning of the psalm. The literary context may be more significant than the original historical context.

[169]McCann, 'Psalms,' 4:1210. For an analysis of the Songs of Ascent that treats them as a unity with the theme of Yahweh's restoration of Zion, see Philip E. Satterthwaite, 'Zion in the Song of Ascents,' in *Zion, City of Our God* (eds. Richard S. Hess and Gordon J. Wenham; Eerdmans, 1999), 105-28.

[170]McCann, 'Psalms,' 4:1212.

[171]Kim, *Psalm 110*, 297.

[172]Delitzsch ('Psalms,' 5:316) points out the possible connections between the sprouting of the horn in Psalm 132 and the passages in the prophets that speak of the branch (Isa. 4:2; Jer 23:5; Zech 3:8 and 6:12), which reinforces the Messianic connections of Psalm 132.

[173]Allen (*Psalms 101–150*, 289) calls Psalm 144 a mixed form and Gerstenberger (*Psalms, Part 2*, 427) points out the curious mixture of form elements ranging from praise and blessing to urgent petition, complaint, and vow. Even Calvin (*Psalms 93-150*, 259) calls it a mixture of praise and prayer.

[174]Mays, *Psalms*, 435-36.

[175]For the following discussion, see McCann, 'Psalms,' 4:1254-56 and Kim, *Psalm 110*, 135-36.

[176]Allen, *Psalms 101–150*, 290. Delitzsch ('Psalms.' 5:379) accepts the LXX heading and sees Psalm 144 as a prayer of David before he faced Goliath.

[177]Both McCann and Kim use the term eschatological to refer to Psalm 144, the latter showing connections between Psalm 144 and Zechariah 14 to emphasize the eschatological motifs.

[178]The transition from the first part of the psalm (vv. 1-11) to the second part (vv. 12-15) is seen in the word '*ăšer*, which begins verse 12. This word can express purpose or result (VanGemeren, 'Psalms,' 5:859 and Harman, *Psalms*, 441).

[179]McCann, 'Psalms,' 4:1255.

[180]Kraus, *Psalms 1–150*, 2:542.

[181]Harman, *Psalms*, 443.

[182]For connections between Psalm 144 and prior royal psalms, see McCann, 'Psalms,' 4:1256 and Kim, *Psalm 110*, 135-36.

[183]Many commentators want to emend the Hebrew from 'my people' in verse 2 to a plural 'peoples', with the translation 'who subdues peoples under me', because the violence of the verb 'subdue' suggests that other nations are in view (Allen, *Psalms 101–150*, 287 and Kraus, *Psalms 1–150*, 2:542). Calvin (*Psalm 93-150*, 261) does not think the verb refers to violent domination but that it is affirming that the kingdom was given to David by God. Delitzsch ('Psalms,' 5:381) thinks the verse refers to the time when the whole kingdom was not yet under David's rule. The Hebrew makes sense in light of the ministry of Christ because most of his deceitful enemies were among God's covenant people, many of whom had to be subdued, but not in a military sense.

Chapter 8. Direct Messianic Psalms

[1]This list is based on a comparison of Walter Kaiser, *The Messiah in the Old Testament* (Zondervan, 1995), 92-94; J. Barton Payne, *Encyclopedia of Biblical Prophecy* (Harper & Row, 1973), 76; and Gerard Van Groningen, *Messianic Revelation in the Old Testament* (Baker Book House, 1990), 332.

[2]Willem VanGemeren ('Psalms,' in *The Expositor's Bible Commentary* [12 vols.; Zondervan, 1991], 5:109) calls it a hymn of praise, or more specifically, a hymn of creation praise.

[3]John Calvin, *Institutes of the Christian Religion* (2 vols.; Library of Christian Classics; The Westminster Press, 1977), 1:37.

[4]James L. Mays, *Psalms* (Interpretation; John Knox Press, 1994), 65.

[5]VanGemeren, 'Psalms,' 5:110.

[6]Hans-Joachim Kraus, *Psalms 1–150* (2 vols; A Contintental Commentary; Fortress Press, 1993), 1:180.

[7]The Hebrew terms for children in verse 2 emphasize small children, especially when the two terms are used together. The second term, a participle of the verb *yānaq* (ינק), refers to nursing children. This includes infants, but children could nurse until they were two or three years old (W. R. Domeris, 'ינק (*ynq*),' *NIDOTTE* [5 vols.; ed. Willem VanGemeren; Zondervan, 1997], 2:472-73).

[8]Kraus (*Psalms 1–150*, 1:181-82) notes that this thought is unique in the Old Testament. However, a similar idea may occur in Isaiah 7–12 with the emphasis on children in the context of Ahaz' decision as to whether to trust God or call on Assyria for help.

[9]Peter C. Craigie, *Psalms 1–50* (WBC; Word Books, 1983), 108.

[10]The LXX translated Elohim with angels. Elohim is a plural form, which when used of the God of Israel is translated as a singular. It can also be used of other gods, and then it is translated as a plural, 'gods.' Elohim can refer to divine or heavenly beings (Ps. 82:1, 6-8), which is the way the LXX translates it. It is possible the LXX translation of Elohim as 'angels' rather than 'God' is to avoid elevating human beings too high (Craigie, *Psalms 1–50*, 108).

[11]VanGemeren, 'Psalms,' 5:113.

[12]Mays (*Psalms*, 70) comments, 'With sin dominion has become domination, rule has become ruin, subordination to the divine purpose has become subjection to human sinfulness.'

[13]Mays, *Psalms*, 64.

[14]The Hebrew word for strength ('*ōz*) can mean praise, possibly in the sense of power ascribed to God in praise (Exod. 15:2; Ps. 29:1; 96:7). F. Delitzsch ('Psalms,' *Commentary on the Old Testament in Ten Volumes* [ed. C. F. Keil and F. Delitzsch; Eerdmans, 1978], 5:152) notes that this meaning occurs only when used with verbs of giving, as in Psalms 29:1; 96:7. It is also possible that the LXX uses a tradition of bringing Exodus 15:2 and Psalm 8:2 together. This tradition had children praising God at the Red Sea, a view reflected in the Wisdom of Solomon 10:21 (W. D. Davies and Dale C. Allison, *The Gospel According to Matthew* [3 vols.; T & T Clark, 1997], 3:142).

[15]Craigie, *Psalms 1–50*, 109-10.

[16]There is some ambiguity in Hebrews 2:8b concerning whether it refers to man's original role before the fall or to Jesus Christ. Simon J. Kistemaker (*The Thessalonians, The Pastorals, and Hebrews* [NTC; Baker, 1984], 65-66) argues the former view and Philip E. Hughes (*A Commentary on the Epistle to the Hebrews* [Eerdmans, 1977], 86-87)

argues the latter view. Perhaps the ambiguity is purposeful, allowing reference to both. Jesus came to restore the original dominion of Adam over creation.

[17]Dan G. McCartney, 'Ecco Homo: The Coming of the Kingdom at the Restoration of Human Vicegerency,' WTJ 56 (1994), 8.

[18]J. Clinton McCann, Jr., 'Psalms,' in New Interpreter's Bible (Abingdon Press, 1996), 4:736 and VanGemeren, 'Psalms,' 5:153.

[19]This structure is adapted from A. A. Anderson, The Book of Psalms (NCB; 2 vols.; Eerdmans, 1972), 1:141, and Gerard Van Groningen, Messianic Revelation, 338.

[20]There is little agreement on the setting of Psalm 16 or whether the psalmist is facing a crisis situation that is immediate or has already passed.

[21]The introductory statement, translated 'I say' in the ESV, actually reads 'you say' in the Hebrew (second feminine singular). The difference between the first person and the second person is the difference between seeing verses 2-3 as the confession of the psalmist (first person), or as the statement of an idolater who claims allegiance to the Lord (second person). According to Craigie (Psalms 1–50, 154), most translations follow the first person, but he opts for the second person (either masculine or feminine). Some accept the second feminine singular of the Hebrew text and understand the subject to be the soul of the psalmist, which is feminine in Hebrew (nepeš). This would make verses 2-3 a confession of the psalmist (see John Calvin, Psalms 1-35 [Calvin's Commentaries; trans. Henry Beveridge; 22 vols; Baker, 1996 reprint], 4:216).

[22]Kraus, Psalms 1–150, 1:236.

[23]See Craigie, Psalms 1–50, 155.

[24]Allan Harman (Psalms [Christian Focus, 1998], 102) argues that the words in verses 2-3 are those of an idol worshipper who claimed allegiance to the Lord but who followed other gods. He also believes the second feminine singular of verse 2 ('you say') supports this view (see footnote 21).

[25]Delitzsch, 'Psalms,' 5:221-22; VanGemeren, 'Psalms,' 5:154, 156; and Van Groningen, Messianic Revelation, 344.

[26]On the basis of the inheritance ideas Kraus (Psalms 1–150, 1:236) believes the speaker is a Levite and that the Levites are identified here with the saints; however, such terminology does not have to be limited to the Levites because God was the portion of each Israelite (Anderson, Psalms, 1:143).

[27]Cup can be used figuratively for experiencing God's blessings (Ps. 23:5) or God's judgment (Jer 25:15).

[28]Kraus, *Psalms 1–150*, 1:238 and Anderson, *Psalms*, 1:144.

[29]Craigie, *Psalms 1–50*, 158 and Kraus, *Psalms 1–150*, 1:240.

[30]Mays, *Psalms*, 89.

[31]See Desmond T. Alexander, 'The Old Testament View of Life After Death,' *Themelios* 11 (1986): 41-46. He discusses the meaning of Sheol.

[32]VanGemeren, 'Psalms,' 5:159 and Van Groningen, *Messianic Revelation*, 347.

[33]S. R. Driver, 'The Method of Studying the Psalter: Psalm 16,' *Expositor*, Seventh Series, 10 (1910): 37, quoted in Walter Kaiser, *The Uses of the Old Testament in the New* (Moody Press, 1985), 27.

[34]Kraus, *Psalms 1–150*, 1:242.

[35]Craigie, *Psalms 1–50*, 158-59.

[36]Kaiser, 'The Promise to David in Psalm 16 and Its Application in Acts 2:25-33 and 13:32-37,' *JETS* 23 (1980): 219-29; also reprinted in *Uses of the Old Testament*, 25-42.

[37]Mays, *Psalms*, 105.

[38]Many in the early church argued that Christ was the exclusive subject of Psalm 22 (see Richard D. Patterson, 'Psalm 22: From Trial to Triumph,' *JETS* [2004], 218, who mentions 1 Clement and the Epistle of Barnabas). Others include Augustine, and E. W. Hengstenberg, *The Christology of the Old Testament* (Kregel Publications, 1970), 80-89. On the other side, some argue that the original meaning of the psalm was not Messianic but that it is appropriate now to read the psalm in a Messianic way as related to Jesus (Craigie, *Psalms 1–50*, 202; Kraus, *Psalms 1–150*, 1:300-01; and Anderson, *Psalms*, 1:185). Such a disjunction between the original meaning of the psalm and the later meaning in the New Testament is troubling. For a good discussion of the relationship between the Old Testament meaning and the New Testament meaning, with Psalm 22:13-18 as an example, see Vern S. Poythress, 'Divine Meaning of Scripture,' *WTJ* (1986): 241-79.

[39]Gerald H. Wilson, *Psalms Volume 1* (NIVAC; Zondervan, 2002), 413, 425. Patrick D. Miller, Jr. (*Interpreting the Psalms* [Fortress Press, 1986], 111) emphasizes the implications of the incarnation and the cross for those who are suffering.

[40]There is no agreement on the origin of Psalm 22. The title reads 'A Psalm of David' and many have argued for the legitimacy of Davidic

authorship (see Delitzsch, 'Psalms,' 5:303-05 and Patterson, 'Psalm 22,' 214-15). Calvin (*Psalm 1-35*, 357) argues that David does not just refer to one experience of persecution but comprehends all the persecutions he experienced under Saul. Craigie (*Psalms 1–50*, 198) and Kraus (*Psalms 1–150*, 1:294) argue that Psalm 22 arises out of the experience of a particular individual but that it reflects use in a liturgy for people severely threatened by sickness and death. Mays (*Psalms*, 106) argues that the psalm was composed for use in the liturgy and that the experience it describes is a typical case. Our view is that Psalm 22 originated in an experience of David but when it was included in the Psalms it was understood to be a typical or model experience for God's people to meditate on (see Poythress, 'Divine Meaning,' 270).

[41]Mays, *Psalms*, 106-07.

[42]McCann, 'Psalms,' 4:762. Notice how both Mays and McCann want to see something in the text that transcends the text itself and points forward to a greater fulfillment, which in our view is only made possible by a divine author.

[43]Mays (*Psalms*, 107) uses the phrase 'typical event' and mentions the views of Calvin and Delitzsch. Calvin especially understands Psalm 22 in light of the experience of David before making connections to Jesus Christ.

[44]VanGemeren, 'Psalms,' 5:198 and Wilson, *Psalms Volume 1*, 412.

[45]Mays, *Psalms*, 109 and McCann, 'Psalms,' 4:762.

[46]VanGemeren, 'Psalms,' 5:201.

[47]Miller, *Interpreting the Psalms*, 104.

[48]VanGemeren, 'Psalms,' 5:202. Wilson (*Psalms Volume 1*, 415) comments concerning the phrase 'I am a worm', that the worm is significant because of its insignificance.

[49]Van Groningen, *Messianic Revelation*, 355-56.

[50]VanGemeren, 'Psalms,' 5:202.

[51]The phrase in verse 16 [17], 'they have pierced my hands and my feet' (esv), is a problematic phrase. A series of articles have been published in *JBL* on it: Gregory Vall, 'Psalm 22:17B: "The Old Guess"' *JBL* 116:1 (1997): 45-56; John Kaltner, 'Psalm 22:17b: Second Guessing "The Old Guess"' in *JBL* 117:3 (1998): 503-14; Brent Strawn, 'Psalm 22:17b: More Guessing' *JBL* 119:3 (2000): 439-51; and Kristin M. Swenson, 'Psalm 22:17: Circling around the Problem Again,' *JBL* 123.4 (2004): 637-48. The article by Swenson tries to solve the problem by retaining the Hebrew text but dividing it differently. Also check the commentaries for a variety of proposals.

[52]Dogs in the ANE were not like our pets but were scavengers who moved around in packs looking for food (VanGemeren, 'Psalms,' 5:206).

[53]Delitzsch ('Psalms,' 5:321) notes that by casting lots for the garments the enemies assume the certain death of the sufferer.

[54]Anderson, *Psalms*, 1:189 and Craigie, *Psalms 1–50*, 200.

[55]VanGemeren, 'Psalms,' 5:205-06.

[56]Anderson, *Psalms*, 1:191.

[57]Kraus, *Psalms 1–150*, 1:292. The LXX takes this phrase as a noun, 'my afflicted one.' For a discussion of this option and an argument in support of the Hebrew, see Craigie, *Psalms 1–50*, 197.

[58]Craigie, *Psalms 1–50*, 201.

[59]Patterson, 'Psalm 22,' 216.

[60]Mays, *Psalms*, 111.

[61]Miller, *Interpreting the Psalms*, 108.

[62]Wilson, *Psalms Volume 1*, 425.

[63]According to typology, the antitype must be greater than the type. Delitzsch ('Psalms,' 5:310) comments that the abandonment experienced by Christ is unique and goes beyond what David experienced.

[64]Calvin (*Psalms 1-35*, 361-62) comments that because Christ was our representative and took upon himself our sins he appeared before the judgment seat of God as a sinner, from which proceeded the terror and dread that constrained him to pray for deliverance from death. Although subject to human passions and affections, he never fell into sin through the weakness of the flesh.

[65]Delitzsch, 'Psalms,' 5:305.

[66]Kaiser, *The Messiah*, 117, n 13.

[67]Delitzsch, 'Psalms,' 5:328.

[68]Delitzsch, 'Psalms,' 5:324.

[69]Hengstenberg (*Christology of the Old Testament*, 90-93) is one of the few who argues that Psalm 40 has no 'lower reference' to David but should be understood only as the words of the Messiah. This view is based partly on his understanding that in Psalm 40 the speaker already offers himself as a sacrifice in place of the sacrificial system, which cannot refer to David. But such a meaning of 40:6 is highly suspect.

[70]For a discussion of this problem, see Anderson, *Psalms*, 1:314; Craigie, *Psalms 1–50*, 313-14; and Kraus, *Psalms 1–150*, 1:424.

[71]For the verbal connections between the two parts, see Walter Brueggemann, *The Message of the Psalms* (Augsburg Publishing House, 1984), 130-31; Craigie, *Psalms 1–50*, 314; and McCann, 'Psalms,'

4:842. Brueggemann also shows the connections between the beginning and ending of the psalm.

[72]Mays, *Psalms*, 167.

[73]McCann, 'Psalms,' 4:842. Craigie (*Psalms 1–50*, 314) and Erhard S. Gerstenberger (*Psalms Part 1* [FOTL; Eerdmans, 1988], 169) argue for the unity of Psalm 40 based on liturgical reasons.

[74]This is Brueggemann's translation. Both Brueggemann (*The Message of the Psalms*, 128) and Harman (*Psalms*, 173) think the translation 'I waited patiently' is too passive.

[75]McCann, 'Psalms,' 4:842.

[76]Kraus, *Psalms 1–150*, 1:425.

[77]VanGemeren, 'Psalms,' 5:320 and Craigie, *Psalms 1–50*, 315.

[78]The difficulty surrounds the meaning of the verb *kārāh*. Does it mean 'to dig' with the translation 'ears you have dug for me' (McCann, 'Psalms,' 4:843), meaning that God made the ears (Kaiser, *Uses of the Old Testament*, 134)? Or does the verb mean 'to pierce' with the translation 'you bored ears for me' (Mays, *Psalms*, 168), or 'ears Thou hast pierced for me' (Delitzsch, 'Psalms,' 5:38)? Kaiser (*Uses of the Old Testament*, 134) argues against any connection to Exodus 21:16 because the verb is different. Whatever way the verb is translated, there is agreement that the meaning of the phrase refers to willing obedience.

[79]Wilson (*Psalms Volume 1*, 641) lists most of these with Kaiser (*Uses of the Old Testament*, 136) stressing 2 Samuel 7 and revelation up to the time of David.

[80]Craigie, *Psalms 1–50*, 315; Delitzsch, 'Psalms,' 5:39; Harman, *Psalms*, 174; and VanGemeren, 'Psalms,' 5:320. The psalm does not have to be a royal psalm for this view.

[81]Poythress, 'Divine meaning,' 270.

[82]Kraus (*Psalms 1–150*, 1:426) and Mays (*Psalms*, 168) understand the scroll to contain an account of the deliverance and the song of thanksgiving that the psalmist is offering to God in place of the sacrifice. This view is possible but there is very little evidence to support it other than some stele inscriptions in Asia Minor. Hardly any modern commentaries follow Calvin (*Psalms 36-92*, 103) who argues that the scroll refers to the book of life.

[83]VanGemeren, 'Psalms,' 5:360, and Brueggemann, *Message of the Psalms*, 129.

[84]Brueggemann, *Message of the Psalms*, 130.

[85]McCann, 'Psalms,' 4:844.

[86]Kaiser, *Uses of the Old Testament*, 131. Harman (*Psalms*, 174) denies the psalm is primarily Messianic because of the confession of sin. Kaiser takes a different approach to Psalm 69, where there is also a confession of sin. He explains that a piecemeal approach, where only some verses refer to the Messiah, is a step backward in the history of interpretation. He handles the confession of sin in Psalm 69 in connection with the promise of 2 Samuel 7:14b, where the warning is given that, if any of the Davidic sons sins, he will not participate in the blessings of the promised plan. He distinguishes the sinfulness of the Davidic line from the purity of the Messiah. It is hard in this view to see how Christ could pray the psalms.

[87]Hengstenberg, *Christology of the Old Testament*, 92.

[88]This is mentioned by Hengstenberg, *Christology of the Old Testament*, 92.

[89]Hughes, *Hebrews*, 398.

[90]Hengstenberg (*Christology of the Old Testament*, 91) comments that Christ presents himself as the true sacrifice of whom Moses had written.

[91]Kaiser, *Uses of the Old Testament*, 126.

[92]McCann, 'Psalms,' 4:944.

[93]Kraus, *Psalms 1–150*, 2:47 and Tate, *Psalms 51–100*, 170.

[94]Kaiser, *Messiah*, 130.

[95]Anderson (*Psalms*, 1:482) argues post-Davidic and Tate (*Psalms 51–100*, 174) argues postexilic, although he acknowledges that the history of the development of the psalm is impossible to reconstruct.

[96]Kraus (*Psalms 1–150*, 2:49) here is reflecting on Mowinckel's views.

[97]Kaiser, *Messiah*, 130 and Delitzsch, 'Psalms,' 5:246. The latter even explains how the looking forward to future victory in Psalm 68 fits the way the Syro-Ammonite war played out.

[98]See Kraus (*Psalms*, 2:49-51) and Tate (*Psalms 51–100*, 172-75) for a full discussion of the issues related to the structure of the psalm.

[99]Kraus (*Psalms*, 2:49) makes this comment related to Mowinckel's view that the psalm was used in an Autumn New Year festival.

[100]Anderson, *Psalms 1–150*, 1:481; McCann, 'Psalms,' 4:944; and Wilson, *Psalms Volume 1*, 935.

[101]The following analysis of the structure adapts material from Mays, *Psalms*, 225-26.

[102]There is little doubt in verse 33 that God is the one who rides in the heavens, but in verse 4 there is debate surrounding the phrase that uses

'God rides.' Some connect the Hebrew phrase *lārōkēb bā'ărābôṭ* with a Ugaritic phrase *rkb' rpt*, used of Baal, to mean that God is the one who 'rides on the clouds,' not Baal. This would parallel verse 33. But the Hebrew word is a common word that refers to deserts or wilderness, with God as the one 'who rides through the deserts,' which fits the context of verse 4 better (see the discussion in Tate, *Psalms 51–100*, 163, 176).

[103]The verb in verse 1 is an imperfect form (God will arise) but it is translated in the NIV, NKJV, and the NASB as a jussive (let God arise). Wilson (*Psalms Volume 1*, 935) notes that the jussive expresses the hope that God will arise, and the imperfect affirms the present reality of God's arising. Because there is a separate jussive form of this verb, it is better to take it as an imperfect expressing an affirmation of what God will do.

[104]VanGemeren, 'Psalms,' 5:444.

[105]McCann, 'Psalms,' 4:945.

[106]Tate, *Psalms 51–100*, 176.

[107]It is beyond the scope of this book to deal with the problems of verses 13-14 in any detail. A common view of verse 13 is that it is praising the warriors who returned from battle victorious with spoils but that others who did not participate lost out (VanGemeren, 'Psalms,' 5:447-48; Anderson, *Psalms 1–150*, 2:489). The 'wings of a dove' (v. 13) have been explained as the spoils of war (a jeweled object or an image of Astarte), a symbol of Israel herself who has captured the wealth of the opposing kings, or the release of birds to celebrate the victory (see McCann, 'Psalms,' 4:945). The 'snow in Zalmon' (v. 14) has been taken as a snowstorm used to defeat the enemy, or the bleached bones of the fallen warriors that look like snow from a distance (Harman, *Psalms*, 241; Delitzsch, 'Psalms,' 5:256).

[108]Anderson, *Psalms 1–150*, 2:941.

[109]VanGemeren, 'Psalms,' 5:449 and Anderson, *Psalms 1–150*, 2:941.

[110]Wilson, *Psalms Volume 1*, 939.

[111]Although Delitzsch ('Psalms,' 5:260) denies that the phrase *bā'ādām* can refer to people given as gifts to the king, others note this possible use of the preposition *beth* (Tate, *Psalms 51–100*, 166). There seems to be some ambiguity in this phrase so that the gifts might include tribute or people.

[112]The statement in Psalm 68:22, 'I will bring back from Bashan,' has no object. Many take it to refer to the enemies of God in order to assure their complete destruction rather than to the people of God

(VanGemeren, 'Psalms,' 5:450; Anderson, *Psalms 1–150*, 2:494; Tate, *Psalms 51–100*, 182; and Wilson, *Psalms Volume 1*, 940). Concerning verse 23 Wilson (*Psalms Volume 1*, 941) comments: 'The scene depicts the execution of captives from the defeated nations in the streets of Jerusalem so that the general populace can participate in the humiliation of the enemies and know personally the great victory Yahweh has accomplished for them.'

[113]Delitzsch, 'Psalms,' 5:272.

[114]Many who use the term 'midrash' do not define it precisely. Andrew T. Lincoln (*Ephesians* [WBC; Word Books, 1990] lvii) uses it in the sense of the reuse of authoritative tradition. For a discussion of midrash, see Jacob Neusner, *What is Midrash?* (Guides to Biblical Scholarship; Fortress, 1987) and E. Earle Ellis, 'Biblical Interpretation in the New Testament Church,' in *Mikra* (ed. Jan Mulder; Fortress, 1990), 702-09.

[115]Lincoln, *Ephesians*, 225-26, 242. He does affirm that what the writer says about Christ in Ephesians 4:8 lines up with what he has said in Ephesians 1:20-22. Kraus (*Psalms*, 261) also comments that Psalm 68 is wrongly applied based on the Old Testament context, but he admits there is a correspondence between the ascension of Yahweh and the exaltation of Christ.

[116]Markus Barth, *Ephesians 4-6* (AB; Doubleday, 1974), 472-76. Note the assumption here that we would not follow the example of the New Testament authors in how they interpret Scripture. Some think there may be an oral tradition behind the use of Psalm 68 because the Targums (Aramaic paraphrases of the Old Testament) also have 'gave gifts to men'. But the Targums understand the psalm in relationship to Moses and there are problems related to the dating of the targums of the psalms and whether such a tradition would make any sense to the audience of Ephesians (see Barth, *Ephesians 4-6*, 475 and Ernest Best, *Ephesians* [ICC; T & T Clark, 1998], 379-80).

[117]Gary V. Smith, 'Paul's Use of Psalm 68:18 in Ephesians 4:8,' *JETS* 18 (1975): 186-87. He does not discuss the change of person in 4:8.

[118]Other arguments by Kaiser (*Messiah*, 131-32) in support of the direct Messiah reference are the person 'ascends' rather than processes in some line of march on earth, the place this person ascends to is 'on high,' which never means anything less than heaven, this theophanic person takes captives, and he both receives and gives gifts.

[119]Kaiser, *Messiah*, 132-33.

[120]The 'descent' is best understood to be the humiliation of Christ, which could include the incarnation, but focuses on the crucifixion. For a discussion of other views of the descent, such as it refers to Christ's burial, his descent into the underworld, and the descent of the Spirit at Pentecost, see William Hendriksen, *Exposition of Ephesians* (Baker, 1967), 192-93 and Lincoln, *Ephesians*, 245-47.

[121]Calvin, *Psalms 36-92*, 26-27. Even Kaiser (*Uses of the Old Testament*, 108-09) recognizes the importance of the intent of the divine author when it comes to typology.

[122]Van Groningen (*Messianic Revelation*, 397, n 67) comments that Calvin is one of the few who takes the whole psalm as messianic.

[123]Leslie Allen, *Psalms 101–150* (WBC; Word Books, 1983), 122 and McCann, 'Psalms,' 4:1153.

[124]Allen, *Psalms 101–150*, 122. The processional nature of the psalm and the shifting speakers makes the psalm difficult to classify, even though the elements of the thanksgiving psalm are fairly prominent (Kraus, *Psalms 1–150*, 2:394; VanGemeren, 'Psalms,' 5:730; and McCann, 'Psalms,' 4:1153).

[125]Mays (*Psalms*, 375) has the best discussion of the structure of Psalm 118 and my analysis is dependent on him to a large degree.

[126]Harman, *Psalms*, 377.

[127]Mays (*Psalms*, 374) notes that the term 'steadfast love' (*ḥesed*) does not occur in the body of the psalm, but that it is a key element because it frames the psalm.

[128]McCann, 'Psalms,' 4:1154.

[129]See Allen (*Psalms 101–150*, 124) and VanGemeren ('Psalms,' 5:734) for a discussion of the translation of verse 13. The Hebrew literally reads 'you pushed me hard.' The 'you' could refer to God or to the enemy. In the context of the psalm it probably refers to the enemy. Many follow the passive of the LXX and translate 'I was pushed hard,' an emendation of the Hebrew that requires dropping the final *nun* on the verb.

[130]The word translated 'set free' refers to a broad, roomy place and contrasts with the confinement of the distress the psalmist faced (McCann, 'Psalms,' 4:1154).

[131]Allen, *Psalms 101–150*, 121; Delitzsch, 'Psalms,' 5:228; and Kraus, *Psalms 1–150*, 2:399. VanGemeren ('Psalms,' 5:734) comments that only the righteous, those who meet the requirements of covenant

loyalty and trust in the Lord, are permitted to enter the presence of the Lord, symbolically guarded by the gates of righteousness (see Psalms 15 and 24).

[132]Mays, *Psalms*, 377.

[133]Allen, *Psalms 101–150*, 125. For other possibilities, see VanGemeren, 'Psalms,' 5:735-36.

[134]VanGemeren, 'Psalms,' 5:735; Allen, *Psalms 101–150*, 125; and McCann, 'Psalms,' 4:1155.

[135]McCann, 'Psalms,' 4:1155. See Allen (*Psalms 101–150*, 122) for a discussion of the problems of verse 27b, which begin with the fact that there is not an attested practice of binding the sacrifice to the horns of the altar with cords. This leads to the discussion of other possibilities, like some kind of processional dance with the altar being covered with boughs.

[136]Allen, *Psalms 101–150*, 123-24.

[137]Van Groningen, *Messianic Revelation*, 402; Kaiser, *Messiah*, 100; and Calvin, *Psalms 93-150*, 376. Calvin assumes Davidic authorship rather than setting forth the arguments for it. Harman (*Psalms*, 376) connects the psalm to Jehoshaphat's victory over Moab and Ammon (2 Chron. 20:1-30).

[138]Allen, *Psalms 101–150*, 125. He does not state specifically how Psalm 118 came to have Messianic meaning.

[139]Van Groningen, *Messianic Revelation*, 402-03; Kaiser, *Messiah*, 101-02; and Calvin, *Psalms 93-150*, 392-93.

[140]Some connect the origin of the psalm to a festival, such as the Feast of Tabernacles, rather than an historical victory or setting (Anderson, *Psalms*, 2:797). In such a view the psalm could be preexilic or postexilic and could have a Messianic connection if the king is the main speaker.

[141]Delitzsch, 'Psalms,' 5:224.

[142]Ibid., 5:229-30.

[143]Kraus, *Psalms 1–150*, 2:396 and McCann, 'Psalms,' 4:1153.

[144]Mays, *Psalms*, 378.

[145]McCann, 'Psalms,' 4:1154.

[146]Ibid.

[147]Allen, *Psalms 101–150*, 125.

[148]William Hendriksen, *Exposition of the Gospel According to Matthew* (New Testament Commentary; Baker, 1973), 785-86.

[149]Mays, *Psalms*, 379-80.

9. Conclusion: The Majesty of Christ in the Psalms

[1]It is also true that the three offices of prophet, priest, and king cannot be separated from each other. W. A. Visser 't Hooft comments, 'The three offices are so related to one another that Christ is Prophet in a priestly and royal manner; Priest in a prophetic and royal way; King, but King as priest and prophet. The three offices can be distinguished; they cannot be separated' (*The Kingship of Christ* [Harper & Brothers, 1948], 16-17), quoted in Robert Sherman, *King, Priest, and Prophet: A Trinitarian Theology of Atonement* [New York: T & T Clark, 2004], 21).

[2]A general review of the psalms covered in this book follows as a way to focus on the psalms and their relationship to Christ. For a detailed discussion of each psalm see the exposition of the psalm.

[3]The Westminster Shorter Catechism, question 28, identifies Christ's exaltation 'in his rising again from the dead on the third day, in ascending up into heaven, in sitting at the right hand of God the Father, and in coming to judge the world at the last day'.

[4]This book has focused on how the psalms relate to Christ, but other uses of the psalms are also appropriate. For example, a psalm that focuses on the law can relate to Christ as prophet and as the Word of God. It would also be appropriate from a psalm that emphasizes the law to stress the second use or the third use of the law. A redemptive historical emphasis and a systematic theology emphasis are both important and can be utilized profitably in preaching. For an analysis of the relationship between redemptive historical themes and systematic theology categories and the various ways scholars bring these together, see Robert J. Cara, 'Redemptive-Historical Themes in the *Westminster Larger Catechism*,' in *The Westminster Confession of Faith in the 21st Century*, Vol. 3 (ed. Ligon Duncan; 3 vols.; Christian Focus, 2007).